FOREIGN MISSIONS:

THEIR

RELATIONS AND CLAIMS.

BY

RUFUS ANDERSON, D.D., LL.D.,

LATE FOREIGN SECRETARY OF THE AMERICAN BOARD OF COMMISSIONERS FOR FOREIGN MISSIONS.

THIRD EDITION REVISED.

BOSTON:
CONGREGATIONAL PUBLISHING SOCIETY,
CONGREGATIONAL HOUSE,
BEACON STREET.
1874.

Entered according to Act of Congress, in the year 1869, by
Charles Scribner and Company,
in the Clerk's Office of the District Court for the Southern District of New York.

BV
2060
.A55
1874

Riverside, Cambridge:
Stereotyped and Printed by
H. O. Houghton and Company.

Chicago Theol. Sem.
Exch.
7-20-1927

TO THE TRUSTEES

OF THE

THEOLOGICAL SEMINARY IN ANDOVER,

UNDER

WHOSE APPOINTMENT THIS WORK WAS PREPARED.

PREFACE.

THE work now offered to the Christian public had its origin in a series of Lectures on Foreign Missions, delivered in the Theological Seminary at Andover, under appointment from the Trustees; and subsequently, by request, before the Theological Seminaries at Bangor, Hartford, Auburn, and Princeton, and the Union Seminary in New York City. It was fitting that the oldest of our theological seminaries, and the first to send missionaries into foreign heathen lands, should take the lead in establishing, for its students, a permanent Lectureship on Foreign Missions. This was created by a vote of the Trustees early in the year 1866; and the needful pecuniary endowment was secured to the Seminary by HENRY H. HYDE, Esq., a citizen of Boston. The statutes of the endowment require the course to embrace as many as ten lectures; but it is left for the Trustees to decide, whether they shall be delivered annually, to the Middle Class, or triennially, before the entire Seminary.

In February, 1866, the author was appointed by the Trustees lecturer on this foundation, and was requested to deliver, at his early convenience, a course of lectures on Foreign Missions. The appointment had reference to his intended retirement from official life; which was effected that year, at the age of threescore and ten, after a connection of more than forty years with the Foreign Correspondence of the American Board of Commissioners for Foreign Missions. It was with the hope, however, of being enabled, through the divine blessing, to devote the residue of his life to embodying the results of his experience in forms that should be useful to the missionary cause.

The duty first in order was to select topics for the lectures, and to make the needful investigations, which required longer time and greater labor than had been expected. The aim was to embody practical views of the missionary work in its largest sense, contemplated from the missionary stand-point, and to draw illustrations from every part of the great field where they seemed most appropriate.

The lectures were delivered to three successive Middle Classes in the Andover Seminary; and the author takes pleasure in acknowledging his obligations to Dr. EDWARDS A. PARK, of the theological department, having special charge of that class, for his kind and efficient support, as also to the other Professors, and to the Students. At the five other seminaries, the Lectures were delivered before the body of Professors and Students. It may not be improper to say, that at Auburn the delivery was on nine successive evenings, and at Princeton on ten, and that this unbroken succession seemed to be with the happiest effect. The last six lectures of the course at Hartford were delivered on successive days, and with the like result.

The author thankfully acknowledges his obligations to the Trustees of the Andover Seminary, for the formal expression of their earnest desire for the publication of the lectures; and also to the Professors in the several institutions where he had the privilege of lecturing, for their very kind manner of communicating the same sentiment. And he the more confidently appears before the Christian public by reason of the frequent expressions of this sentiment by students in the different seminaries. The present work is in compliance with these wishes; though in a form that is deemed better adapted to the taste of the reading public. The text is unaltered, except so far as was rendered necessary by the change of form; and hence the reason why the writer is more prominently before the reader, than he is desirous of being.

As reference is occasionally made to the author's personal intercourse with missions, it may be well to state, that he made an official visit to the missions of the American Board, bordering on the Mediterranean, in the years 1828 and 1829; again, in 1844 and 1845, when he had the friendly companionship of the late Dr. Joel Hawes, of Hartford; and again, in 1855, on his way home from India. He visited the India missions, with Dr. Augustus C. Thompson as an associate, in 1854 and 1855; and in the year 1863, he spent four months, in an official visit, on the Sandwich Islands. Each of these visits involved much travel by land and sea; yet, under the protection of a kind Providence, not a single accident was anywhere experienced.

It will at once be seen what is the object of this work. It is to show the extent of the field that has been providentially opened for foreign missions; the providential preparation otherwise made for such missions; the peculiar nature of the work of missions; the extent to which it has been carried; its success; the hindrances at home and abroad, and how they may be removed; and the claims of foreign missions upon the churches, and upon young ministers of the gospel.

The appeal is to those, who look upon the gospel as the only hope of this lost world. To this view the author's experience has brought him with a power he is unable to resist. His theory of missions is substantially that of the Apostle to the Gentiles. And he has the more confidence in his exposition of it, because of the ample scope it allows for the exercise of discretion in the use of subordinate means. Whatever exalts the cross, whatever impressively sets forth the gospel, must be within the scope of the great commission given by our Lord.

But the use to be made of subordinate means, is a subject of much difficulty, on which the best and most intelligent men are not yet fully agreed. Should this volume have the effect to stimulate secretaries, missionaries, or others specially interested in the subject and conversant with it, to efforts for solving the yet unresolved problems, even should their opinions differ from his own, the author will greatly rejoice; believing that, in so mighty an enterprise, entered upon so recently, we must yet be far from a complete apprehension of the agencies that ought to be employed.

While the value of local native churches as a prominent instrumentality for renovating the heathen world, is set forth with earnestness, the word church is used only in the sense of an associated, local body of Christians, whether governed by the popular vote, by elders chosen for the purpose, or in some other way. The necessity of native pastors is indeed insisted upon; and also of a pastorate confessedly modified from that of the apostolic churches, though in strict conformity with the present usage of all evangelical denominations. Into the minor details of church polity, the author has not deemed himself called to enter.

Some may be ready to regard the theory of missions here described as being self-evident, seeing it is so very simple. But such an impression would betray much ignorance of the history of modern missions. It is even now a controverted point with not a few friends of missions, to say nothing of others, whether civilization must not precede Christianity, or, at any rate, what is the precise relation of the two. Recent publications show, also, that the relative place of preaching in the missionary work, as compared with education, is not quite settled, though the difference is perhaps somewhat more theoretical than practical; and the question seems to have no great interest beyond the caste-regions of India. Scarcely fifteen years have elapsed since it was deemed advisable to send a Deputation to India, with one of its leading objects to persuade the missionaries of the American Board in that country to commence the practice of ordaining native pastors. There is printed evidence, much of which has not been published, that the theory of missions advocated by the Deputation when in India, was substantially the same which is embodied in this work; and the unexpected discussion at the annual meeting of the American Board in 1855, as to the proceedings of that Deputation, and the holding of a special meeting to inquire into their proceedings, was in great measure the result of misapprehension; as was abundantly shown, at the annual meeting in 1856, by the Report of the "Committee of Thirteen." Yet the numerous columns of the religious newspapers, occupied with this subject previous to the report of that committee, would convince any one, that the theory of missions was then by no means determined. Seven years later, a Deputation was sent to the Sandwich Islands, largely to induce the missionaries on those islands to put the native church-members generally under a native pastorate, and to place the native pastorate of the islands on an independent footing, which there was an apparent backwardness to do. And so far as information is yet attainable, it is only a few years since the discovery was made, that native pastors form an essential element in native churches, to make them healthful, vigorous, self-supporting, and aggressive.

In point of fact, the principles and methods of foreign missions embodied in the seventh chapter, were wrought out with painstaking, and through much conflict of opinion.

The author's aim, throughout, has been to give an honest presentation of what may properly be called the science of missions, as it is understood by himself, and never in a controversial form; and he ventures the hope that this result of his labors may serve, in future times, for a landmark to those who shall perform the service for their generation, which he has endeavored to perform for his.

It is proper to say a word as to the classification and arrangement of topics. The first chapter presents the field of the world, as it is opening to the foreign missions of our day, and the second the preparations for occupying it. The seven following chapters illustrate, in various forms, the nature of the work. The hindrances existing at home to the propagation of the gospel in heathen lands are next considered; and then there are two chapters setting forth the extent to which modern missions have been prosecuted, and the success which has attended them. It was natural to discuss the claims of the work on young ministers of the gospel, which is the topic of the thirteenth chapter. Nor could the great subject of missions, avowedly for the conversion of the heathen world to the evangelical faith, be dismissed without an inquiry into the strength of the opposing force there is in the Romish missions. The last chapter contains a résumé of the volume, with concluding reflections. Articles will be found in the Appendix, that are believed to add materially to the value of the work.

CONTENTS.

APPENDIX.

FOREIGN MISSIONS.

CHAPTER I.

AN OPENING WORLD.

Objects of Inquiry. — Why restricted to Asia. — Importance of India. Problems to be solved. — How the Possession of India by Great Britain opened the Way into Turkey. — How into China. — Combination of the Great Christian Powers for opening China to Commerce. — Remarkable Change in the Diplomatic World. — How India was opened. — Openings in other Parts of the World.

It is proper that I enter upon my subject by showing, in the first place, how the unevangelized world has of late been providentially opened to Christian missions; secondly, how Christendom, meanwhile, has been in a process of unconscious preparation for evangelizing it; and, thirdly, the consequent development, in the Evangelical Church, of a missionary spirit, and of missionary organizations, with the avowed expectation and purpose — for the first time since the apostolic age — of laboring for the conversion of the whole heathen world.

The first branch of the subject is too extended for an exhaustive discussion. I shall therefore attempt only to show how the portions of the unevangelized world were opened that are most populous. I refer to Southern, Eastern, and Western Asia, containing a population of more than six hundred millions. It has for many years been my official duty to give attention to this process; and it has seemed to me to be one of the most impressive indications of an all-embracing Providence, preparing the way for the great work now claiming the attention and efforts of the Christian Church. Preliminary to this, it will be necessary to state the great problems that were to be practically solved.

I begin with India, because that was the pivot on which the lever of Providence (so to speak) seemed to move in opening so large a portion of the heathen world. Here, in a population of nearly two hundred millions, it was necessary, first, to break down the Mohammedan power, extending over most of the country; secondly, to break down the Brahminical power, resting upon caste, and having the sanction of ages; and, thirdly, when the East India Company had answered its purpose, it was needful to bring that great selfish corporation to an end. India was not fully prepared for the entrance of the gospel, until these results were all substantially attained.

In Western Asia, it was necessary, first, that England should secure a predominant influence in the governments of both Turkey and Persia; secondly, that the persecuting ecclesiastical rulers of the Oriental churches should somehow be so far restrained, as to secure a tolerable protection for Protestant converts; thirdly, that the death-penalty in Mohammedan law should be practically nullified; and, fourthly, that Western and Central Asia should be protected against the encroachments of the late ambitious and bigoted autocrat of Russia.

In Eastern Asia it was necessary, that the great Christian powers of the world should combine to secure a free commercial and religious access to the vast population of China and the neighboring countries.

We at once see, that only the hand which moves the world could accomplish all this. Fifty years ago, no well-informed man would have said that any part of Western, Southern, or Eastern Asia was fairly opened to Christian missions; and no well-informed man can doubt that these countries are now open, with only a few partial exceptions.

How was the opening for the gospel into these extended and populous regions effected?

The discovery of the way to India by the Cape of Good Hope, in 1498, was the first step. The second was the chartering of a small company of Englishmen by Queen Elizabeth, in the year 1600, for trading in India, which afterwards took the name of the East India Company. The next step was twelve years later, when the Grand Mogul was persuaded to authorize this Company to form a commercial post in India. This was the beginning of the British empire in the East. Then came the struggle, first with the Portuguese, and then with the French, which was to determine whether Popery or Protestantism should govern India; and the triumph of Protestantism. The Mohammedan powers of India were partially subdued by means of successive wars. The celebrated battle of Plassey, in 1757, with Clive in command, more than a hundred and fifty years after the chartering of the Company, first gave it dominion; and this dominion was constantly extended by similar measures, until it covered thirty degrees of latitude, and as many of longitude, embracing every variety of climate, scenery, and soil, and nearly two hundred millions of people, speaking twelve or fifteen polished languages.

The possession of this Indian empire by the English nation, — the opening of which to the gospel I shall illustrate after tracing its influence in the west and east of Asia, — made it necessary to keep open a highway between India and England, the mother country. Here is a point of special interest; for were it not for this, the whole political influence in Turkey, if not the absolute dominion (so far as we can now see), would have been divided between France and Russia, — the one Roman Catholic, the other of the Greek Church, and both hostile to Protestant missions.

The security of the English empire in India made it imperative with England to acquire and to exercise a paramount influence in the government of Turkey. For this purpose she kept her ablest diplomatist at the Porte. Her war with Egypt in 1840, with Russia in 1855, called the Crimean war (in which France found it for her interest to unite), and with Persia in 1856, — from which the immortal Havelock returned just in time to act his important part in saving India to England and to the cause of missions, — all these wars grew more or less directly out of the necessity of keeping this great highway open; and also of restraining the progress of Russian power across Central Asia towards the Indian empire.

Moreover, as Russia was the acknowledged protector of the Greek Christians in Turkey, and France of the Roman Catholics, the question naturally arose with the enlightened English Ambassador at the Porte, and with English statesmen, whether England would not strengthen herself in Western Asia, by becoming the protector of the Protestant Christians, then multiplying in those regions through the labors of Protestant missionaries. A Parliamentary "Blue Book" contains the proof of this. Thus it came about that the English embassies, both at Constantinople and in Persia, were providentially induced, if they were not really instructed, to extend that protection to the American missionaries, and their converts, among the Armenians and Nestorians, without which neither Turkey nor Persia would have been really open to the gospel. Through the influence of Lord Stratford de Redcliffe, the British Ambassador at Constantinople, the death-penalty in Mohammedan law for abjuring the Moslem faith, was virtually abolished; and the Protestant Christians of the empire were recognized by the Sultan as a distinct body, independent of all the other Christian sects, and entitled to the protection of the government in their persons and religious privileges. We owe all this, under God, to the providential fact, that England had gained an empire in India, and must needs preserve an unincumbered way to it.

Next, as to the great and vastly populous countries lying eastward of India. The East India Company had a trading-post in China, at Canton, and one of their most profitable articles for sale was opium. It was, and is now, a rich source of revenue. As this was exerting a pernicious influence on the health and morals of the people, the Chinese government wisely sought to put a stop to the trade. Finding no other way to prevent the introduction of the poison into the empire, they destroyed a large quantity of it at Canton. The result was a war, — an iniquitous war, doubtless, on the part of the East India Company, — but still a war; and this was the beginning of a series of warlike aggressions, in which, ultimately, for the purpose of opening China to the commercial world, not only England, but France, Russia, and even the United States, became more or less involved; until, in 1858, treaties were made by the Chinese with each of the four great powers, — England, France, Russia, and America, engaging, among other things (I quote the words of the treaty), that "any person, either citizen of the country with which the treaty is made, or Chinese convert to the faith of the Protestant or Roman Catholic churches, who, according to these tenets, peaceably teaches and practices the principles of Christianity, *shall in no case be interfered with, or molested.*"[1]

As this was a stipulation made with each and all of those powers, for not less than four hundred millions of pagans, it must be regarded as one of the most important transactions of modern times. Subsequent events have shown that the treaty was not a vain form. Every important port of China is accessible, and so is almost every part of the interior, not in a state of rebellion; and China is now seeking, through an embassy, at the head of which is one of our own countrymen, to establish peaceful and honorable relations with the Christian world.

It should be added that, after China had been made thus accessible to the commerce and religion

[1] *Report of Am. Board,* 1859, p. 111; *Miss. Herald,* 1858, p. 338

of Christendom, it was not possible for its near neighbor, Japan, to be much longer in determined non-intercourse with other nations; and Japan is now being opened, though reluctantly, to the light and influence of Christian truth, as well as to the commerce of the world.

The remarkable union of the plenipotentiaries of the four great Christian nations, in stipulating with the Chinese emperor for the entrance and protection of Christian missionaries, and for the protection also of their converts in every province of the empire, reveals an astonishing change in the public sentiment of the diplomatic world, as regards the value of missionaries, and of Christian missions.

It may be well to add, that these treaties were negotiated in 1858, a year memorable as the one in which the East India Company closed its existence.

We shall be more impressed with the magnitude of this revolution (for it was such, as regards religious toleration), if we now go back to the beginning of the century, and observe what indications of hostile feeling to missions existed in the high places, not of India alone, but even of England, and how the hostile feeling was at last overcome.

The well-known English Baptist missionaries, Carey, Marshman, and Ward, arrived at Calcutta in 1799, and were ordered by the East India government to leave India; but found a refuge, for a time, in the Danish town of Serampore, sixteen miles above Calcutta, which was not then subject to the East India Company. On a subsequent arrival of missionaries, orders were given by the authorities at Calcutta, not to preach to the natives, nor to allow their converts to preach, nor to distribute books or tracts, nor to take any step to induce the people to embrace Christianity.[1] In 1812, the first American missionaries, — Hall, Judson, Newell, Nott, and Rice, — arrived at Calcutta, and were ordered away, though they somehow found means to evade the order. An English missionary, who accompanied them from America, was actually forced by the government to return to England.

How strangely the East India government was long in sympathy, and even partnership, with Hindu idolatry, is strikingly set forth by Dr. Mullens, now Foreign Secretary of the London Missionary Society, whose valuable acquaintance I formed while he was a missionary at Calcutta. He says: —

"There was a time when, through the extensive preaching of the gospel by the Tranquebar and Tanjore missionaries and other causes, the temples in the Madras Presidency began to be deserted, and to fall into decay. Then it was that the government of Madras took them under its own protection,

[1] Marshman's *Life and Times of Carey*, etc., vol. i. p. 260.

appointed the officiating priests, received the offerings, disbursed the expenses, publicly presented gifts, and restored new vigor to the dying system! The government of Madras made itself trustee of the pagoda-lands. In times of drought, the Collector ordered the Brahmins to pray to the gods for rain, and paid money for their expenses. European officers joined in salutes to the idols. Some, of their own accord, would make their obeisance, and others would ride in front of the cars, shouting with the multitude, 'Hari Bol!' Villagers were summoned to draw the cars by order of the Collector, and were whipped by the native officials, if they refused. The temples were kept in repair by the government, and the illuminations at the festivals were paid for from the treasury."[1]

Another authority states than more than eight thousand temples in the Madras Presidency, with all their estates, were entirely managed by the English officers of government. In 1852, they paid out $750,000 for repairs of temples, for making and consecrating new idols, and for priests, idol cars, musicians, painters, watchmen, and dancing women.[2]

"The same guilty course," Dr. Mullens continues, "was adopted at the other Presidencies. In Ceylon, all the chief Buddhist priests were appointed by government, and expenses for 'devil

[1] *Result of Missionary Labor in India*, p. 44.

[2] *Christian Work*, July, 1864.

dancing,' continued at Kandy for seven days, were paid, as per voucher, 'For Her Majesty's service'!"

There were members of the government, and some of the Governor Generals, to whom this heathenish policy was far from being acceptable; but such was the prevailing spirit of the ruling powers. Such, too, was the spirit of the "Old Indians," as those were called who had retired to opulence and ease in England. A mutiny of native troops at Nellore, in 1806, occasioned the loss of five hundred English lives; and this mutiny the "Old Indians" attributed — as indeed they afterwards did the larger one of 1857 — to the presence and influence of Christian missions. A great controversy arose at length in England, in which nearly thirty different publications were issued. This did something towards preparing the public mind for the question of a new charter for the East India Company, which came before Parliament in 1813, and which the friends of missions were determined should be made to secure religious toleration in India. This was three years after the formation of the American Board, thirteen years after that of the Church Missionary Society, and eighteen after that of the London Missionary Society. There was then an energetic renewal of the controversy. And it is painful to see how indifferent, how hostile even, what was in fact the most Christian government in Europe then was to the diffusion of the glorious gospel of Christ among the millions of its subjects in the East. The great bulk of the Anglo-Indians insisted, that any attempt to evangelize India would cost England a loss of the Indian empire. Mr. Wilberforce believed that nine tenths of the members of the House of Commons would vote against any motion the friends of religion might make. The periodical press was almost universally opposed to introducing the gospel into India; and the high ministers of state were believed to be utterly devoid of sympathy with missionary efforts.[1] Nothing could have overcome all this, and secured freedom to the missionaries in India, except such an unlooked-for development of interest in missions in the English churches, as was evinced by nine hundred petitions, from all parts of the country, which came in as the result of an appeal from Wilberforce, Grant, and others, together with the addition of two of Wilberforce's eloquent speeches during the progress of the debate in Parliament. The charter was finally made substantially conformable to the wishes of the friends of missions, and thus, in the good providence of God, India was thrown open to missionaries; that is to say, English missionaries could no longer be debarred by the East India government from entering that country.

But the connection of the government with the

[1] Marshman's *Life and Times*, etc., vol. ii. p. 3.

idolatry of that country continued to be active, and its spirit more or less hostile to missions, for nearly thirty years longer; and the full preparation of India for the gospel was not before the year 1857, — the year of the great mutiny and rebellion, — and was the immediate consequence of that terrible convulsion. Caste was the last idol in India which the English rulers ceased to dread. Its terror lay mainly in the Sepoy army, of some two or three hundred thousands, which they could not trust, and did not know how to disband. At length this great native army rebelled, and made war alike upon English rulers and native Christians. Everywhere English dwellings were burned down, and the bodies of more than fifteen hundred English men and women, many of rank and culture, "lay unburied upon the wastes, the food of dogs and jackals, and of foul birds of prey; and riot, plunder, and murder strode wildly over the land."[1] Yet this storm, after it had passed, was found to have been a rich blessing, though terribly disguised. The Sepoy army had been disbanded. Caste was no longer a terror. The Moslem power was broken. And, what was perhaps most important of all, it was found that two thousand native converts had endured persecution firmly, some of them unto death; and the missionaries thus learned to hold such converts in much higher estimation, and became more

[1] Mullens' *Ten Years in India*, p. 8.

ready to repose confidence in them when formed into churches, and to entrust to them the pastoral office. To crown all, the reign of the East India Company was brought to a most desirable close, and Sir John Lawrence, one of the ablest and best of the Christian men in India, was placed on the vice-regal throne.

This opening of a population of more than six hundred millions in India and Western and Eastern Asia, to the missionaries of the gospel, may all be said to have occurred (excepting the earlier wars with the Moslem and Pagan powers) after the year 1812, or within the space of about fifty years, and since the formation of the American Board. I believe the change, for magnitude and importance, is without a parallel in the history of the world. And who can fail to see the hand of Him, who, with all power in heaven and earth, is preparing the way for His people to carry out the grand purpose of His redemption.

Were I to pursue this illustration of a world opening to the gospel, I might point to Western and Southern Africa, to Italy, to South America, and to the Isles of the Pacific. I might speak of the Protestant ascendency recently gained in Central Europe, of the recent change in Spain, and of the four emancipated millions in our own country.

But enough has been said. The providence of

God, in so marvelously opening the uncivilized world for the propagation of the gospel, naturally leads to the inquiry, whether corresponding changes have meanwhile occurred in the Christian world. This will be the topic of the next chapter.

CHAPTER II.

AN UPRISING CHURCH.

Preparations in the Christian World. — Development of a Missionary Spirit. — What is meant by it. — How differing from that of Former Ages. — Missionary Development in England, and its Early Characteristics. — When the several Evangelical Denominations of Europe entered upon the Work. — Missionary Developments in the United States. — Characteristics. — The Time come for attempting the Conversion of the World.

THE providential changes in the Christian world, of which I am now to speak, did not severally awaken any great attention at the time of their occurrence, but we now see in them the hand of God. Volumes would not exhaust the subject; and I can merely glance at the more important topics. Nor is it needful that I do more, as the reader must already be so familiar with this part of the subject, that a simple utterance of the propositions will suggest the needful illustrations.

Since the Reformation, the human mind in the Christian Church has been continually becoming more free for examining, embracing, and promulgating the truths of the gospel. The Bible has been set at liberty, to be translated into all languages, and to be read by all the world. The apostolic idea of the local, self-governed church, for many ages in great measure lost to the world, has been recovered, as one of the great results of the Reformation. A Christian literature has been created. And, finally, while the churches remain in the full exercise of their ecclesiastical prerogatives, with what facility do their members, whose hearts beat in unison with the Saviour's command, form themselves into associations, in harmonious coöperation with the churches, and really a part of their organization, for collecting and managing the funds which are needed to fill the world with preachers, with the Scriptures, and with intelligent readers of the same. These are all immense results, and of inestimable value.

In a general view, embracing the Christian world at large, the preparation is even more striking. We see it in all the domains of literature, science, art, commerce, and geographical discovery; in the rebellions and revolutions of nations; in the history of civilization from the Reformation until now. As compared with the Roman world, in the first ages of Christianity, or with the Christian world, in the Early and Middle Ages, everything is greatly changed. The tendency among Christian nations now, is more and more to the forming of international relations, which is a new and most hopeful feature. Life, thought, labor, all have a greatly increased value, because of the immense increase of facilities for the intercommunication of man with man. With our railroads, steamships, and telegraphic wires; with our electrotyping, and power-presses; our sciences, arts, and commerce; with neither Hun, Vandal, nor Moslem to set back the tide of civilization, who does not see that the time for blessing the whole earth with the gospel has come, and that this is the grand business of the churches in our day?

We should not be surprised, then, if, as a consequence of this, and the result of divine agency, we find also a new and strange development of the missionary spirit, and a strange uprising for the missionary work, throughout the evangelical churches.

This suggests our third and last topic, namely,— the development, in the Evangelical Church, of a missionary spirit, and of missionary organizations, with the avowed expectation and purpose of laboring for the conversion of the whole heathen world.

To avoid misapprehension, I define what I mean by the missionary spirit. It is really the same thing in foreign missions, and in home missions; being the earnest response of a believing heart to the Saviour's last injunction. I of course use the phrase in its special relation to foreign missions. Yet it is not the foreign missionary alone, who illustrates this spirit. It is as really illustrated by the home missionary, and by every pastor who labors to call forth the prayers and contributions of his people for the conversion of the world.

It will at once be seen, that the modern development of the missionary spirit must needs differ in many respects from that of all past ages. This is owing to the vastly changed condition, already described, both of the unevangelized world, and of Christendom. The missionary spirit is now intensely social and enterprising, seeking to enlist and organize Christians in large bodies, with the declared and earnest purpose of a universal diffusion of the gospel. We saw it not in this form in the apostolic age, nor do we in any of the subsequent ages. Indeed, the missionary spirit is possible in this form only in a considerably advanced Christian civilization.

I am not able distinctly to trace a historical connection between either the Danish mission to India, commenced in 1705, or the Moravian mission to Greenland, commenced in 1733, or the missions to the American Indians previous to 1750, with the modern development of the missionary spirit, of which I am now treating; though each of those is worthy of all honor, and of a grateful commemoration.

The missionary development, in its modern form, would seem to have had its rise about the year 1789, in the efforts of William Carey, a Baptist minister in the interior of England, who afterwards became a distinguished missionary in India. The project of personally effecting a mission among the heathen, and of an organized movement in the churches at home for that purpose, seems to have taken full possession of his soul. Yet he found little encouragement among his ministerial brethren. Marshman, in his "Life and Times" of Carey and his associates, relates the following singular occurrence at a meeting of Baptist ministers in Northampton. He says: "Mr. Ryland, senior, called on the young men around him to propose a topic for discussion; on which Mr. Carey rose, and proposed for consideration 'The duty of Christians to attempt the spread of the gospel among heathen nations.' The venerable divine received the proposal with astonishment; and, springing on his feet, denounced the proposition with a frown, and thundered out, 'Young man, sit down; when God pleases to convert the heathen, he will do it without your aid, or mine.'" [1]

It is difficult to account for this feeling of the good old minister, even should we suppose him strongly tinctured with the antinomianism then so prevalent among his brethren. But Mr. Ryland was not thus tinctured, and was not alone in this feeling; for we are told, that "the aged and more influential ministers generally" endeavored to dissuade Mr. Carey from what they deemed "so visionary a scheme." [2] His ultimate success was with men nearer his own age and standing; such as Andrew Fuller, Sutcliff, John Ryland, and Pearce.

[1] Marshman's *Life and Times*, etc., vol. i. p. 10.

[2] Marshman, vol. i. p. 14.

What I now relate, as having occurred in the Scottish Church, is on the same authority, and is corroborated by other testimony.

In the year 1796, after the Baptist and London Missionary Societies had both been formed, a proposition to establish a foreign mission was made in the General Assembly of the Church of Scotland; and "was treated," we are told, "not only as an unnatural, but a revolutionary design." A clergyman by the name of Hamilton asserted, that "to spread abroad the knowledge of the gospel among barbarous heathen nations, seemed to him highly preposterous, inasmuch as it anticipates, nay, reverses the order of nature." "Men," he said, "must be polished and refined in their manners, before they can be properly enlightened in religious truths. The venerable Dr. Erskine earnestly opposed those views. But Dr. Hill pronounced missionary societies to be highly dangerous in their tendencies to the good order of society; and Mr. Boyle declared his apprehension that their funds would in time be turned against the constitution, and therefore the General Assembly ought to give the overtures recommending them its most serious disapprobation, and its immediate and most decisive opposition.[1]

Yet in that very year a missionary society of moderate size was formed in Edinburgh, by Presby-

[1] Marshman, vol. i. p. 19. See also Dr. William Brown's *History of the Propagation of Christianity*, vol. ii. p. 474.

terians and others, which afterwards took the name of the Scottish Missionary Society, and another was formed in Glasgow; both of which sent missionaries to Western Africa. It was nearly thirty years after the debate just mentioned, before the General Assembly of Scotland entered on foreign missions, but the Church of Scotland has since done good missionary service.

I must state, in the briefest manner, at what time the different European evangelical denominations entered the field. The English Baptists, as we have seen, in 1792; the English Independents in 1795, in the London Missionary Society; the Scottish and Glasgow Missionary Societies in 1796; the Dutch, in the Netherlands Missionary Society, in 1797; the Evangelical English Episcopalians, in the Church Missionary Society, in 1800; the Swiss, in the Basle Missionary Society, in 1816; the English Wesleyans in 1817; and the Church of Scotland in 1824. Since then, five missionary societies, on a small scale, have been formed in England; five in Scotland; one in Ireland, one in France; eight in Germany and Switzerland; one in Holland; one in Norway, and two in Sweden. And the annual aggregate income of these thirty-three European missionary societies, in the year 1866, exceeded $3,500,000.

I come now to the development of the foreign missionary spirit in our own country.

It was a leading object with the 'Pilgrims' in migrating to this western continent, to extend the Redeemer's kingdom in lands where Christ had not been named. They worked under great disadvantage; but the age of John Eliot, from 1646 to 1675, is said, with probable justice, to have been as really a missionary age in New England, as is the present; and that portion of our country is believed to have done as much then for the conversion of the heathen, in proportion to its ability, as it is doing now.[1] Of Eliot's translation of the Bible, a single copy of which (because so few copies are in existence) is now worth a large sum, three thousand five hundred copies were printed at Cambridge; and these were the only Bibles printed in America for a long time. In 1675, as the result of the labors of Eliot and perhaps a dozen other missionaries, there were fourteen settlements of "praying Indians," with a population of three thousand and six hundred, and twenty-four regular congregations, with as many Indian preachers. The whole formed a partially civilized Christian community. It suffered greatly in King Philip's war, which commenced in 1675. But the missions were continued, and in 1696 there were thirty Indian churches in Massachusetts alone, some with Indian pastors; and the number of Christian Indians was somewhat over four thousand.[2] The missions were

1 Tracy's *History of the American Board,* p. 21.

2 See Tracy's *History of the American Board,* for a more extended account of the early missions to the Indians.

nearly suspended in the revolutionary war; but were revived early in the present century.

Missions to the Indians have, therefore, been always sustained in this country. It remains for me to show, though in the briefest manner, how the American missions were revived on a much broader scale.

The Foreign Missionary Societies now existing in our country, were formed in the following order. The American Board of Commissioners for Foreign Missions, in 1810; the American Baptist Missionary Union, in 1814; the Methodist Episcopal Missionary Society, in 1819; the Board of the Reformed Dutch Church, in 1832; the Free-will Baptist Foreign Missionary Society, in 1833; the Presbyterian Board of Foreign Missions, in 1833 (though the Presbyterian Church properly dates its entrance upon foreign missions as far back as the year 1812, when it commenced that associated operation through the American Board which a portion of it still continues); the Protestant Episcopal Board of Missions, in 1835 (though Episcopal missionaries had been sent to Greece five years before); the Evangelical Lutheran Missionary Society, in 1837; the Reformed Presbyterian, the Associate Presbyterian, and the Associate Reformed Presbyterian, in 1844; the Southern Baptist Board, in 1845; the American Missionary Association, in 1846; the American and

Foreign Christian Union, in 1850; the United Presbyterian (by union of the Associate and Associate Reformed), in 1859; the American Church Missionary Society, in 1860; and the Southern Presbyterian Board, in 1861.

Two or three of the more important characteristics in the development of our present missionary spirit, should receive a brief notice.

1. It had a small beginning and many discouragements in this country, as it had in England. So far as is known, the idea of a personal consecration to a foreign mission was first entertained by a few students in Williams College, in 1808, and afterwards by those and others in the Andover Theological Seminary. But they found so little sympathy in the religious community, that they long kept their intention a secret. When at length they ventured to ask advice at Bradford of the General Association of Massachusetts, two of the six names on their paper were stricken off, lest so many candidates for a foreign mission should alarm the clerical body. Our Christian community, as a whole, was then far from being ready to approve of their mission. The Rev. Mr. Sanborn, of Reading, in Massachusetts, a good man, expressed the widely extended sentiment of the community when, at a conference with the young candidates in Professor Stuart's study in Andover, he said, — after expressing his sense of the importance of the object, — that the project seemed to

savor of infatuation; that the proposal was premature; that we had more work at home than we could do; and that it would be impossible to meet the expense.[1]

It is the opinion of some good men, now, that the American Board, the first foreign missionary society formed in this country, ought to have been constituted by a vote of the individual Congregational churches, rather than by that of a General Association. But the Congregational churches, as a body, were not then interested enough to vote generally on the subject. A general vote could not have been obtained. And if it could, the vote would doubtless have been against going forward, at that time, in missions to foreign heathen nations.

2. That the missionary spirit is yet far from being an all-pervading sentiment in the churches, is evinced by the large number of church-members — from a fourth to one third — who are known to give nothing in support of the cause.

3. There has, however, been an encouraging progress. The most spiritual, prayerful, active, and intelligent members of the evangelical churches have, to great extent, been at length partially enlisted; and they are acting on principle, and have enlisted for life. The contributions are an evidence of advance. Those in this country, for foreign missions,

[1] *Memorial Volume of the American Board of Commissioners for Foreign Missions*, p. 52.

in the year 1811, amounted to only $1,667; but in the year 1868, their sum total exceeded $1,600,000.

In a review of the facts which have passed under survey, the conclusion seems irresistible, that the time for all friends of the Redeemer to pray, plan, and labor for the speedy conversion of the world, has come. How do we account for all this? What does it mean? Within the memory of many who are now living, the world has been strangely opened, as by a miracle, and made accessible to the gospel. Why is this? And why has such a vast, systematic organization of associations grown up over the Christian world, with the specific and declared purpose to publish the gospel to every creature? Never was such a thing seen before. Why has the great and blessed God crowded so many and such stupendous results into our day? I am unable to answer these inquiries, except on the supposition that the "fullness of time" has come for the commanded and predicted publication of the gospel through the world. Surely there has never been an age like the present. Never did churches, never did individual Christians, never did any man with the gospel in his hands, stand in such a relation to the unevangelized world, as we now do. Not only is that world accessible, but it lies on our very borders. Men sometimes complain of the frequency and the urgency of the calls on their religious benevolence, or upon their missionary service. But do they not see that these calls result from the character which God has impressed upon our age, and from the relations we stand in to the surrounding world? Our fathers of the last century had no such calls from nations beyond the limits of Christendom; and they had not, because those nations were then comparatively unknown, or else were unapproachable. But God has been pleased to lift the pall of death from off the heathen world; to bring it near; and to fill our eyes with the sight and our ears with the cry of their distress. He has leveled mountains and bridged oceans, which separated the benighted nations from us, and made for us a highway to every land. To us he says, "Go!" — with an emphasis and a meaning such as this command never had to ministers and Christians in former ages.

CHAPTER III.

DEVELOPMENT OF THE IDEA OF THE CHRISTIAN CHURCH.

The Apostles Missionaries. — Their Missions the Model for all Missions. — Theirs a Missionary Age. — Surveyed from a Missionary Stand-point. — A New and Great Idea. — Developed in the Face of Jewish Prejudices. — Jewish Notion of Messiah's Reign. — Idea underlying the Prediction of Messiah's Kingdom. — Backwardness to receive Gentile Converts simply as Christians. — The Judaizing Doctrine disowned by the Apostles. — Why they were so long in Jerusalem. — Reserve of the Supernatural. — Unrecorded Years of St. Paul. — Mission to Cyprus. — Labors at Antioch. — Ritualists. Matters referred to Jerusalem. — The Church Idea developed, and St. Paul enters on his Mission. — Why the Intellectual Christian Life was so slowly developed.

Experience has brought me to the conclusion, that the apostolic missions ought to be regarded as substantially the model for Christian missions to the heathen in all subsequent ages. I may then be allowed, thus early in the discussion, to ask attention to those missions, as they are set forth in the New Testament, and beheld from a missionary stand-point.

The apostles were really missionaries, though with an inspiration and authority peculiar to themselves, and with miraculous powers that were not transmitted. Timothy, Titus, and others their companions, usually called Evangelists, were missionaries in the ordinary sense. The apostolic age was preëminently a missionary age, and will best be understood when contemplated as such; and it is as such that I propose now to view it, presenting the facts as I find them in the inspired record. That record being inspired, it is of course infallibly correct, and whatever there is in it of doctrine or duty, is from God. But it does not follow, that the first missionaries did not profit by the teachings of experience in the prosecution of their missions. It will appear as we proceed, I think, that they did thus profit, and that there is therefore, much in their experience which we may use for our own instruction and encouragement.

The first thing claiming our attention, is the process by which the CHRISTIAN IDEA OF A CHURCH was originally developed. It was a remarkable process. And it is the more important for us to consider it, and the time it took to develop that idea, because we have been much longer in modern missions, as I shall have occasion to show hereafter, in working out the true, spiritual idea of missions. Considering the strength and prevalence of the Judaizing spirit and prejudices in the apostolic age, we must not wonder that there was a tardy development of so new and great an idea, as a CHURCH FOR

THE WHOLE WORLD; involving baptism, to take the place of circumcision; the relation sustained to Abraham, as the Father of the Faithful, to be no longer one of descent, or of blood, but simply one of faith; and the promises of the Old Testament to be no longer understood as applicable exclusively to the Jews as such, but to the Christian Church. This grand idea — the hope of a perishing world — was wrought out through years of strife, imprisonments, and blood. This process I am now to consider in its several aspects. And, —

1. The apostles, when chosen to be such, were thoroughly imbued with the Jewish notion, that the Messiah was to reign personally on earth — to have a temporal kingdom, and to elevate the Jews to the rank of a royal nation. And the evidence that they retained this notion until after the resurrection of Christ, appears in the question put by them to their Lord before his ascension. We are told that they then asked him, "Lord, wilt thou *at this time* restore again the kingdom to Israel?"[1] As there is ample proof that this error of the apostles prevented them, while entertained, from clearly apprehending the spiritual nature of the kingdom their Lord had come to set up, he might perhaps have been expected to eradicate it while he was with them. But he did not, and his reply to the question proposed was: "It is not for you to know the times

[1] Acts i. 6.

or the seasons which the Father hath put in his own power; but ye shall receive power after that the Holy Ghost is come upon you."[1] And no doubt they did at length arrive at a correct apprehension of this subject, under the teachings of the Spirit. Paul fully comprehended the grand idea underlying the predictions of Messiah's kingdom. Writing to the Galatians, and to the Romans, during his second visit to Corinth, he boldly sets forth the purely spiritual nature of Messiah's reign. He declares, that under that reign, — that is, under the Christian dispensation, — "there is neither Jew nor Greek, neither male nor female," but that all are "one in Christ Jesus." He affirms, that all who are Christ's, Gentiles as well as Jews, "are Abraham's seed, and heirs according to the promise;"[2] that the middle wall of partition between Jews and Gentiles is broken down by the gospel.[3] This was what so especially roused the enmity of the Jews. "He is not a Jew," says the apostle, "which is one outwardly; neither is that circumcision, which is outward in the flesh; but he is a Jew, who is one inwardly, and circumcision is that of the heart, in the spirit, and not in the letter."[4] Meaning, that Jewish descent and circumcision were no longer to be considered, in gathering a Christian church. Again, he declares Abraham

[1] Acts i. 7, 8.
[2] Gal. iii. 28, 29.
[3] Eph. ii. 14.
[4] Rom. ii. 28, 29.

to be "the father of all them that believe, though they be not circumcised." "For," he adds, "the promise that he should be the heir of the world, was not to Abraham, or his seed, through the law, but through the righteousness of faith."[1] Which can mean no less than that the promises and blessings connected with the covenant made with Abraham, are the common inheritance of all who possess his faith, to whatever age or nation they may belong.

Thus broadly did the holy apostle lay the ever-enduring foundations of the Christian Church. But the chronological development, and full acceptance of this grand idea by the apostles, was not until years after the day of Pentecost.

2. A remarkable fact, considering the positive nature of the Saviour's parting command, was the apparent backwardness of the apostles and their Jewish brethren to receive heathen converts into the church simply as Christians, without their being first circumcised. Notwithstanding the tongues of fire, notwithstanding the vision of Peter, notwithstanding the conversion of Gentiles to Christianity, but not to Judaism, and the gift of the Holy Ghost to them, notwithstanding the voice of the ascending Lord, commanding to go into all the world, and preach the gospel to every creature; baptizing all who believe in the name of the Father,

[1] Rom. iv. 11, 13.

and of the Son, and of the Holy Ghost; no formal decision on this subject appears to have been reached by the apostles, until after the memorable discussion at Jerusalem, in which Paul and Barnabas assisted, and declared the "miracles and wonders God had wrought among the Gentiles by them."[1] It was not until then, that the ritualistic doctrine, so obnoxious to those missionaries and to their Gentile converts, was authoritatively and publicly disowned. This was as many as ten or twelve years after Paul's conversion.

3. Another fact worthy of attention is, the probable cause of the long abode of the twelve apostles at Jerusalem. They had been instructed by their Lord to remain there until they were endowed with power from on high;[2] but they appear to have remained there much longer, and we are left by the sacred historian without any certain information *when*, and *how far*, any of them went forth to preach the gospel to Gentile nations.

It is nowhere intimated in the Scriptures that the apostles were wrong in this. We know that they were active in their ministry among the Jews. They "gave themselves continually to prayer and to the ministry of the word."[3] St. Paul, in his Epistle to the Galatians, testifies to the effective mission of Peter to his own countrymen. At the same time he informs the Galatian church that James, Peter, and

[1] Acts xv. 12. [2] Luke xxiv. 47, 49. [3] Acts vi. 4.

John, the three leading apostles, gave to him and Barnabas the right hand of fellowship when they were at Jerusalem, that they should labor among the Gentiles, while the three apostles and their immediate associates devoted themselves to the Jews.[1]

This apparently disproportionate amount of labor among the Jews, probably arose from the extreme danger to which the Jewish-Christian churches, and the Gentile churches, were exposed from the ritualistic Judaizing members of the church. Those erring but zealous brethren were everywhere an annoyance to the Apostle Paul during his whole missionary life. They were so even among churches gathered from the Gentiles; and how much worse must the case have been in Judea. Hence the necessity, at that time, of having an acknowledged human authority in matters ecclesiastical; and since the apostles alone possessed such authority, it may have been deemed important for most of them to reside where their advice and decisions could have the weight of the collective body, until the Christian commonwealth should have settled upon its true foundation. In this way we account for the prolonged residence of the apostles in Jerusalem. The necessity arose from that mysterious economy of sovereign grace, by which the gifts of the Holy Spirit were so restricted in their influence upon Jewish opinions and prejudices. And this may have

[1] Gal. ii. 8, 9.

been among the principal reasons, in the providence of God, why the original band of the apostles had no more opportunity for engaging in missions in the Gentile world.

This reserve of the illuminating agency of the Spirit is more noticeable from its having been in an age so conspicuous for the supernatural; but it is only the development of a permanent law of grace — namely, to put forth no more of supernatural agency than is needful — which we shall find in every age of the church, and to which we need to give heed.

4. It is due to the Apostle Paul, that I offer a few suggestions on the six or seven unrecorded years of his early Christian life, since they stand connected with the subject under consideration. I believe it is a common opinion, that his missionary life commenced with his tour to Cyprus and Asia Minor. But there is a strong improbability in such an assumption. From St. Paul's bold and zealous preaching of Christ in the synagogues of Damascus, "straightway" after his conversion, I think it right to infer, that he could not have been silent during the three years of his comparative retirement in Arabia; though we are not informed how he was employed. We may suppose it was in those years he received some at least of the abundant revelations of which he speaks so emphatically in his Epistle to the Corinthians.[1] At the expiration of

[1] 2 Cor. xii.

that time he went to Jerusalem to see Peter, and abode with him fifteen days. He saw, also, James, the Lord's brother.[1] And it is pleasant to think how large a part of this visit, both with Peter and James, must have been employed, by this young candidate for the foreign missionary service, in drawing from their well-stored memories the facts in the history of the blessed Saviour. It was probably at this time he was entranced while praying in the temple, and was directed by the Lord to leave Jerusalem at once, and go "far hence to the Gentiles," since the people of Jerusalem would not receive his testimony.[2]

He withdrew to his native province of Cilicia. And now we have as many as four more unrecorded years. But was not the apostle true to his original calling, and to the injunction to preach to the Gentiles, so lately received from his Master? I have no doubt that he was. This I infer from his decisive character; from his previous history at Damascus and Jerusalem; and from the fact that Barnabas, when overburdened with ministerial labors at Antioch, and needing a helper, went down to Tarsus to obtain the aid of Paul. Doubtless he had been successfully employed in planting those churches in Cilicia, and the adjoining districts of Syria, of which mention is made in the subsequent history.[3] And we may presume it was here and now he was sub-

[1] Gal. i. 18, 19. [2] Acts xxii. 18, 21. [3] Gal. i. 21.

jected to some of the Jewish scourgings, the beatings with Roman rods, the journeyings, and the perils of waters and robbers, in the city and in the wilderness, of which he speaks, fourteen years later, when writing to the Corinthians.[1]

It is recorded of Paul and Barnabas, that, in this reunion at Antioch, "they assembled themselves with the church, and taught much people, for a whole year." [2] These words of Scripture would seem to restrict their labors to the great heathen city of Antioch; but while I was travelling through that region, in the year 1855, and beheld the remains of ancient cities and villages all easy of access from Antioch, I could not resist the impression, that these two popular and enterprising preachers found time to make their voices heard over no small part of the then heathen country, now so usefully occupied by American missionaries.

About the year forty-five or forty-eight, the "prophets and teachers" in the church of Antioch were directed by the Holy Ghost, as they ministered to the Lord and fasted, to separate Barnabas and Saul, two of their number, and the most eminent and useful among the few who were laboring in that only partially Christianized metropolis of the East, for a more distant service than any hitherto performed. This was a new and important step in advance; and thus originated the mission to Cyprus

[1] 2 Cor. xi. [2] Acts xi. 26.

and Asia Minor, which occupied a year or more. And here it should be remarked, that their selection for this foreign mission was by the Holy Ghost; that their formal recognition by the laying on of hands, with prayer and fasting, was by their ministerial associates, the prophets and teachers; that this was in no sense an introduction to the gospel ministry, for they had both been in that ministry, and prominently so, for years; that there is no evidence of their having been in any proper sense then sent forth as missionaries by the church at Antioch; and no evidence of that church having done anything for their support on that mission, except what may be inferred from the fact that, on their return, they "gathered the church in that city together, and rehearsed" to it "all that God had done with them, and how he had opened the door of faith unto the Gentiles." And for two years or more after this, or (as the sacred narrative has it) "for a long time," there is no evidence of a movement in that metropolitan church to renew the mission.[1]

A principal cause of this apparent weakness of the Christian spirit in the Antiochian church may have been the influence of high-church teachers from Judea, who created no small dissension there by their notions of the constitution of the Christian Church; holding that all, who would enjoy its privileges, must first be circumcised after the Mosaic

[1] Acts xiv. 27, 28.

law. To be consistent, they must have held, that there was no true church in which this principle was not followed. Indeed, they went so far as to teach that none could be saved who were not circumcised after the manner of Moses, and thus entered the church.[1] They of course met with strenuous opposition from the two missionaries; and it was finally decided to refer the matter to the apostles at Jerusalem. Paul and Barnabas, with others, were accordingly sent thither for that purpose. The event shows that those two brethren must have gone with the determined purpose of having the principles on which churches among the Gentiles were to be constituted, fully and formally decided. Such, happily, was the result; and after laboring somewhat longer at Antioch, the two missionaries resolved to revisit the churches they had planted on their former missionary tour.

This meeting at Jerusalem was in after ages, and is still, called a Council. But it was not such, in the common acceptation of that term. It was simply a reference of an ecclesiastical question, which had awakened feeling and prejudices, and divided the opinion of the churches, to the judgment of the only body of men recognized as having authority in such matters, namely, the apostles; who, in an assembly of the whole Jerusalem church, gave a full hearing to the two missionary brethren.

[1] Acts xv. 1.

The constitution of the Gentile Christian churches was now settled by apostolic authority, and on a spiritual basis; and the needful preliminaries were completed for the regular prosecution of the life-work of the great apostle to the Gentiles.

With the apostle's second tour, — which gave the gospel to Europe, and to us, — about the year fifty-one, began his uninterrupted career as a foreign missionary; which terminated only with his martyrdom at Rome, between the years sixty-two and sixty-eight. A short time, truly, for so great a work.

Some of the facts, to which I have briefly adverted, are among the most notable in the history of the church, and doubtless involve principles worthy of our serious attention. For that age of marvelous divine interpositions, they certainly involve a reserve we should not have expected, in the use of supernatural agency on the minds of men. The spiritual illumination of the apostles, excepting the matter of inspiration, though extraordinary, differed only in degree from the ordinary spiritual illuminations. There was no coercion of the mind. Prejudice, error, conflicting opinions, were as possible in that age of miracles as they are now, and the triumphs of faith over sin were wrought in the same manner. "Miracles," as has been well said, "did not convert; inspiration did not sanctify. Then, as now, imperfection and evil clung to the members, and clogged the energies of the kingdom of God."[1] The slowness of the first missionaries in apprehending the spiritual nature of Christ's kingdom, and afterwards the spiritual nature of the Christian Church; their backwardness to receive Gentile converts into the church on a purely Christian basis; and finally the wonderful fact, as recorded in the New Testament, that nearly the whole of what may properly be called the foreign missionary work of that age, was performed by a single apostle and his assistants, must of course have been foreseen and intended by our Lord, and formed a part of his all-wise plan; and there must have been a fitness in these his chosen instruments, and in his manner of treating them, to the ends he had in view. Had he seen fit, how easily might he have given every one of his apostles, and every Jewish disciple, an immediate and thorough insight into the spiritual nature of his kingdom, so that the constitution of the Christian Church, for Gentiles as well as Jews, might have been settled without delay. This reserve of supernatural agency, at a time when it was so frequently exerted upon the minds of men, leaving the grand results to be wrought out more slowly by the operation of natural causes, may have been necessary to the best permanent development of the church. Had the apostles, James, Peter, and John, and their associates at Jerusalem, been carried forward as

[1] Conybeare and Howson's *Life of St. Paul,* vol. i. p. 456.

rapidly in the intellectual development of the Christian life, as was the Apostle Paul, it is easy to see that, without a constant miracle, they would all have been driven from Judea, as St. Paul actually was.

I should here repeat the remark, that in view of this tardy development of the exclusively spiritual nature of the apostolic missions, we shall be less surprised when we shall see, that a much longer time was occupied in developing the purely spiritual nature of the modern missionary work.

CHAPTER IV.

CHARACTERISTICS OF THE APOSTOLIC MISSIONS.

Silence of Inspired History as to Apostolic Missions. — Small Credit given to Uninspired Accounts. — Why the Mission of St. Paul is alone considered. — His Relation to the Lord Jesus. — His Understanding of Christ's Commission. — His Use of Local Churches, and Care for them. — His Confidence in them. — The Idea of the Local Church afterwards lost. — Its Importance. — How the Apostolic Missionaries appeared to their Contemporaries. — How supported. What Classes composed their Churches. — Influence of Pious Females. — Character of Primitive Churches. — Apostolic Success. — Summary.

It is among the mysteries of Providence, that the book of Acts gives no account of the closing labors of the Apostle Paul, and none of the labors of the other apostles bearing directly on the heathen world; if we except the mission of Peter to the Roman centurion, and of Philip to the Ethiopian eunuch. From a remark in the First Epistle of Peter it has been inferred, that he preached the gospel to the Jews eastward as far as Babylon; and from the superscription to the same Epistle it has been supposed, that his labors may have extended into Asia Minor. The zealous efforts of the Judaizers at Corinth suffice to account for the party formed in that church bearing Peter's name, without supposing that he was ever there. The evidence that Peter was never at Rome, preponderates over the evidence that he was. The reference in the Apocalypse to the seven churches of Asia gives support to the early tradition, that the Apostle John resided among them in his old age. Little credit is given, however, by the best ecclesiastical historians, to the uninspired accounts of the missions of the twelve apostles into distant regions of the unevangelized world, or to the stories of the martyrdom of any of them, except Peter, Paul, and James.

Of course in treating of the missions to the heathen after the year 50, our chief attention must be given to the Apostle Paul and his immediate associates. What I have to say concerning his mission, will be under distinct heads.

1. The Apostle Paul claimed to sustain a very high and intimate relation to the Lord Jesus, the foundation doubtless of his great courage and spiritual strength. It was nothing less than that he was Christ's ambassador, authorized to speak in his name when calling upon men to be reconciled to God.[1]

2. We learn what were the apostle's views of his responsibilities under Christ's commission, from the following emphatic declaration: "I have planted, Apollos watered, but God gave the increase; so neither is he that planted anything, neither he

[1] 2 Cor. v. 20.

that watereth, but God that giveth the increase."[1] His responsibility was for the faithful use of the prescribed means. In the spiritual culture of the world, it was for planting and watering. Then with respect to his views as to how far those means were to be employed, we learn that opportunity was to be given to all, so far as possible, to hear the gospel. This having been done in Pisidia, the sacred historian affirms, that "as many as were ordained to eternal life believed."[2] It was of course necessary for them to have opportunity to hear the gospel in order that they might believe, and herein lay the duty of the apostle and his fellow-laborers. This general publication of the gospel, with the gathering of the converts into churches (of which I shall speak under the next head), illustrates St. Paul's understanding of the import and obligation of Christ's command.

3. The kind of instrumentality, on which the apostle depended for success in his mission, clearly appears in his description of his ministrations at Corinth. He says, that when he came from Athens to Corinth, there to declare the testimony of God, it was not with any surpassing skill of eloquence, or philosophy. For it was no earthly knowledge, which he desired to display among them, but the knowledge of Jesus Christ alone, and him crucified. And in proclaiming this message, he had not used the

[1] 1 Cor. iii. 6, 7. [2] Acts xiii. 48.

persuasive arguments of human wisdom, but set forth the proofs of the might of the Holy Spirit, so that their faith might not rest on the wisdom of men, but on the power of God.[1]

Such was the eminently spiritual nature of the instrumentality employed by the apostle, in his personal ministry among the Gentiles.

But his stay in most places was generally and necessarily short. At Corinth it was indeed extended to nearly two years, and at Ephesus to nearly three. But in most places he could have spent only a few weeks, or months, though he may often have left behind him Silas, Timothy, or Titus, "to set in order the things which were wanting."

His grand means, as a missionary, was the gathering and forming of local churches. These appear to have been formed wherever there was a sufficient number of converts, each with its own presbyters, to whom must have been committed the pastoral oversight of the church, whatever may have been their other duties. In every church there appears to have been more than one, — an idea apparently borrowed from the Jewish synagogue, — and thus was formed the early pastorate. Such would seem to have been his practice; for it is expressly declared that, in his first recorded missionary tour, presbyters were ordained in every church; and in the great island of Crete, where he had not

1 *Life of St. Paul*, vol. ii. p. 36; 1 Cor. ii. 1–5.

time to do it himself, he left Titus, and required him to ordain them in every city.[1]

Such was the apostle's custom. He thus in each place put in requisition the power of association, organization, combination, of a self-governed Christian community; and the churches must necessarily have been self-supporting. They were formed for standing without foreign aid; and that they possessed a singular vitality, that they were self-propagating, as well as self-governing and self-supporting, is evident from the tenor of the Epistles addressed to them by their founder. Indeed, Christian churches are among the most vital of organizations. They are spiritual agencies, deriving their nature and motive power from the spiritual world. They are among the most indestructible of agencies. When the apostle had fully organized a church, he boldly left it. If he could, he visited it, and he wrote to it. To the larger churches, as I believe, he wrote repeatedly. How else could he have "daily" exercised, as he claims to have done, "the care of all the churches?"[2] Looking at the subject in the light of experience, and at the Apostle Paul as a man, with eminent epistolary powers, and freely acting out his nature, I come to no other conclusion, than that he wrote many letters; though Divine Providence was pleased to allow only certain of them to come down to us. Perhaps St.

[1] Titus i. 5. [2] 2 Cor. xi. 28.

Paul's short Epistles to Timothy, Titus, and Philemon, and St. John's to "the Elect Lady," and "the well-beloved Gaius," are specimens of their ordinary missionary correspondence. Added to all, was a constant habit of commending his churches to God in his prayers. It appears to have been a settled point with him, that a church once fairly planted and organized, with a proper arrangement for the pastoral care, might be safely left to itself, under the supervising grace of God. This, as will readily be seen, is a point of vital importance in the missionary work. Had not the apostolic idea of self-governing, self-supporting, self-propagating churches dropped out of the Christian mind so soon after the age of the apostles, not to be fully regained until modern times, how very different had been the history of Christendom, and of the world!

4. The apostolic missions belonging to a remote antiquity, and to an age of miracles and inspiration, we almost instinctively clothe the apostles, in our conceptions of them, with somewhat of the supernatural, or at least with the extraordinary. Let us then briefly consider the manner in which they must have appeared to their contemporaries.

For some years the name of Paul is mentioned in the Acts after that of his senior, Barnabas. The bold, dashing persecutor must have been singularly transformed by his conversion. He is modest and retiring; and, until he entered fully upon the great purpose of his life, was probably regarded as no more than a zealous, eloquent, promising young preacher, and, by the Judaizing Christians, as of decidedly radical tendencies. By many of the Jewish converts, if not for a time even by some of the apostles, he was looked upon with more or less of distrust. In his last ten or twelve years, he may be supposed to have moved among the churches he had gathered from the Gentiles much as Wesley did among the churches of his connection; and sometimes — as at Ephesus, where his miraculous powers were marvelously exercised — the enthusiasm he awakened may have more resembled that which attended the apostolic Whitfield.[1] His miraculous powers were of course less appreciated in that age, than such powers would be in our own. Unconverted Jews and heathens did not at all recognize the signs of his apostleship, and they generally looked upon him with aversion. In short, I suppose that the first Christian missionaries to the heathen were regarded very much as Christian missionaries are now; and that even the apostles, beyond a limited circle, inspired but little of the reverence which we so justly award to them.

5. It is interesting to inquire as to the manner in which the apostles and their missionary associates were supported in their travels and labors. The information we have on this subject is mostly inci-

[1] Acts xix. 11, 12.

dental. Their voyages in ships owned by heathen, their food and clothing, the animals on which they rode, — how were these and other expenses met during St. Paul's long and active career? No missionary society existed, to raise and remit funds. The churches of Judea were so poor, that they looked for relief in their poverty to churches gathered among the heathen. The apostle, in his letters, insists upon a principle, which he says was propounded by the Lord; "that they who preach the gospel should live by the gospel;" and he intimates that Peter and the other apostles acted on this principle in their mission to the Jews. But it was among the characteristics of this wonderful man, that he, in his mission to the Gentiles, declined doing so, and preferred laboring with his own hands to being dependent on his converts. He also intimated, that the other apostles having their field of labor especially among the Jews, and so being differently situated from himself, and more at home, had wives, who travelled with them; and he claimed the right to do the same thing. Nevertheless, in his peculiar circumstances and relations, he had not used that liberty, lest he "should hinder the gospel of Christ."[1] He doubtless refers to his itinerant life, and to the necessity of not deriving his support from churches gathered among the heathen. At Ephesus he claims to have labored not only for his own support, but also for the support of his assistants.[2]

[1] 1 Cor. ix. 4, 5, 14. [2] Acts xx. 34.

St. Paul's liberal education, and his high social position in early life, warrant the supposition that he inherited property to some extent; and this was doubtless used by him in defraying his early expenses. Then Barnabas, a native of Cyprus, who had contributed largely to the church-fund at Jerusalem, was probably able to defray the united cost of their first mission. The history states, that when the Apostle Paul started from Antioch, on his second grand missionary tour, the church of that city had made such progress in the missionary spirit, that they "recommended him unto the grace of God."[1] Having done so much, they could hardly have sent him away empty. But whatever were his means, they seem to have been exhausted soon after entering Europe. At Philippi, he and his companions enjoyed the hospitality of that noble woman, Lydia.[2] At Thessalonica, for some unexplained reason, he declined receiving anything from his converts there, and labored "night and day," because, as he says, he would not be chargeable to them;[3] while, at the same time, he allowed the Philippian church to supply his necessities. That church did this "once and again," while he was at Thessalonica; and afterwards at Corinth; and again, when he was a prisoner at Rome.[4] At Athens, after his speech on Mars' Hill, he would be joyfully entertained by his patrician convert, Diony-

[1] Acts xv. 40.
[2] Acts xvi. 15.
[3] Thess. ii. 9.
[4] Phil. ii. 25; iv. 15, 16; 2 Cor. xi. 9.

sius the Areopagite; who, I cannot doubt, afterwards took pleasure in seeing him over the Isthmus to Corinth. During the year and a half of his abode in Corinth, he declares to the church in that city, that he "was chargeable to no man;" for what was lacking to him the messengers from the distant Philippian church supplied, and he meant to keep himself from being burdensome to them. It must have been a matter of notoriety at Corinth, that he labored for his own support in the tent-factory of Aquila and Priscilla, having learned the craft at Tarsus, as a part of his Jewish education; though I imagine that one object he had in view, both there and at Ephesus, was to set an example of self-support to the native presbyters.

It is due, however, to the primitive Gentile churches to presume, that the Christian community, which was growing up under the self-denying labors of this holy apostle, became at length alive to the duty and privilege of carefully looking after his wants; and that while, for special reasons in the infancy of the churches, he refused to receive aid from certain of them, he was not ordinarily accustomed to refuse the hospitalities and kindly proffered benefactions of personal friends, as he passed from place to place. That love, which hung on his lips at Troas "even till break of day;" which received him in Galatia "as an angel of God, as Jesus Christ;" which fell weeping on his neck at Miletus, because they should see his face no more; and which wept at Cesarea over his approaching sufferings so as to break his heart, — would not have permitted him to want, when there was the power to prevent it.

Yet there is a passage in the Apostle John's brief letter to the "well-beloved Gaius," which seems to intimate the general usage, not only of St. Paul, but also of his associates, not to depend for their support on mission churches among the Gentiles. St. John expressly declares, that, for Christ's sake, "they went forth, taking nothing from the Gentiles."[1]

6. It is important, in a missionary point of view, to observe what classes of persons were gathered into the apostolic churches. Our Saviour evidently sought, in his private instructions, to guard his disciples against expecting great success among the rich and noble of the earth. The foundations of his spiritual kingdom were not to be laid among such. "Verily I say unto you," was his emphatic declaration, "that a rich man shall hardly enter into the kingdom of heaven." That this declaration made a strong impression at the time, is evident from its being recorded, with the addition of its more emphatic reduplication by three of the Evangelists.[2] There are indeed names of rich and noble converts on the pages of the New Testament; but the great

[1] 3 John v. 7. See 2 Cor. xii. 13.

[2] Matt. xix. 23, 24; Mark x. 23–27; Luke xviii. 24–27.

body was from the middle and poorer classes. It was eminently so among the Greeks at Corinth. "Ye see your calling, brethren," the apostle wrote to them, "how that not many wise men after the flesh, not many mighty, not many noble, are called; but God hath chosen the foolish things of the world, to confound the wise; and God hath chosen the weak things of the world, to confound the things that are mighty; and base things of the world, and things which are despised, hath God chosen, yea, and things which are not, to bring to nought things which are; that no flesh should glory in his presence."[1] One of the ancient historians of the church,[2] speaking of the early Christians, says,—"They were neither rich nor learned, but workers in brass, builders, house-slaves, laborers, tree-fellers, and women." In an age of the world when wealth and power were never held in higher estimation, the leaven of the gospel was cast into the lower and middle strata of society, and worked upwards, till the whole was leavened. It is interesting to notice,—

7. That the influence of pious females is a conspicuous fact in the Gospels, the Acts, and the Epistles. There is no need that I illustrate this. Pious women, as is well known, have a noble record in the missionary life of the great apostle, as they also have in that of our blessed Lord.

8. The tardy development of the *Ecclesia*, the

[1] 1 Cor. i. 26–29. [2] Theodoret, A. D. 420.

church, in the apostolic age, has been already illustrated. Not till after nearly a score of years was it fully settled, that Gentile churches should not be required to conform to Jewish customs and prejudices. While we nowhere find distinct traces in the New Testament of the associated, organized denominationalism of our times, it is not on that account to be condemned, when not opposed to the spirit of the gospel. It is obvious, that neither Presbyteries, Consociations, Associations, or Conferences could be formed, until there were churches enough of which to form them, churches sufficiently trained and near together to be advantageously associated. It may be that the sacred history closed before there was a full ecclesiastical development in any direction.[1] But the local church in its principles and outline is there; and modern missionaries from the several evangelical communities are at no loss for an example as regards such churches.

[1] "Neither in the New Testament, nor in any ancient document whatever, do we find anything recorded, from whence it might be inferred, that any of the minor churches were at all dependent on, or looked up for direction to those of greater magnitude or consequence; on the contrary, several things occurred therein, which put it out of all doubt that every one of them enjoyed the same rights, and was considered as being on a footing of the most perfect equality with the rest. Indeed it cannot, — I will not say be proved, but even be made to appear probable, from any estimony divine or human, — that in this age it was the practice for several churches to enter into and maintain amongst themselves that sort of association, which afterwards came to subsist amongst the churches of almost every province." — Mosheim, *Commentaries*, vol. i. p. 196.

It is more to my purpose to inquire into the character of the apostolic churches, than into their method of organization and government. The common opinion, that those churches excelled the churches of modern times in their Christian development, is not sustained by a thoughtful reading of the inspired documents, nor could such a thing be reasonably expected. The work of the Holy Spirit, in its permanent results on the hearts and minds and lives of men, appears not to have differed materially then, from what it is in our day. St. Paul seems to have had as many and as great trials with his mission churches, as do modern missionaries with theirs. In the church of Corinth, on which the apostle had bestowed so much labor, he had to lament the many carried away by false teachers, disorders in their worship, irregularities at the Lord's Supper, neglect of discipline, party divisions, litigations, "debates, envyings, wraths, strifes, backbitings."[1] And how soon were the Galatians seduced from their loyalty to the truth, even to what seemed "another gospel;" so that the apostle feared he had labored among them in vain.[2] He thought it needful to exhort the Ephesian church to put away lying, to steal no more, and to have no more to do with fornication and coveteousness.[3] He also exhorts the Colossians not to lie one to another;[4] and

[1] 2 Cor. xii. 20.
[2] Gal. i. 6; iv. 11.
[3] Eph. iv. 25, 28; v. 3.
[4] Col. iii. 9.

the Thessalonians to withdraw from such of their brethren as walked disorderly.[1] He cautions Timothy against fables, endless genealogies, and profane and vain babblings, as if such were prevalent in some of the churches; and speaks of preachers who, after making shipwreck of their faith, added blasphemies to their heresies.[2] And the Apostle John declares, somewhat later, that many "antichrists" had gone out from the church.[3]

As there were great defects, so there were also great excellences coexisting in the churches gathered by the apostles. At the very time of St. Paul's censures of the Corinthians, he declares that church to be "enriched by Jesus Christ in all utterance and in all knowledge," so that it came behind in no gift.[4] While he so seriously cautions the Ephesians, he ceases not to give thanks for "their faith in the Lord Jesus, and their love unto all the saints."[5] He thanked God upon every remembrance of the Philippians;[6] and when he wrote to the Colossians, he gave thanks for their faith in Christ Jesus, and their love to all the saints.[7] And how abundant his commendations of the Thessalonians, whom he declares to be "ensamples to all that believe in Macedonia and Achaia."[8]

[1] 2 Thess. iii. 6.
[2] 1 Tim. i. 19, 20; vi. 3–5.
[3] 1 John ii. 18, 19.
[4] 1 Cor. i. 5, 7.
[5] Eph. i. 15, 16.
[6] Phil. i. 3.
[7] Col. i. 3, 4.
[8] 1 Thess. i. 3, 7.

We come to this result as to the character of the apostolic churches: that while the primitive converts were remarkable, as a class, for the high tone of their religious feelings, and the simplicity and strength of their faith, they were deficient in a clear, practical apprehension of the ethical code of the gospel. All things considered, this was not strange; and we should always remember this, when we contemplate the character of modern mission churches.

9. Finally, I must make some estimate of the amount of success, on the whole, which resulted from the apostolic missions; though the materials for this are imperfect, owing to the brevity of the sacred narrative.

The Jews had synagogues, the pagans had temples; but there is no reason to suppose that church-buildings were erected anywhere in connection with the apostolic missions. The religious assemblies were private. No separate and distinguished edifice attracted attention; and ecclesiastical history affirms, that there were no Christian houses of worship erected before the third century.[1]

There is no reason to suppose that the Apostle Paul was privileged to see any one district, or even any one city, so much as nominally Christianized. Antioch was not for at least two centuries. The people in Lesser Asia, both Jews and Greeks, are said all to have heard the word of the Lord Jesus;

[1] Neander, vol. i. p. 291; Mosheim, vol. i. p. 134.

but though the worship of Diana is declared to have suffered much decline in consequence, the mob at Ephesus drove the apostle away at last, and showed that paganism was still the dominant power.

The most that can be said — and that is saying very much — is that self-supporting, self-governing, and self-propagating churches had been planted in all the principal cities of the Roman Empire; as far West, certainly, as Rome, and as far East as Mesopotamia; each under the instruction and care of its own presbyters. Fabricius has collected from the New Testament the names of more than fifty places, which must have had churches.[1] Doubtless the whole number was greater. Judea, Samaria, Syria, Asia Minor, Macedonia, Greece and its Islands, and perhaps a portion of Western Italy, had churches. The great apostle planted them "from Jerusalem round about unto Illyricum."

These churches were lights shining amid a general and deep spiritual gloom. We may compare the whole process to the lighting up of some great metropolis. Night is not thereby converted into day. A distant observer would not perceive that any impression was made upon the darkness. Yet the wayfarer in the street, or crossing a public square, would find his path illuminated, and go on his way rejoicing.[2] But this illustration, however

1 *Salutaris Lux Evangelii,* etc., p. 83.

2 This illustration first occurred to me at Calcutta, while looking out

expressive, is inadequate. For each one of those churches, scattered over the empire, was a growing influence, and growing the more rapidly for the frequent and cruel persecutions, and was constantly extending its illumination; until, through the divine blessing, under the combined influence of the whole, the Roman Empire bowed to the supremacy of the gospel, and assumed the Christian name.

Such were the apostolic missions. Such were the efforts made for propagating the gospel among the heathen by missionaries under a special divine guidance. It was by gathering converts into churches at the centres of influence, and putting them under native pastoral inspection and care. The means employed were spiritual; namely, the gospel of Christ. The power relied upon for giving efficacy to these means was divine; namely, the promised aid of the Holy Spirit. The main success was among the middle and lower classes of society; and the responsibilities for self-government, self-support, and self-propagation were thrown at once upon the several churches.

Another chapter will show how far the apostolic missions to the heathen reappear in missions of the present day.

one dark night upon the large, gas-lighted public square. I thought, this dark yet illuminated space is India, and the lights are her missions.

CHAPTER V.

IRISH MISSIONS IN THE EARLY AGES.

Nestorian Missions. — Irish Missions. — The Present and Past of Ireland contrasted. — Hume's Statement. — D'Aubigne's. — McLauchlan's. — Ireland distinguished for its Learning, Piety, and Missions. A Refuge for the Church. — Its Situation favorable. — Early History of Patrick. — A True Missionary. — Not connected with Rome. His Mission to Ireland. — Followed by a Native Ministry. — Prevalence of Religion. — Monasteries and Schools. — Why not spoken of as a "Culdee" Mission. — Columba's Mission. — Monastery of Iona. — Mission of Columbanus. — His Character. — Among the Pagans of Burgundy. — His Schools and Co-laborers. — Teachings. — Banishment, and Subsequent History. — Gallus, the Apostle of Switzerland. — Missionaries from Ireland. — Extent and Nature of their Labors. — Defects in their Missions. — Iona. — Irish Missions connected with the Reformation of Luther. — Melancholy Decline. — Reflections and Inferences.

The most remarkable of the missions in the ages subsequent to the apostles, was doubtless that of the Nestorians in Central and Eastern Asia, begun in the fourth century, and extending onward — it may be with prolonged interruptions — through the greater part of a thousand years. But the missions most interesting to us, are those which went forth from Ireland to Continental Europe, in the sixth and seventh centuries. So little were they known to me when I began to investigate their history, that I pursued the investigation with increasing wonder and delight.

In a religious point of view, Ireland of the present day is painfully contrasted with Ireland as it was a thousand years ago. Yet one would scarcely think so, on reading what Hume says of it, previous to its conquest by Henry II. in the year 1172.

"The Irish," he says, "from the beginning of time, had been buried in the most profound barbarism and ignorance; and as they were never conquered, or even invaded by the Romans, from whom all the Western world derived its civility, they continued still in the most rude state of society, and were distinguished by those vices alone, to which human nature, not tamed by education or restrained by laws, is forever subject."[1] He adds, indeed, that "the Irish had, by precedent missions from the Britons, been imperfectly converted to Christianity; and, what the Pope regarded as the surest mark of their imperfect conversion, they followed the doctrines of their first teachers, and had never acknowledged any subjection to the See of Rome."

How remote the first of these extracts is from historic truth, in respect to Ireland before its subjection to the Pope of Rome, will appear as we proceed.

But Ireland has suffered more from the errors of

[1] Hume's *History of England*, vol. i. p. 328.

ecclesiastical historians, than from those of mere secular writers. The excellent D'Aubigné, in his history of the "Reformation in England," misled by his authorities, has done much injustice to the ancient Irish Christians; and Irish authors very properly take exception to his statement concerning the propagation of the gospel on the continent of Europe. "The missionary bishops of *Britain*," he says, "traversed the low countries, Gaul, Switzerland, Germany, and even Italy. . . . . Columbanus (whom we must not confound with Columba), feeling in his heart the burning of the fire which the Lord had kindled upon earth, quitted Bangor in 590, with twelve other missionaries, and carried the gospel to the Burgundians, Franks, and Swiss. . . . . Thus was Britain faithful in planting the standard of Christ in the heart of Europe." Again: "The British Church, which, at the beginning of the seventh century, carried faith and civilization into Burgundy, the Vosges mountains, and Switzerland, might well have spread them both over Britain." Once more: "At that time there existed at Bangor, in North Wales, a large Christian society, amounting to nearly three thousand individuals, collected together to work with their own hands, to study, and to pray, and from whose bosoms numerous missionaries (Columbanus was among the number) had from time to time gone forth."[1]

[1] *History of the Reformation*, vol. v. pp. 29, 34.

It will be seen that the honor of one of the most protracted, influential, and noble missions subsequent to the apostolic age, which belonged chiefly to Ireland, is here given to Britain.

The Rev. Thomas McLauchlan, a recent historian of the Church of Scotland, has fallen into a similar error. He assumes (what to a certain extent is true) that the ancient Scots, emigrating from Ireland, inhabited a part of Albania (the present Scotland), as well as Ireland. He also assumes, that the monastery of Iona was a Scottish institution; and calling the missions Scottish missions, and rarely, if ever, Irish, he leaves an impression very like to that of D'Aubigné. His unqualified use of the word "Scottish" is somewhat remarkable; and the Irish biographer of Archbishop Usher charges the Scottish writers with claiming, without hesitation, for their country everything that is said of "Scotia," utterly disregarding the teaching of all the ancient historians.[1]

I shall not find it difficult to show, that the historians above mentioned all wrote under a misapprehension.

[1] Usher's *Works*, vol. i. p. 144. It is due to Mr. McLauchlan to say, that his error originated in no desire to gain authority for his own system of church polity; for he cordially acknowledges, that it would be vain to look among the establishments in the early "Scottish Church," for anything like what is called a Presbyterian organization. *Early Scottish Church*, pp. 171, 172.

D'Aubigne quotes the following from the celebrated Alçuin, of the court of Charlemagne, in support of his first assertion: "Antiquo tempore doctissimi solebant magistri de Hibernia Britanniam, Galliam, Italiam venire, et multos per ecclesias Christi fecisse profectus." Now the declaration here is, that the most learned teachers in ancient times were accustomed to come from Ireland to visit the churches in Britain, Gaul, and Italy. Nor was Columbanus from Bangor in Wales, as is asserted, but from one of the most renowned of the Irish monasteries, at Bangor in Ireland, founded by the Abbot Comgall, early in the sixth century, and embracing at one time a community numbering three thousand.[1] In a life of Columbanus, still extant in the Latin language, written in the seventh century by Jonas, his contemporary and countryman, his birth is declared to have been in Hibernia. It is added that Ireland was "then inhabited by the Scots, who, though without the laws of other nations, yet in the worthiness of the Christian faith exceeded the piety of all other people."[2] The venerable Bede, writing in the eighth century, calls Hibernia by the name of Scotia, and the inhabitants he calls Scots. And Archbishop Usher affirms that no author, before the eleventh century, has described Albania under the name of Scotland, and that the name of Ireland

[1] Neander's *Memorials*, p. 434.

[2] Webb's *Annotations on D'Aubigne*, p. 41.

until then was Scotia, and its inhabitants were called Scots.[1] The famous monastery of Iona was founded by a native of Ireland, and was claimed as an Irish institution by the Synod of Ulster, as late as the thirteenth century.[2] Neander, speaking of the fifth and sixth centuries, represents the wild parts of Ireland as covered with monasteries, that were distinguished for Christian discipline, industry, knowledge of the Scriptures, and such general knowledge as could be obtained from Britain and France.[3] Henry, Bishop of Auxerre, writing to Charles the Bald, about the middle of the ninth century, informs him that Ireland, notwithstanding the dangers of the sea, was sending crowds of philosophers to their shores. Under the successors of Charlemagne, Hibernians were extensively engaged in the work of education throughout the empire, and were the chief Biblical translators and commentators of Europe. Mosheim, writing concerning the ninth century, says of the Irish, that they "were lovers of learning;" and "distinguished themselves in those times of ignorance by the culture of the sciences beyond all other European nations." He adds, that "so early as the eighth century, they illustrated the doctrines of religion by the principles of philosophy," and "were the first teachers of

1 Usher's *Works*, vol. i. p. 144.

2 Webb's *Annotations*, p. 35.

3 Neander's *Memorials*, p. 434.

the scholastic theology in Europe."[1] Neander, speaking of the theological teaching in the ninth century, declares the Irish monasteries to have been "the seat of science and art, whence, and for a long time afterwards, teachers in the sciences and useful arts scattered themselves in all directions." He says, moreover, that there issued from the Irish Church "a more original and free development of theology, than was elsewhere to be found, and was thence propagated to other lands."[2]

These testimonies are applicable to Ireland for the space of about four centuries, from the fifth to the ninth, and present us with a very interesting view of the Irish people. Ireland then served, under Divine Providence, as a convenient refuge for the church, in a very disordered and dangerous period of the nominally Christian world; being the remotest of the European islands, secured by distance, and by having England and Scotland as a rampart, from the destructive inroads of Goths and Huns, and, for a long time, from those also of the sea-roving Northmen. For many ages it was a sanctuary for Scriptural instruction and scholarship, in the intellectual night that followed the downfall of the Roman Empire. It was also the source of gospel missions, which sowed the seeds of the great Reformation in Germany, Eng-

[1] Webb's *Annotations*, pp. 40, 141, 142, 148

[2] Quoted by Webb, p. 143.

land, and Scotland, that came as a blessing to the world, eight or nine centuries afterwards.

The gospel was planted in Ireland by a single missionary, self-moved — or rather divinely moved — and self-supported. His historic name was Patrick, and the Roman Catholics (claiming him, without reason, as their own) call him St. Patrick. He was born about the year 410, and most probably in some part of Scotland. His parents were Christians, and instructed him in the gospel. Patrick's first visit to the field of his future mission was in his youth, as a captive of pirates, who carried him away, with many others, as a prisoner. Patrick was sold to a chieftain, who placed him in charge of his cattle. His own statement is, that his heart was turned to the Lord during the hardships of his captivity. "I prayed many times a day," he says. "The fear of God and love to him were increasingly kindled in me. Faith grew in me, so that in one day I offered a hundred prayers, and at night almost as many; and when I passed the night in the woods, or on the mountains, I rose up to pray in the snow, ice, and rain, before daybreak. Yet I felt no pain. There was no sluggishness in me, such as I now find in myself, for then the spirit glowed within me." This is extracted from what is called the "Confession" of Patrick, written in his old age.

Some years later, he was again taken by the

pirates, but soon regained his liberty, and returned home. His parents urged him to remain with them; but he felt an irresistible call to carry the gospel to those among whom he had passed his youth as a bondman. "Many opposed my going," he says in his "Confession," "and said, behind my back, 'Why does this man rush into danger among the heathen, who do not know the Lord?' It was not badly intended on their part; but they could not comprehend the matter on account of my uncouth disposition! Many gifts were offered me with tears, if I would remain. But, according to God's guidance, I did not yield to them; not by my own power, it was God who conquered in me, and I withstood them all; so that I went to the people of Ireland to publish the gospel to them, and suffered many insults from unbelievers, and many persecutions, even unto bonds, resigning my liberty for the good of others. And if I am found worthy, I am ready to give up my life with joy for His name's sake."[1]

In such a spirit did this apostle to Ireland commence his mission, about the year 440; not far from the time when Britain was finally evacuated by the Romans.

A papal legend makes Patrick to have visited Rome, and to have received his appointment as a missionary from Pope Celestine. This, though apparently credited by Mosheim, is rejected by Neander

[1] Neander's *Memorials*, pp. 426–428.

as incredible. The oldest of what profess to be the Lives of Patrick, is believed to have been written at least four hundred years after his time. The one by Joceline, in his "Acta Sanctorum" (Lives of the Saints), dates as late as the twelfth century, and all are regarded as very doubtful authority. What is commonly known as his "Confession" (already quoted) is almost universally received as authentic. It was written in his old age. The "Epistola ad Coroticum," and the hymn known as his "Lorica," are regarded as his. Of high authority, as claiming to be contemporary with him, or nearly so, is the "Hymn of Sechnal" or "Secundinus," and a biographic poem in his praise, called the "Hymn of Fiace," composed not more than eighty years after his death.[1]

Patrick being acquainted with the language and customs of the Irish people, as a consequence of his early captivity, gathered them about him in large assemblies at the beat of a kettle-drum, and told the story of Christ so as to move their hearts. Having taught them to read, he encouraged the importation of useful books from England and France. He established cloisters after the fashion of the times, which were really missionary schools, for educating the people in the knowledge of the gospel, and for training a native ministry and missionaries; and he claims to have baptized many thousands of the people.

[1] *London Quarterly Review*, April, 1866, p. 252.

It is perhaps needful to a just appreciation of the case, that I quote the discriminating remarks of Dr. Todd, one of his ablest Protestant biographers. After stating that Patrick always addressed himself, in the first instance, to the kings or chieftains, Dr. Todd says: "The people may not have adopted the outward profession of Christianity, which was all that, perhaps, in the first instance they adopted, from any clear or intellectual appreciation of its superiority to their former religion; but to obtain from the people even an outward profession of Christianity was an important step to ultimate success. It secured toleration, at least, for Christian institutions. It enabled Patrick to plant in every tribe his churches, schools, and monasteries. He was permitted, without opposition, to establish, among the half pagan inhabitants of the country, societies of holy men, whose devotion, usefulness, and piety soon produced an effect upon the most barbarous and savage hearts.

"This was the secret of the rapid success attributed to St. Patrick's preaching in Ireland. The chieftains were at first the real converts. The baptism of the chieftains was immediately followed by the adhesion of the clan. The clansmen pressed eagerly around the missionary, who had baptized the chief, anxious to receive that mysterious initiation into the new faith, to which their chieftain and father had submitted. The requirements preparatory to baptism do not seem to have been very rigorous; and it is, therefore, by no means improbable that in Tirawley, and other remote districts, where the spirit of clanship was strong, Patrick, as he tells us himself he did, may have baptized some thousands of men."

I cannot forbear also quoting a summary view of the life and labors of the Irish apostle.

"On the whole, the biographers of St. Patrick, notwithstanding the admixture of much fable, have undoubtedly portrayed in his character the features of a great and judicious missionary. He seems to have made himself 'all things,' in accordance with the apostolic injunction, to the rude and barbarous tribes of Ireland. He dealt tenderly with their usages and prejudices. Although he sometimes felt it necessary to overturn their idols, and on some occasions risked his life, he was guilty of no offensive or unnecessary iconoclasm. A native himself of another country, he adopted the language of the Irish tribes, and conformed to their political institutions. By his judicious management, the Christianity which he founded became self-supporting. It was endowed by the chieftains without any foreign aid. It was supplied with prelates [ecclesiastics?] by the people themselves; and its fruits were soon seen in that wonderful stream of zealous missionaries, the glory of the Irish Church, who went forth in the sixth and seventh centuries to evangelize the barbarians of Central Europe."[1]

When this zealous missionary died, about the year 493, his disciples, who seem all to have been natives of Ireland, — a native ministry, — continued his work in the same spirit. The monasteries became at length so numerous and famous, that Ireland was called *Insula Sanctorum*, the "Island of Saints."[2]

It gives a wrong idea of these institutions to call them monasteries, or to call their inmates monks. "They were schools of learning and abodes of piety, uniting the instruction of the college, the labors of the workshop, the charities of the hospital, and the worship of the church. They originated partly in a mistaken view of the Christian life, and partly out of the necessity of the case, which drove Christians to live together for mutual protection. The missionary spirit, and consequent religious activity, prevailing in the Irish monasteries, preserved them for a long time from the asceticism and mysticism incidental to the monastic life, and made them a source of blessing to the world."[3] The celibacy of the clergy was not enjoined in those times.[4] Married men were connected with the cloisters, living, how-

[1] *Life of St. Patrick*, pp. 499, 514.

[2] Neander's *Church History*, vol. iii. p. 103; and *Memorial*, p. 434.

[3] Walsh's *Christian Missions*, p. 74.

[4] Usher's *Works*, vol. i. p. 137; vol. iv. p. 294.

ever, in single houses. The Scriptures were read, and ancient books were collected and studied.

The missions which went forth from these institutions, as also those from England and Wales, are frequently called "Culdee" missions; but as that term is of uncertain import, and appears to add nothing to the significance of the history, but rather the contrary, it is not here used.

Neither have I deemed it necessary to discuss the ecclesiastical position and relations of Patrick and his three hundred and fifty Irish associates. Episcopal writers call them all bishops; but are naturally perplexed by their great number. In my apprehension, they have their counterpart in the foreign missionaries of modern times and their native clerical associates, — more especially the latter; the one class (including Patrick himself) being neither more nor less bishops than the other. In this manner, we are not incommoded with the difficulty of accounting for the acknowledged fact, of the very slight reference made to Patrick by the Irish missionaries of subsequent ages; and I find no reason in that fact for assuming, as some have done, that those missionaries were connected with the British and not with the Irish churches.

The names of Columba and Columbanus are familiar to the readers of ecclesiastical history. Both were Irish missionaries, and both were from the institution at Bangor, in Ireland.

Columba's mission was to the Picts of Scotland, and was entered upon at the age of forty-two, in the year 563. This was thirteen hundred years ago, and about seventy years after the time of Patrick. He was accompanied by twelve associates, and was the founder of the celebrated monastery on Iona, an island situated to the north of Scotland, now reckoned one of the Hebrides. This school of the prophets, which has had an enduring fame, became one of the chief lights of that age. Continuing thirty-five years under Columba's management, it attained a high reputation for Biblical studies, and other sciences; and missionaries went from it to the northern and southern Picts of Scotland, and into England, along the eastern coast to the Thames, and to the European continent.[1]

Columbanus entered on his mission to the partially Christianized, but more especially to the pagan portions of Europe, in the year 589. That he was an evangelical missionary may be confidently inferred from the tenor of his life, and from the records of his Christian experience.

He thus writes: "O Lord, give me, I beseech thee, in the name of Jesus Christ, thy Son, my God, that love which can never cease, that will kindle my lamp but not extinguish it, that it may burn in me

[1] Neander's *Church History*, vol. iii. p. 10; McLauchlan's *History of the Church of Scotland*, pp. 225, 226.

and enlighten others. Do thou, O Christ, our dearest Saviour, thyself kindle our lamps, that they may evermore shine in thy temple; that they may receive unquenchable light from thee, that will enlighten our darkness, and lessen the darkness of the world. My Jesus, I pray thee, give thy light to my lamp, that in its light the most holy place may be revealed to me in which thou dwellest as the eternal Priest, that I may always behold thee, desire thee, look upon thee in love, and long after thee."[1]

Columbanus went first to France, taking with him twelve young men, as Columba had done, to be his co-laborers; men who had been trained under his especial guidance. Here, as a consequence of continual wars, political disturbances, and the remissness of worldly-minded ecclesiastics, the greatest confusion and irregularity prevailed, and there was great degeneracy in the monastic orders. Columbanus preferred casting his lot among the pagans of Burgundy, and chose for his settlement the ruins of an ancient castle in the midst of an immense wilderness, at the foot of the Vosges mountains.[2] There they often suffered hunger, until the wilderness had been in some measure subdued, and the earth brought under cultivation. The mission then became self-supporting, but we are not informed by what means the previous expenses were defrayed. Preaching was a part of their duty, though there

[1] Neander's *Memorials*. [2] Neander's *Memorials*, p. 35.

is less said of this, than of their efforts to impart the benefits of a Christian education to the children of the higher classes. The surrounding poor were taught gratuitously. All the pupils joined in tilling the fields, and such was their success in education, that the Frankish nobles were forward to place their sons under their care. It was the most famous school in Burgundy, and there was not room in the abbey for all who pressed to gain admittance; so that it became necessary to erect other buildings, and to bring a large number of teachers over from Ireland to meet the demand.

Here the eminent missionary pursued his labors for a score of years. As he represents himself to have buried as many as seventeen of his associates during twelve years, the number of his co-laborers must have been large. The discipline which Columbanus imposed on the monastic life was severe, but perhaps scarcely more so than was required by the rude spirit of the age; and he took pains to avoid the error so prevalent in the Romish Church, of making the essence of piety to consist in externals. The drift of his teaching was, that everything depended on the state of the heart. Both by precept and example he sought to combine the contemplative with the useful. At the same time he adhered, with a free and independent spirit, to the peculiar religious usages of his native land. As these differed in some important respects from what were then prevalent among the degenerate Frankish clergy, he had many enemies among them who sought to drive him from the country. This they at length effected, with the aid of the wicked mother of the reigning prince. Columbanus was ordered to return to Ireland, and to take his countrymen with him. This he did not do, but repaired first to Germany, and then to Switzerland. He spent a year near the eastern extremity of the Lake Constance, laboring among the Suevi, a heathen people in that neighborhood. The territory coming at length under the dominion of his enemies, he crossed the Alps, in the year 612, into Lombardy, and founded a monastery near Pavia; and there this apostle to Franks, Swabians, Bavarians, and other nations of Germany, passed the remainder of his days, and breathed out his life on the twenty-first of November, 615, aged seventy-two years.[1]

Gallus, a favorite pupil and follower of Columbanus, remained behind in consequence of illness, and became the apostle of Switzerland. He also was an Irishman, and was characterized, as was his master, by love for the sacred volume. In what was then a wilderness he founded a monastery, "which led to the clearing up of the forest, and the conversion of the land into cultivable soil, and it afterwards became celebrated under his name, St. Gall." Here he labored for the Swiss and Swabian population till

[1] Webb's *Annotations*, p. 71.

his death, in the year 640.[1] This monastery was preëminent for the number and beauty of the manuscripts prepared by its monks; many of which, and among others, some fragments of a translation of the Scriptures into the Alemanni language, about the year 700, are said to be preserved in the libraries of Germany.

There is no special advantage in going further into the details of these missions. Neander is of the opinion, that the number of missionaries who passed over from Ireland to the continent of Europe must have been great; though of very few is there any exact information. Wherever they went, cloisters were founded, and the wilderness soon gave place to cultivated fields. According to Ebrard, there were more than forty cloisters in the vicinity of the Loire and Rhone, which were governed according to the rules of Columbanus, and to which emigrants came from Ireland as late as the close of the seventh century. He also affirms, that Germany was almost wholly heathen when that missionary entered it. But before the year 720, the gospel had been proclaimed by himself and his countrymen, from the mountains of Switzerland down to the islands in the delta of the Rhine, and eastward from that river to the river Inn, and the Bohemian forest, and the borders of Saxony, and still farther on the

[1] Neander's *History*, vol. iii. p. 36.

sea-coast. All the really German tribes within those borders were in subjection to the Christian faith as it had been taught by the Irish missionaries.[1]

It was in 723 that the English Winfred, better known as Boniface, began his well-intentioned and successful labors to reduce the Germanic Irish Church to the Roman rule. But into that part of the history — the subjection of the German Church to the Romish See — I cannot now enter, as it does not come within my proper range.

Ebrard's earnest testimony to the evangelical nature of the Irish missions, should not be overlooked. He declares, that they read the Scriptures in the original text; translated them wherever they went; expounded them to the congregations; recommended the regular and diligent perusal of them; and held them as the living word of Christ. The Scriptures were their only rule of faith. They preached the inherited depravity of man; the atoning death of Christ; justification without the merit of works; regeneration as the life in Him who died for us; and the sacraments as signs and seals of grace in Christ. They held to no transubstantiation; no purgatory; no prayers to saints; and their worship was in the native language. But though they used neither pictures nor images, they seem to have been attached to the use of the simple cross;

[1] Ebrard's *Manual*, vol. i. pp. 409, 410, 415, 416.

and Gallus, the distinguished companion of Columbanus, is said, when marking out a place on which to erect a monastery, to have done it by means of a cross, from which he had suspended a capsule of relics.[1] Complete exemption from superstition, was perhaps among the impossibilities of that age.

The statement of evangelical truths in the ancient Irish Church, may be enlarged. The life of Columbanus, by his friend and successor Jonas, somehow escaped destruction under the papal interdict, and is our fullest record of individual Irish missionaries. We have also a statement of the doctrinal views of two distinguished missionaries from Ireland, in the eighth century, named Clement and Virgilius; and of another, still more distinguished, named Claude, in the ninth century, two hundred years after Columbanus. From these and other sources it is inferred, that the early Irish Church did not inculcate adoration of relics and images; nor pilgrimages; nor auricular confessions, penances, or absolution; nor masses; nor works of supererogation; nor adoration of the Virgin Mary; nor baptismal regeneration. And Mosheim declares the Irish divines to have been the only ones in the ninth century, who refused to submit implicitly to the dictates of authority.

Yet there were defects in the Irish missions, grow-

[1] Ebrard's *Manual*, vol. i. p. 396; Neander's *History*, vol. iii. p. 36.

ing out of the times, and such as were not easily avoided.

1. They did not fully recover the apostolic idea, which had been lost, of the local, self-governed church. Their churches were, so to speak, monasteries or colleges, held together by the authority of priest or abbot. Hence the perpetual pupilage of their missionary communities, and the consequent protracted need in those communities of foreign culture and aid. In our own sense of the term, they appear to have had no local, self-governed churches. Nor was religious freedom of thought and action a current idea in those ages, even in the Irish cloisters.[1] Then the Irish missions were too protracted. Irish missionaries continued to be needed, and to follow each other into Germany for successive ages. And so it must be in missions where the church of the Apostle Paul is not a primary element in the working of the mission.

2. The leading instrumentality employed by the Irish missionaries, appears to have been education. Light and influence were thus diffused, and the education was an essential thing. But though the Scriptures appear to have been freely used by the missionaries, so far as was possible in an age of costly manuscripts, and though there was preaching, and often no doubt much of it, yet schools would seem to have been the predominant agency. These

[1] Neander's *Memorials of Christian Life*, p. 438.

were so in the monastery; and while they may have been essential to the life of such institutions as grew out of the Irish missions, they had not, in themselves, the renovating, life-giving power essential to the creation and preservation of the organized, self-propagating church. And the predominance of school instruction over preaching, if such were the fact, was an error.

3. Another defect in these missions was their want of intimate connection with the churches at home. The missionaries appear not to have been sent forth by home churches acting in any capacity, not even by the cloisters, nor to have derived their support from their native land.[1] We do not know how they met the expense of travelling into what must have been to them remote regions. But when once they were there, they became associated in schools, or cloisters, and were soon self-supported. And having abundant occupation, and no strong motive for keeping their work before the attention of Christians at home, and there being few facilities for correspondence, the missionaries must have been soon in great measure forgotten. Hence Ireland lost an invaluable reaction from its missions; and hence, probably, one cause, along with the destruc-

[1] McLauchlan believes there were contributions made in Ireland for the continental missions under direction from Iona. But these were probably for those missionaries only who went from Iona, and it is also probable, that the contributions were made only in Ulster.

tive invasions of the Northmen in the ninth and tenth centuries, of the apparent decline of vital Christianity in that island before the more general desolation of the Norman and Papal invasion.

The missionary institution at Iona, which dates from the sixth century, held out against Romish aggression until the eighth; and Ireland, though sadly ravaged by the roving Danes in the ninth century, maintained its religious independence three or four hundred years longer, until conquered by Henry the Norman. In that conquest, which was avowedly made in the interest of the Pope, and for a long time afterwards, an exterminating war is said to have been waged against such of the old manuscripts of the Irish Church as had escaped the ravages of the Danes; and also against the schools, which, for several hundred years, had supplied Europe with her brightest examples of Christian life, and her most efficient literary teachers.[1]

But the seed which had been sowed over Central Europe, though long buried, sprang up in the Reformation of the sixteenth century. And it is a fact of some interest that Luther, the great leader of the Reformation, came from the convent of Erfurth, one of those founded many ages before by the Irish missionaries, and said to have been the very last of their

[1] Webb's *Annotations*, p. 177.

German convents which survived.[1] He was a monk of the order of St. Augustine, and it may be said that the two streams of theological influence, having their rise a thousand years before — the one from Augustine, in Northern Africa, the other from Patrick, in Ireland — were here united, to flow on together for ages we know not how many.

It is a question deserving of more consideration than I have the means of giving, how the early and truly Protestant Christian and missionary spirit of the Irish people came to so melancholy an end. The invasions of the Danes must have exerted a disastrous influence, both upon the learning and the religion of the island. A Roman Catholic historian asserts, that these sea-rovers destroyed the Irish monastery at Bangor, in the year 821, and massacred nine hundred of its inmates.[2] The middle of the ninth century was specially distinguished for these inroads, but they extended into the tenth. The Irish Church retained its independence longer than the Church of England, and its missionary light in consequence burned longer and brighter. But this spirit gradually declined, until her sons, while they continued to travel in numbers through foreign countries, went rather as teachers of the Frankish clergy, than as preachers.[3]

[1] Walsh's *Christian Missions*, p. 82.

[2] Brenan's *Eccl. Hist. of Ireland,* Dublin, 1864, p. 158.

[3] Walsh's *Christian Missions,* p. 82.

The bull of Pope Adrian IV., in the twelfth century, authorizing Henry II. to invade Ireland, for the purpose, as he said, of "extending the boundaries of the church," shows that, up to that time, Rome had no control of the island. The frightful carnage and desolation occasioned by these Norman invaders, and the subsequent stout opposition of the Irish clergy and the people to the papal decrees, are admitted by papal historians.[1] But the unremitted efforts of the Romish Church to subvert the ecclesiastical constitution of Ireland, were at length successful; and the Reformation of the sixteenth century, the seeds whereof had long before been planted by Irish missionaries, seems not to have exerted much influence in Ireland. It was repelled by the native Irish, out of their intense hatred of England. Richard Baxter, a contemporary witness, says, that Papists, in the days of Charles I., rising at once all over the island, massacred two hundred thousand Protestants within the space of a few weeks.[2] The Irish Jesuit, O'Mahoney, confessed, in 1645, that his party had cut off one hundred and fifty thousand heretics in the space of four years.[3] The retribution by Cromwell, eight years after the massacre, was terrible. Forty thousand Irish soldiers were transported to Spain, France, and Poland,

1 Brenan's *Eccl. Hist. of Ireland,* pp. 232, 237, 238.

2 *Jesuit Juggling; or, Forty Popish Frauds Detected and Disclosed,* New York, 1835.

3 *Edinburgh Review,* Oct. 1845, p. 264.

where they were drafted into the armies of those kingdoms; and the "Irish nation" was compelled to vacate ten of the most fertile counties, and crowd itself into the counties of Connaught and Clare. The whole island, excepting those counties, and also a part of Ulster, which was already occupied by Scottish settlers, was assigned to the English army and to English colonists. The Scotchmen of Ulster brought with them families, and obtained godly ministers from Scotland, who remained through the prelatic persecutions of after times, and the good results are still seen. The Cromwell soldiers, on the other hand, felt obliged to intermarry with the natives, and were thus absorbed, in a few generations, into the mass of the unenterprising, unimproving Roman Catholic population. It should be added, that most of the one hundred and thirty Independent and Baptist ministers, who had been sent to look after the spiritual interests of this class of settlers, returned to England when their salaries were withdrawn at the Restoration, having no means of support, leaving their people without provision for their spiritual wants. The Episcopal establishment, which took the place of these, though it was and is richly endowed, seems never to have exerted a decided religious influence; [1] and its disestablishment is now one of the exciting questions in the British Parliament and nation.

[1] See *Edinburgh Review*, for Oct. 1865, p. 270; *North British Review*, Dec. 1866.

In a review of the Irish missions in the early ages of the Christian Church, I have been not a little interested in the reflections and inferences with which I close this statement.

It surely is wonderful, that those missions continued in operation so long. For, unlike papal missions, they had no strong central government to urge them forward, and to lean upon. Indeed the Irish missions had nothing of the kind. Just think of missions, with such defective agencies, and moved only by the voluntary principle, being prosecuted continuously for successive centuries! There must have been a good degree of Christian principle back of all this. And whether we regard the missionary spirit as the normal condition of piety in the true church of God or not, we must admit that the missionary work, when once fairly entered upon by a large body of true Christians, is not likely to be of transient duration; and especially that it will not be so in our day. This seems to be a legitimate inference from the wonderfully protracted missions now under consideration, and it may well encourage us. Surely if the Irish missions of those early ages had so much of life and duration, we may expect the missions of our times, with their purer theology, their freer spirit, their great extent, and their numerous other advantages both in the church and the world, will have an enduring existence. If the Protestant nations which send them forth do not relapse into a worldly formalism — and the missionary enterprise of our times is one great defense against such a result — the Protestant missions may be expected to grow and extend until their great work is accomplished.

CHAPTER VI.

HISTORICAL DEVELOPMENT OF MODERN MISSIONS.

Importance of the Subject. — No Difference of Opinion as to the Object of Missions. — Diversity as to Modes of Operating. — Number to be Evangelized. — Not a Hopeless Work. — How to be accomplished. Method proposed by Gordon Hall. — Why not rely on such Calculations. — Great Providential Results usually exceed our Calculations. — Analogy between Apostolic and Modern Missions. Missions a Work of Faith. — Use of Agriculture and the Arts. Of the Language, Literature, Science, and Manners of Western Civilization. — St. Paul's Dealing with Churches. — Why Native Churches should engage in Foreign Missions. — Result of Experience.

I PROPOSE, in this chapter and the next, to give a practical illustration of the nature of modern missions. The subject is vitally important, and I would present it so as at the same time to secure the attention of the reader, and to satisfy his judgment. I shall be expected to develop the missionary work in connection with its principles, and shall treat the case historically, so far as may be, giving the facts needful for the forming of opinions.

I know of no diversity, in the views of different portions of the Evangelical Church, as to the proper objects of missions; for there is no mistaking the command, on which the enterprise is founded, which is so to make known the gospel to perishing men as to induce them to repent and believe on the Lord Jesus Christ. So far as there has been diversity of opinion, it has had respect to the most effectual methods of bringing the gospel to bear on the hearts and lives of the unevangelized, in their different conditions and countries. Here there has been considerable difference of opinion and of practice, in the different missionary societies, and in the same missionary society at different stages of its progress.

We have already seen how more than six hundred millions of heathen were made accessible to the gospel, who were not accessible forty years ago; and how the Evangelical Church is beginning to rouse itself to the work of sending them the gospel. I must add two hundred millions to the six hundred, for parts of the unevangelized world not distinctly embraced in that survey, and we have at least eight hundred millions to be somehow evangelized.

A work of such magnitude would be appalling, were it not expressly enjoined upon us by divine command, with the promise of all needed divine aid; and were it not brought before the church by almost miraculous interventions of Providence, and with the facilities for doing it multiplied a hundred fold.

There must be a possible way of accomplishing the work, however vast; and the question now presents itself, What is that way?

Gordon Hall, one of the first and ablest of the American missionaries, writing fifty years ago in the celebrated tract entitled "Claims of Six Hundred Millions," held that the work was to be done by sending one missionary for every twenty thousand souls. He says: "One missionary for every twenty thousand souls may be considered a tolerable supply, because that wherever the gospel is preached, and its power experienced, native preachers will be raised up on the spot, to aid missionaries, and ultimately to take the work off their hands." With one missionary to every twenty thousand souls, and as many as nine native preachers to every missionary, he says, the heathen world would have as great a proportion of Christian teachers as the United States was supposed then to have. He also shows the possibility of bringing all these missionaries on the ground in twenty-one years.

But I have ceased to place much reliance on such calculations. Great results depending on the providence and grace of God, come about much easier and more rapidly than our previous calculations would lead us to expect. Was it not marvelously so with the liberation of our four millions of slaves? It will doubtless be so with the conversion of the world. Let one reflect how soon the old Roman Empire was compelled to receive the Christian name, notwithstanding the whole force of that mighty empire was in determined resistance, and he will see how little human calculations have to do with such matters. The very wonderful opening of the unevangelized world to the gospel, and the preparation in Christendom for sending it forth, as already described, lead to the same conclusion. I therefore go into no general calculations as to the time, or the number of missionaries, necessary for the whole work. My belief is, that "the Lord will hasten it in his time."[1]

There is a striking analogy, in one respect, between the apostolic missions and those of modern times. The apostles, as a body, were a considerable time in coming to the conclusion, that Gentile Christian churches ought not to be subjected to the Jewish ritual; that is to say, they were so long in securing an acknowledged purely spiritual basis for their foreign missions. We, also, have had substantially the same difficulty in respect to the purely spiritual nature of the missionary work itself, and we have been longer in surmounting that difficulty, if we have even yet fully surmounted it. The main cause of our difficulty, however, is not one that affected the apostolic missions. It has been the higher civilization of the Christian Church, as compared with that of modern heathen nations. This has tended to confuse our conceptions of the religion we were to propagate. From our childhood our idea of the Christian religion has been identified with education, social

[1] Isa. lx. 22.

order, and a certain correctness of morals and manners; in other words, with civilization. It is even true of us all, that the civilization of centuries forms a part of the hourly manifestations of our piety; and we seldom reflect how our personal religion would appear to casual observers, were we divested of a culture which we share in common with the world around us.

This composite idea of the gospel (if I may so describe it), this foreign intermixture, has placed the missionaries of our day under a disadvantage, as compared with missionaries in the apostolic age. It has weakened their faith in that perfectly simple form of the gospel as a converting agency, in which it was apprehended by the apostles; and also their reliance on the divine power, upon which the apostles so exclusively depended for success.

This faith in God, and in his appointed means for the conversion of the world, is now the grand desideratum in the Christian Church, and in Christian missions. And it is remarkable, through the whole recorded history of the church, what a demand God has ever been pleased to make upon it for an exclusive faith in the divine presence and power. The church of the old dispensation stood on the defensive, with a hostile world around it. Yet it was forbidden to trust in chariots and horsemen, and only in Jehovah. The forty-sixth Psalm, beginning, "God is our Refuge and Strength," was the jubilant song of piety with the ancient theocratic people, in view of their entire safety under the protection of Almighty God.

The church of the new or Christian dispensation, on the other hand, is an aggressive body, with institutions all shaped for conquest and extension. It exists for the spiritual subjugation of the world. And in the use of its spiritual weapons, it is as much required to rely on the Almighty Saviour and the "Spirit of Truth," as the church of the old dispensation was on Jehovah. It would seem to be no more allowable for the Christian Church or for its missionaries to trust in chariots and horsemen, and go to Egypt for help, than it was for God's ancient people.

Experience has, with the grace of God, been bringing us gradually into more spiritual conceptions of the end we should have in view, and of the means by which that end is to be attained. This I am now to illustrate in several particulars.

1. A question often mooted at the outset of modern Christian missions, and sometimes mooted now, is, Whether savages must be civilized before they can be Christianized. I shall be excused for drawing illustrations of this point from missions with which I have been most conversant. Our fathers, in their earlier missions to savage peoples, acting with the light they had, avowedly sent Chris-

tianity and civilization forth together, as coöperating forces. For instance, ordained missionaries to the North American Indians were accompanied by farmers and mechanics; and a farmer was sent with the first mission to the Sandwich Islands. The American Board, in its Report for 1816, declared it to be the object of the missions to the Indians, "to make them English in their language, civilized in their habits, and Christian in their religion." And, three years later, the pioneers of the Sandwich Islands mission were instructed, "to aim at nothing short of covering those Islands with fruitful fields and pleasant dwellings, and schools and churches, and of raising the whole people to an elevated state of Christian civilization."

What now have been the results of experience? In the year 1823, the missions of the American Board to the Indians, with ten preaching missionaries, numbered fifteen farmers and mechanics. In 1842, with twenty-four preaching missionaries in those missions, the farmers and mechanics had been reduced to nine; and in 1852, thirty-six years from the commencement of the missions, with twenty-five preaching missionaries, not a single farmer or mechanic remained. You understand the import of these facts. The honest aim in sending these secular helpers was to aid the preaching missionaries. But the means were found to be inappropriate. A simpler, cheaper, more effectual means of civilizing the savage, was the gospel alone.

I should add, that the missionary farmer sent to the Sandwich Islands remained there only a short time; and never since has there been a thought of sending another.

Thus ended the experiment by the American Board, of connecting agriculture and the arts with the missionary agencies.

2. It was supposed that, in the spiritual conquest of modern heathen nations, the gospel would be essentially aided by the languages, literature, science, and manners of Western civilization. The English language being the chief repository of this civilization in its evangelical form, it has been more or less used as a medium. The Report of the American Board for 1816, already quoted, declared — and it was then the general belief — that if the Indians should learn the English language, their sources of knowledge and means of improvement would be vastly greater than they could be with only their own language; and that, being thus assimilated in language to their white neighbors, they would more readily become assimilated to them in habits and manners. But the venerable Dr. Kingsbury, the first missionary sent to the Indians by the American Board, and still living among the Choctaws, writing in 1861, forty years after entering the field, bears

the following testimony: "With a few interesting exceptions," he says, "those who acquired the most knowledge of the English language seemed the farthest from embracing the gospel, and the least disposed to attend on the means of grace. They regarded themselves as elevated above their parents, and the mass of their people, and became vain in their imaginations, and their foolish hearts were darkened." At the same time, while Dr. Kingsbury believed it would have been more for the moral and religious interests of the Indians had the schools been taught wholly in their own vernacular, he did not hesitate to pronounce the Choctaws a Christian nation.

Another illustration I derive from the experience in Syria. A high school was established by the American Board, at Beirût, in 1835, and was continued in operation seven years. The literature of Western civilization was taught through the English language, and the boarding, lodging, and clothing had a Western type. The pupils were faithfully instructed in the Scriptures; but it was found, that the tendency of their training, on the whole, was to make them foreign in their manners, foreign in their habits, foreign in their sympathies; in other words, to denationalize them. In 1842 that seminary was disbanded, and another was formed on Mount Lebanon, on a more simple plan, and with a thoroughly Biblical instruction. It was Arabic in its language, clothing, boarding, and lodging, and discountenanced all aspirations after foreign habits and customs.[1]

I shall be understood as now speaking of missions, and of what is strictly appropriate to them. There is a stage of advancement — as, perhaps, at Constantinople, Beirût, Calcutta, and the Sandwich Islands — where a portion of the native mind demands a broader, higher culture than even the mission can give; where it is the part of wisdom to afford it through a college, distinct from the mission, and deriving its support from other sources.

I shall state explicitly, further on, what I conceive to be the true place and office of education in missions. What I am now speaking of, is the growth of experience as to the best mode of conducting missions.

The natural order in missions is, "first the blade; then the ear; after that the full corn in the ear." In the earlier missions, this seems not to have been sufficiently observed. The native preachers were sometimes too highly taught in secular knowledge for the incipient stages of the work. Raised too far above the general level of intelligence among their people, they longed for more cultivated hearers than they found in the villages, and for larger salaries than they could receive, or ought to receive, and shrank from pastorates in obscure places, among

[1] *Annual Report*, 1845, pp. 133, 134.

low-caste, ignorant people; and sometimes they were impatient of advice and wholesome restraint from their missionary fathers. In some quarters, they were tempted to contract business relations with the world, and thus the labor and money bestowed on their education were in great measure lost to the cause.

3. We have been slow to admit the extent to which the Apostle Paul's method of dealing with native churches is applicable to the missions of our day. In this remark, I equally include missionaries and their directors. The apostle wrote to Titus, that he had left him in Crete, to "set in order the things that were wanting, and to ordain presbyters in every city;" and with all this in charge, he still required the evangelist to come to him before winter; leaving the churches, thus rapidly organized, to take care of themselves. It will be seen that if the charge to Timothy, to "lay hands suddenly on no man," was equally applicable to Titus (as doubtless it was), it must have had respect more to the judgment to be exercised in the selection of the presbyters, than to haste in the matter of time, as is the common opinion.

Such appears to have been the Apostle Paul's manner with all his churches. In our undue estimate of the influence of civilization, as an auxiliary to the gospel in sustaining the higher Christian life among the heathen, and from an overestimate of the value of Roman civilization in the apostolic age, as an auxiliary to spiritual life in the primitive churches, the apostle's example has by no means had its proper influence. We have been slow to believe, that native churches, or native pastors, with forms of civilization so inferior to our own, or so very unlike it, could stand without foreign aid. Hence the prolonged existence of mission churches with their centre and seat at the residence of the missionary, and their membership spread over a large surrounding district. They often had native preachers, indeed, stationed at some of the more important points in the district, but no native pastors; the whole church membership being long retained under the pastoral supervision of the missionary himself. It is a remarkable fact, that, prior to 1854, forty years after the first entrance of the American Board into India, and until the visit of the Deputation, not one of its missions in that country had a native pastor. Those missions had not then, indeed, even an ordained native preacher. There were, moreover, only a very few native pastors at the Sandwich Islands previous to 1863, more than forty years after the commencement of the mission; though they then had several ordained native missionaries in Micronesia and the Marquesas Islands. And among the missions of that Board to the American Indians, there never was more than one or two native pastors. How far there was a similar experience in the case of other missionary societies, I am not exactly prepared to say; though I find many proofs of the same remarkable short-coming.

In the providence of God, there have been signal rebukes of his people for so unscriptural a policy. In 1842, the French seized the island of Tahiti, and sent the English missionaries away; who, thirty years after the conversion of the people of that island, had not ordained one native pastor. The late eminent Dr. Tidman, Foreign Secretary of the London Missionary Society, adverting to this fact in a speech at Liverpool in 1860, spoke as follows: —

"I must be permitted to say one word concerning the *native pastors* of Tahiti. Why did they become so? Just because our Europeans were sent adrift by French authority. They were thus called forth by the necessities of the situation. These native brethren were not ordained before; but as soon as they were called to the work in the providence of God, they proved quite equal to it. And after twenty years of French misrule, notwithstanding all the influences of Popery on the one hand, and of brandy and wine on the other, there were now living under the instruction and influence of these native pastors a greater number of church-members, than they had had aforetime."

On the same occasion, Dr. Tidman gave another memorable illustration: "With regard to Madagasear," he said, "twenty years ago or more, the European shepherds were all sent away, and a few poor, timid lambs were left in the midst of wolves. And what has been the result? Why men [he means *native* men] had been raised up by God to take the oversight; and instead of tens of Christians under the care of European pastors, there were now hundreds, nay thousands, under the teaching of these men."[1]

Thus the Evangelical Church profits by its experience, and there is progress. Local churches, with a native pastorate, are now being multiplied in the heathen world as never before, after the manner of the apostle to the Gentiles.

It may be asked whether the missionary, thus giving place to the native pastor, is to move from one station to another, as did the Apostle Paul. I answer, by no means to the same extent. But if he be successful in gathering churches, he may find it expedient occasionally to change his position, so as to throw the indispensable responsibility on the native churches and pastors. The child will never stand and walk firmly, if always in leading-strings. The plan of the divine government in the apostolic age, in accordance with which the apostles acted, was in some respects different from what it appears to be now. They were to plant churches only in the central points of the Roman world; they could do no more. But now, as has been shown abundantly,

[1] *Conference on Missions at Liverpool*, 1860, p. 225.

the greater part of the globe, and nearly all the great nations, are open and ready for us; and we are to go for the early and complete conquest of every nation, and for remaining in our several fields so long as there is appropriate work for us to do.

4. There is still another view, which, while it accords with apostolic usage, doubtless lies beyond what the Apostle Paul could have lived to experience. I will illustrate it by a reference to the Sandwich Islands.

In the year 1847, twenty-seven years after the commencement of the mission on those Islands, the Committee and Secretaries of the American Board were surprised, and somewhat disconcerted, by a discovery of what seemed like a threatened collapse of the mission.

It appeared as if the missionary was being absorbed in the parent, and that the foreign laborers on those Islands were all coming home in a few years, to look after the interests of their children. It was soon known that there were a variety of causes for this result. One was the reaction among missionaries and people, consequent upon the great national awakening, which had then reached its crisis. Another was the uncommon number of children in the missionary families, the climate being favorable to their health and life, and the want of arrangements for their education at the Islands; which was met by instituting the Oahu College. But the statement received from the Islands went to show still another influential cause. This was a deficiency of religious stimulus, suited to the sensibilities and habits of a people so low on the scale of intelligence. All the Islands had been alike Christianized. Had one of them remained under the influence of savage paganism, as the whole had been — for instance, the island of Hawaii, — then the four Christianized islands might have been roused to send the gospel to the seventy-five thousand benighted people of Hawaii; and they would have had an appropriate and interesting field near by for their Christian activities. Whereas, there was no such pagan island within less than two thousand miles. To be sure, there was very much of real home missionary work on each of the Sandwich Islands. But it was found there, as it has been in our own country, that the motive-power of the home missionary plea alone, is not of itself sufficiently awakening and powerful. In short, it was painfully certain, that the infant churches on those Islands, regarded as a whole, could not be raised to the level of enduring and effective working churches, without a stronger religious influence than could be brought to act upon them from within their own Christianized islands. It was also evident that the missionaries themselves then needed an additional motive-power, beyond what the Islands any longer afforded.

It was precisely this discovery — for discovery it was — which gave rise to the mission to Micronesia; a group of islands two thousand miles westward; and also to the sending from this country, in the year 1856, of the missionary packet "Morning Star," to facilitate the forming of that mission; and to the employment of native Hawaiians as missionaries on those islands, who should look for their support to their own Hawaiian churches.

I do not mean, that it would have been proper actually to have left any one of the Sandwich Islands in heathenism for such a purpose. I am only illustrating a *principle;* and it is one of high practical importance; namely, that it is impossible for mission churches to reach their highest and truest state, without the aid of what is to them virtually a foreign mission, — without some outside field of labor for them, resembling the "hole of the pit" from which they had themselves been digged.

We have now seen how foreign missions were gradually divested, first of the grosser elements of the world, and then of the more refined elements; how they were contracted, simplified, economized, and brought more and more to depend for success on the cross of Christ, and the "Spirit of truth." The tendency has been directly, though not rapidly, towards the high Christian stand, which the great apostle describes himself to have held as a missionary; determining, with that holy energy of purpose which characterized him, to know nothing among the heathen, and nothing among his converts, "save Jesus Christ and him crucified;" and not to teach "with enticing words of man's wisdom," but in the power and demonstration of the Spirit.

CHAPTER VII.

PRINCIPLES AND METHODS OF MODERN MISSIONS.

What the Apostolic Missions embraced. — Local Churches prominent. Nature of the Mission Church. — Missionaries not to be Pastors. The Missionary System built upon this View of Native Churches. Education and the Press. — English High Schools. — The Object and Work of the Foreign Missionary not peculiar. — Why Funds go further now, than formerly. — Civilization not the Object of Foreign Missions. — Preaching Christ applicable to all False Religion.

I AM now prepared to state, in a concise but positive form, what I believe to be the true and proper nature of a mission among the heathen. The mission of the Apostle Paul, as described in the fourth chapter, embraced the following things: —

1. The aim of the apostle was to save the souls of men.

2. The means he employed for this purpose were spiritual; namely, the gospel of Christ.

3. The power on which he relied to give efficacy to these means, was divine; namely, the promised aid of the Holy Spirit.

4. His success was chiefly in the middle and poorer classes, — the Christian influence ascending from thence.

5. When he had formed local churches, he did not

hesitate to ordain presbyters over them, the best he could find; and then to throw upon the churches, thus officered, the responsibilities of self-government, self-support, and self-propagation. His "presbyters in every church," whatever their number and other duties, had doubtless the pastoral care of the churches.

Prominent, then, among the visible agencies in foreign missions, if we follow the great apostle, are LOCAL CHURCHES. I call them by no denominational name. They may be churches governed by the popular vote, or by elders they have themselves chosen for the purpose. They are local bodies of associated Christians. The first duty of a missionary is to gather such a church. That will serve as a nucleus — and it is the only possible nucleus, a school not being one — of a permanent congregation. A missionary, by means of properly located, well organized, well trained churches, may extend his influence over a large territory. In such a country as India, or China, his direct influence may reach even scores of thousands.

I find nothing in the history of the mission of the Apostle Paul, which seems to me decisive, as to the manner in which these multiplied mission churches should be brought into social relations to each other, and would cheerfully leave that to the good sense and piety of missionaries on the ground.

I now inquire, What should be the nature of the

mission church? It should be composed only of hopeful converts; and should have, as soon as possible, a native pastor, and of the same race, who has been trained to take cheerfully the oversight of what will generally be a small, poor, ignorant people, and mingle with them familiarly and sympathetically. And by a native pastor, I mean one recognized as having the pastoral care of a local church, with the right to administer the ordinances of baptism and the Lord's Supper.

This necessity of a native pastor to the healthful and complete development of a self-reliant, effective native church, is a discovery of recent date. I cannot say, nor is it important to know, by whom this fundamental truth or law in missions was first declared. Like many discoveries in science, it very probably was reached by a number of persons, at nearly the same time, and as the result of a common experience.[1]

[1] "It may be said to have been only lately discovered in the science of missions, that when the missionary is of another and superior race than his converts, he must not attempt to be their *pastor*; though they will be bound to him by personal attachment, and by a sense of the benefits received from him; yet if he continues to act as their pastor, they will not form a vigorous native church, but, as a general rule, they will remain in a dependent condition, and make but little progress in spiritual attainments. The same congregation, under competent native pastors, would become more self-reliant, and their religion would be of a more manly, home character."—Rev. Henry Venn's *Letter to the Bishop of Jamaica*, dated January, 1867. Mr. Venn is Honorary Secretary of the Church Missionary Society, and no one is better informed on missionary subjects.

As soon as the mission church has a native pastor, the responsibilities of self-government should be devolved upon it. Mistakes, perplexities, and sometimes scandals, there will be; but it is often thus that useful experience is gained, even in churches here at home. The salary of the native pastor should be based on the Christianized ideas of living acquired by his people; and the church should become self-supporting at the earliest possible day. It should also be self-propagating from the very first. Such churches, and only such, are the life, strength, and glory of missions.

A foreign missionary should not be the pastor of a native church. His business is to plant churches, in well-chosen parts of his field, committing them as soon as possible to the care of native pastors; himself sustaining a common relation to all, as their ecclesiastical father and adviser; having, in some sense, like the apostle, the daily care of the churches. He might stand thus related to a score of churches, and even more, however they are related to each other; and when he is old, might be able to say, through the abounding grace of God, "Though ye have ten thousand instructors in Christ, yet have ye not many fathers; for in Christ Jesus I have begotten you all through the gospel."[1]

Self-evident as this idea of a mission church may seem on its announcement, it is not yet adopted

[1] 1 Cor. iv. 15.

in all Protestant missions, and until of late, has seemed to gain ground very slowly. Its universal adoption, however, cannot be far distant, and will add immensely both to the economy and the power of missions.

It is upon this view of the nature and relations of native churches, that we build our missionary system.

Education, schools, the press, and whatever else goes to make up the working system, are held in strict subordination to the planting and building up of effective working churches. But though held strictly in such subordination, we see in it the utmost latitude for the exercise of a wise discretion in the conduct of missions. The governing object to be always aimed at, is self-reliant, effective churches,—churches that are purely native. Whatever missionaries believe to be most directly conducive to this end, comes within the scope of their privilege and duty; of course, under reasonable restrictions growing out of their fundamental relations. The use of schools and the press comes under the question, how far they are subservient to the great end, namely, the rapid and perfect development of churches.

We thus perceive the place which education must hold in missions. Without education, it is not possible for mission churches to be in any proper sense self-governed; nor, without it, will they be self-supported, and much less self-propagating. For the church-members there must be common schools. This results from the degraded mental condition of the heathen world, as compared with the field of the apostolic missions. Scarcely a ray of light reaches it from sun, moon, or stars in the intellectual and moral firmament. Mind is vacant, crushed, unthinking, enslaved to animal instincts and passions; earthly, sensual, terribly debased. The common school, therefore, is a necessity among the degraded heathen, to help elevate the converts, and make the village church an effective agency. And the church-members, as far as may be, should be educated within the bounds of their own villages; and in such manner that a large number of them will abide with their people, and help to support their native pastor and schools, and make their Christian village a power in the land. At first, these schools must be sustained by the mission; but it is better for them, not long afterwards, to be sustained by the parents.

The native preachers and pastors come, almost of course, from the same depths of mental degradation; and since they must be enabled to stand alone and firmly in the gospel ministry, and be competent spiritual guides to others, they should of course have a higher training. What this shall be, what it shall include and exclude, must depend on circumstances too various for general rules. But one thing is clear;

our army, liberated from the thralldom of pagan slavery, must be well officered in order to fight bravely.

The printing-press in missions is mainly for the schools and for the church-members, to whom, indeed, books are indispensable. Experience tends to the result of having missions cease to own printing establishments as soon as the needful printing can be secured from presses owned by others.

Wherein, then, do our modern missions differ from those of the apostolic age? They differ in several particulars.

1. Modern missionaries are sent forth and supported by churches in their native lands; by churches, too, of long standing and experience; and, so far at least as this country and Great Britain are concerned, by churches existing and operating in the midst of freedom and high religious intelligence. In this modern missions have certainly a great advantage over the primitive missions.

2. They have not the personal presence and active agency of apostles; but they have the four Gospels, the Acts of the Apostles, and their Letters of Instruction, all written under the guidance of inspiration; and the press, to multiply copies of these documents by thousands. A portion of the modern Evangelical Church, indeed, is coming into the practice of putting their missionaries under the control

of missionary bishops, and regards these as successors of the apostles. But they evidently are not apostles, since they lack the "signs, and wonders, and mighty deeds," which St. Paul, in his Second Epistle to the Corinthians, declares to be the needful "signs of an apostle."[1]

3. The pastorate in modern missions differs from that of the apostolic age, in that it ordinarily has but one pastor for each church; whereas the New Testament always uses the plural in speaking of the pastorate in the churches planted by the Apostle Paul. "They ordained presbyters in every church;" being influenced in this, perhaps (as has been already said), by the usage of the Jewish synagogue. This practice seems to have been lost, with the very idea of the apostolic church, in the great decline of the Early and Middle Ages; and when that idea was recovered, as it was at the Reformation, and put in practice, the usage of having but one pastor in each church was adopted by all evangelical denominations, as being more conformed to the demands of the age. And this is now the general usage in all the evangelical churches; and it has thence been transferred to the mission churches among the heathen. The apostolic principle is retained, but the form is changed. I speak only of the pastorate, in which the evangelical denominations agree; leaving entirely untouched the points concerning which the evangelical denominations differ.

[1] 2 Cor. xii. 12; Rom. xv. 18, 19.

Such is the simple structure of our foreign missions, as the combined result of experience, and of the apostolic example; in all which the grand object is to plant and multiply self-reliant, efficient churches, composed wholly of native converts, each church complete, with its pastors of the same race with the people. And when the unevangelized nations are so filled with such churches, that all men have it within their power to learn what they must do to be saved, then may we expect the promised advent of the Spirit, and the conversion of the world.

It might be deemed a defect in my description of the missionary work, should I not advert to a series of efforts made in the cities of India, and more especially in Calcutta, to gain access for the gospel to the higher classes by means of English schools. In these schools a large number of high-caste Hindus have received a liberal Christian education, through the medium of the English language and literature. The result of the experiment is regarded by those who are making it as very hopeful. There is certainly a development among the higher class of Hindus in Calcutta, and in some other of the India cities, that is worthy of attentive consideration. But the results of the experiments are not yet sufficiently developed to occupy a prominent place in a description of the fundamental nature of the missionary work.[1]

[1] See *Appendices* III. and IV.

I close with a few general remarks.

1. The foreign missionary, the home missionary, and the pastor have each substantially the same object. It is to plant churches, and make them shine as lights in the world. Our leading sentiment is as really applicable to home missionaries, as it is to foreign missionaries. The labors of the home missionary have a direct reference to the forming of self-governed, self-supported churches, and such churches are proofs of his success. The home missionary becomes then a pastor, or gives place to one sustaining that relation.

2. The great simplification in the use of means, and relying more on those which are spiritual, is a principal reason why a given amount of funds now sustains a more extended working mission than it formerly did. The grand object and means are the same; but the working process, becoming more spiritual, bears more effectively on the heart and conscience.

3. The proper test of success in missions, is not the progress of civilization, but the evidence of a religious life.

4. The gospel is applicable equally to all false religions. Generically considered, there can be but two religions: the one looking for salvation by *grace;* the other, by *works.* The principle of evil in all unbelieving men, is the same. The refuges of lies in Popery, in Judaism, in Mohammedanism,

in Brahminism, Buddhism, and every form of paganism, are wonderfully alike. There is one disease, and one remedy. Before the gospel, the unbelieving world stands an undistinguished mass of rebellious sinners; unwilling that God should reign over them, unwilling to be saved except by their own works, and averse to all real holiness of heart and life. There is power in the doctrine of the cross, through grace, to overcome this. The doctrine of the cross — as will more clearly appear when we come to the evidences of success in missions — is the grand instrument of conquest. Not one of the great superstitions of the world could hold a governing place in the human soul, after the conviction has once been thoroughly produced, that there is salvation only in Christ. Be his system what it may, the man, thus convinced, would flee from it, as he would from a falling house in the rockings of an earthquake.

CHAPTER VIII.

VALUE OF NATIVE CHURCHES.

To be illustrated by Native Converts, and the Native Ministry. Value of Native Converts: in Sierra Leone; in Madagascar; in India; in Western Asia. — Value of the Native Ministry: among the Karens; among the Shanars; in the Sandwich Islands; in the Islands of the South Pacific. — How far Native Churches are dependent on the Presence of Missionaries. — How far Revivals of Religion are common in them. — The Prospect.

It was stated in the last chapter, that the grand object of foreign missions is to plant and multiply churches, composed of native converts; each church complete in itself, with presbyters of the same race, left to determine their ecclesiastical relations for themselves, with the aid of judicious advice from their missionary fathers.

The value of native churches must be learned by an estimate of the value of native converts, and of the native ministry. And should it be thought that I produce the richest specimens from our golden mines, it should be remembered that such specimens best illustrate the work of the Holy Spirit in extending Messiah's kingdom. They will best show what can and must be done before the glorious reign of our Lord and Saviour shall extend over all nations.

In estimating the *value of native converts,* I begin with Western Africa. The oldest mission on the West African coast is that of the English Church Missionary Society at Sierra Leone. Here, in the early stage of that mission, we shall find a native church of marvelous interest and power, gathered out of the most unpromising materials, in circumstances the most unpropitious.

It is fifty years since a plain German laborer in London, named William A. B. Johnson, offered himself to the Church Missionary Society to be sent as a school-master to Sierra Leone. He had only a common school education, but was rich in Christian experience. It soon appeared that he was called of God to the gospel ministry, and he accordingly received ordination in Africa. His was a wonderful ministry. When Mr. Johnson first took up his abode at what was afterwards called Regent's Town, in Sierra Leone, the people numbered about a thousand. They had been taken at different times from the holds of slave-ships ; were wild and naked ; and being from twenty-two different nations, were hostile to each other. They had no common medium of intercourse, except a little broken English, had no ideas of marriage, and lived crowded together in the rudest huts. They were devil-worshippers, and most of them lazy, thieving, plundering, brutal savages.

Mr. Johnson was at first exceedingly discouraged. But he resolved to preach Christ to them as the

Saviour of sinners, in the simple manner of the gospel, and to open to them the miserable state of a sinner rejecting such a Saviour. His resolution was the same with that of the Apostle Paul, when he surveyed the desperate pollutions of the Corinthians, — "to know nothing among *them*, save Jesus Christ and him crucified." There is no other adequate power of deliverance. After pursuing this course the greater part of a year, preaching salvation through the Lord Jesus, a remarkable change began to come over the people. Old and young became concerned for their souls. There was, in short, an outpouring of the Spirit. Many sought retirement in the woods for prayer; and soon the neighboring mountains echoed, in moonlight evenings, with the hymns of worshippers. Mr. Johnson has left a record of the experience of many of the converts, in their own simple and broken, but expressive language, when examined, as they all were, for admission to the Lord's Supper. I am impressed by his record of their convictions of sin; their acknowledgments of the divine forbearance; their distrust of their own hearts; their inward conflicts; their tender consciences; their faith and patience; their benevolence; and their love for souls. The outward changes were most striking. The people learned trades, became farmers, attached well-kept gardens to their dwellings. They built a stone church large enough, with the help of galleries, to seat closely nearly two thousand persons; which was regularly filled with decently dressed, orderly, and serious worshippers. They built a parsonage, school-houses, store-houses, a bridge of several arches — all of stone. Most of the adult population were married. Their night-dances and heathenish drumming ceased, and so did their oaths, drunkenness, and stealing; and the schools contained a thousand children.[1]

All this Mr. Johnson lived to see; but he died in 1823, only seven years from the commencement of his mission! Was there ever a more wonderful religious change? It shows the power of the simple gospel, both to convert the savage and to civilize him. It shows the power of the cross of Christ. It shows, also, the illuminating, reforming influence of such a church, regarded as a missionary agency. Would that the same influences could have been continued in all their power. But this was more than forty years ago, and it was then too early for native pastors; their necessity to the full development of a native church not having then been discovered. A worthy missionary successor to Mr.

[1] See *Memoir of Rev. W. A. B. Johnson*, London, 1852, Preface, and pp. 168, 169, 245, 275, 279, 283, 299, 305, 419, 423, 424, 426. Also, *London Missionary Register* for 1819, pp. 5, 378–381, 486–492; and for 1829, pp. 18, 107–113, 197, 252–256, 371. Also, and especially, *Twentieth Report of the Church Missionary Society;* extracts from which are embodied in *Missionary Register* for 1820, pp. 473–476.

Johnson was not soon found, and Regent's Town suffered a decline after his death. But the foundations he had laid were sure, and there was progress on the whole. In the year 1842, twenty-four years after Mr. Johnson began his mission, one fifth of the population of Sierra Leone was at school, and the attendance at public worship was estimated at twelve thousand. In 1862, native pastorates were established, and ten parishes undertook the support of their own pastors; and no less than six different missions were sent by the people to the unevangelized tribes beyond the colony. The present number of nominal Christians in the colony, is said, on high authority, to be eighty thousand, of whom twenty thousand are communicants; and the missionary work at Sierra Leone is regarded as having been accomplished.[1]

I venture to say, to the glory of God in the gospel, that not one of the "seven churches of Asia" shone with a brighter light, than did this one, at that time, gathered from the slave-ships of Western Africa. Were there such churches now along the whole extent of that coast, and in the vast interior, the darkness, crime, and misery of that benighted region would give place to the blessedness of a Christian civilization.

Look, next, at the great island of Madagascar,

[1] *Church Missionary Intelligencer*, 1868, pp. 203, 250.

situated on the eastern coast of Africa. Here we shall see, as of old, infant churches struggling successfully against the utmost efforts of the civil power to destroy them. The London Missionary Society commenced a mission on that island in 1820, under the protection of the King Radama. The missionaries gave the people a written language, a grammar and dictionary, school books, a hymn-book, and the Bible, and taught some thousands to read the Scriptures.[1] The converts were virtually, if not formally, embodied in churches. A pagan queen, the widow of Radama, succeeded her husband in 1828, and, being hostile to the Christian religion, forbade the observance of its ordinances, and the reading of the Bible; and persistence in either was punishable with death. Perceiving that the gospel continued to gain ground, notwithstanding her decree, she, in 1835, banished all the missionaries. The Christians, still increasing, were then subjected to fierce persecution, which continued through twenty-five years, until her death in 1861. They were poisoned; they were hanged; they were speared; they were stoned, and the stoning was a most barbarous mode of execution. They were thrown down a fatal precipice. Loaded with heavy iron collars, and chained together, they were driven into banishment. They were burned at the stake, and some were crucified. Many were sold into slavery. It

[1] Ellis's *Madagascar Revisited*, p. 2.

is believed that more than two thousand persons suffered as Christians, during this persecution, in some cruel form or other.

So far as was possible they associated together as Christian communities; and there were those of their number intelligent and courageous enough to act as pastors and teachers, though always at the peril, and sometimes at the sacrifice of life. The result was a continual growth in numbers through all the persecutions.

The queen was succeeded by her son; who favored the Christians, and invited the return of the missionaries. This was seven years ago; and now, as we have the account from the well-known Dr. William Ellis, in his work recently published, entitled "Madagascar Revisited," dedicated by permission to the Queen of England, and from other sources, there are, within and around the capital of Madagascar, ninety churches, with more than five thousand members; one hundred and one native pastors; and twenty thousand claiming the Christian name. In the space of four years, the number of nominal Christians was more than doubled, and the number of the communicants was increased tenfold.[1] And we hear that a queen, lately come to the throne, has virtually embraced the Christian religion, and that, if she should live, we may expect Christianity to be soon adopted as the national religion.

[1] Ellis's *Madagascar Revisited*, pp. 469, 501.

We may read the history of Roman persecutions from Nero down, and we shall find none more cruel than the one in Madagascar, and none more distinguished for the inflexible firmness of its martyrs; upon whom, it should be remembered, the fiery tempest burst in the very infancy of their religious life. Nor should we forget that these heroic martyrs belonged to the negro race.

Another case illustrating the same thing, but bearing on a more numerous people, is the remarkable steadfastness of native Christians in the great India rebellion of 1857. This was wholly unexpected. The native Christians at the twenty missionary stations which were swept away in that terrible mutiny of the native army, exceeded two thousand in number. A very large portion of these were compelled, as Christians, to flee for their lives. They were beaten, their houses were plundered, and eleven of them suffered death. Everywhere Moslems or Hindus urged them to apostatize, and threatened and persecuted them; but they were firm to their Christian profession. Of the whole number only six yielded, and these returned as soon as the rebellion ceased.[1] Dr. Mullens, long time a leading missionary at Calcutta, and now the able Foreign Secretary of the London Missionary Society, wrote thus, while in India, concerning these native Christians: —

[1] Mullens' *Ten Years in India*, p. 24.

"Drawn, to a very large extent," he says, "from the artificial hot-house system of orphan and boarding schools; helped from first to last by missionaries; not only fed and taught, but in a measure having employments created for them; the community, as a whole, had grown up in the possession of sound principles, but weak in character, with little self-reliance, and a great deal of the petulance of spoiled children. The mutiny has driven all this away; and they who were thrown headlong into the troubled waters, and had to swim for their lives, without the aid of the corks and bladders on which they had relied, gained health and vigor in the process, and landed, not only alive, but *men*. The old system has been flung away forever."[1]

We see in these converts the nature of the materials for Hindu churches. Indeed the examples thus far adduced go to show, that the mission churches of our times are formed of the same material with the churches of the apostolic and martyr ages, and have, through the grace of God, the same power of endurance.

Let us next see what manner of converts, through divine grace, are produced in Eastern Turkey. It is true, that the churches in that empire are not composed of converts from heathenism; but then the knowledge of the way of salvation through faith

[1] Mullens' *Ten Years in India*, p. 25.

in Christ had perished from among them, and they stood, in that respect, very much on a level with Mohammedans and Pagans.

At Harpoot, on the upper waters of the Euphrates, the mission of the American Board formed a station in 1856; and eleven or twelve years ago, a church was gathered there, which, after two years, received a native pastor, and at once guaranteed a portion of his salary, and doubled the amount in the next year. A training-school for the native ministry was opened; and of the eighteen young men in the first class sent forth from that school during 1864, eight were licensed to preach the gospel, and most of the others occupied out-stations as catechists and teachers. Churches were soon formed in the villages, to which these native preachers were sent, which showed great readiness to support their pastors and preachers. As soon as a village became interested in the truth, it earnestly desired a native pastor of its own, and was easily pleased with him, and opposed to a change.

You will bear in mind, that Harpoot is only one of the five stations composing what is called the Eastern Turkey mission; and I have selected it to show how, in the use of appropriate means, with the divine blessing, a mission church may become as leaven thrown into the lump, and how its offshoots, developing into other churches, and they becoming the nuclei of congregations, grow and multiply until they fill the land. At the end of eleven years from the commencement of that church, the work had so extended, that there were connected with it thirteen churches; four hundred and eighteen church-members; eleven native pastors, more than half of them supported by their own people; twelve licensed native preachers; twenty-one native teachers, and forty-one other helpers. The people were very poor; but, as in the Macedonian church of old, "their deep poverty abounded unto the riches of their liberality." Of pupils there were two thousand and forty-one; and scores of unpaid laborers went spontaneously forth every Sabbath-day, as missionaries into the harvest fields around. This was the growth of a single missionary station, and of a single church, in less than twelve years.[1]

The missionary stations at Aintab and Marash, in the Central Turkey mission, are illustrations of the speedy gathering of large mission churches and congregations. It lately became necessary to divide the churches at each of those stations, and the number of members in each of the four churches, thus constituted, was about one hundred and fifty, with congregations of from six to eight hundred. It is not twenty years since the first missionary sent to Aintab was stoned and driven away by the people. Eight years after that time, visiting Aintab, I was

[1] See *Ten Years on the Euphrates*, and *Letters from Eden*, by Rev. C. H. Wheeler.

myself met by a cavalcade of Christian men, several miles from Aintab, who escorted me into the very heart of the city, and I saw nowhere among the people so much as a look of disapprobation. It is only twelve years since a missionary station was begun at Marash; but it was not effected until the messengers of the gospel had been driven away repeatedly by violence. Yet, in 1861, the late Dr. Dwight from Constantinople, being in Marash at a communion season, had the joy of addressing an orderly assembly of twelve hundred people.

Time would fail me to speak of the growth and value of churches elsewhere. Enough has been adduced to show, that the chief work of evangelical Christendom for the conversion of the heathen world, is to plant churches, instinct with gospel life, in all the central and influential districts of the unevangelized land.

I next illustrate the value of a *native ministry.* This also I do by adducing some of the more remarkable cases.

The first is that of a Karen preacher, pastor, and missionary, named Quala (or Sau Quala), a convert of the Baptist mission in Burmah. Quala signifies "Hope," and the name was given him by his parents because of hoped-for relief from Burmese oppression, awakened by the entrance of British ships into Burman ports at the time of his birth; but it was not till the boy was fifteen or sixteen years old, that the British took actual possession of Tavoy. Three years after this, the first Karen convert was baptized by Dr. Judson, and began immediately to preach, and the first sermon of this convert was in the house of Quala's father. That sermon was blessed to the inquiring youth, who was received into the church in the year 1830, thirty-eight years ago.

As with so many of his countrymen, so with him; the first impulse of his spiritual life was "to declare what God had done for his soul, and to invite all whom he could reach to believe and live." His father was an unbeliever almost to the day of his death; but his mother is said to have been a "lovely picture," when sitting under the sound of the gospel, with large beaming eyes, full of intelligence, fixed on the speaker.[1] Quala resembled his mother. He was employed some years by the missionaries in assisting to translate the New Testament into the Karen language. For fifteen years he accompanied the missionary in his jungle-tours in Tavoy and Mergui, tours sometimes extended three or four hundred miles; and they together laid the foundations in those regions of many Karen churches. Thus was this young servant of the Lord prepared for more responsible service.

It is a striking illustration of the excessive cau-

[1] *Gospel in Burmah*, p. 215.

tion of early missionaries in putting native converts into the ministry, that Quala did not receive ordination until fourteen years after his reception into the church.[1] Some time after this, he felt strongly moved to enter on what proved to be the great work of his life, a mission to the Karens in the province of Toungoo. This was a great trial to the churches in Tavoy and Mergui, all of which joined in a written remonstrance to the missionaries against his leaving them. It was like our sending to the heathen our most useful, learned, and valued pastors and ministers. But it was decided to be his duty to go, as may yet perhaps be true of some such men among ourselves. Quala reached Toungoo in December, 1853, the year after that province, by the annexation of Pegu, came under the protection of English law. The first baptism he performed was in the following January. Before the close of that year, the number of converts connected with his labors was seven hundred and forty-one, who were associated in nine churches. In less than three years, the number of churches was increased under his ministry to thirty, with an aggregate of two thousand one hundred and twenty-seven members, more than two thousand of whom were baptized by Quala himself.[2] Nor do those con-

[1] *Gospel in Burmah*, p. 231, 236.

[2] *Gospel in Burmah*, p. 241; also, *Reports of the American Baptist Union* for 1856, pp. 72, 76; and for 1855, p. 86.

verts appear to have been admitted to the church without due consideration. His labors and fatigue were truly apostolical, and such was his success. His singleness of purpose was like that of the Apostle Paul. He received no salary in Toungoo, and, being constantly on the move, he found it necessary, for two years, to leave his lovely wife in Tavoy, who is represented as "the flower of the jungle." One and another of the native disciples gave him a garment when he needed it, and, having no house, he got his food where he labored.

The wild mountain Karens, in "regions beyond," sent a petition, that he would come and tell them of the "Eternal God." The English Commissioner, hearing of this, offered Quala a salary from the English government, if he would become the head and overseer of that wild tribe. Quala gives this very touching account of his conference with the Commissioner. His reply was: "Sir, I cannot do it. I will not have the money. I will not mix up God's work with government work. There are others to do this thing. Employ them. As for me, I will continue the work in which I have been engaged." The Commissioner asked, "Where do you obtain money to live on? Why do you not like money? We will give you money, and you may continue your work as teacher as heretofore. Will it not make it easier for you?" He answered, "No, sir; when I eat with the children of poverty, my heart sleeps. I did not leave my dear wife, and come up hither in search of silver, or agreeable food. I came to this land that its poor people might be saved. Be patient with me, sir. Were I to take your money, the wild Karens would turn against me." Admirable man! Where shall we find his equal in devotion to the cause of Christ?

This servant of God is still living, after a most useful career, in a venerable old age.[1] Though he stands out preëminently above his brethren in the native Karen ministry, we still recognize him as a Karen, and as owing all that he was and is to the grace of God, who can easily raise up many such men from among heathen converts.

Many of the older missions in other heathen countries have also had native ministers of distinguished ability and usefulness, but I shall specify only two more.

The Rev. John Thomas, a distinguished missionary of the English Church Missionary Society in Southern India, having the care of ten thousand native Christians, speaks thus of a native preacher among the Shanars: "Without any exception, he is the most able and eloquent native preacher of the gospel now in India." "I have no hesitation," Mr. Thomas adds, "in saying, that if such sermons as

[1] In the *Annual Report of the Baptist Missionary Union* for 1864, he is called "the Prince of Preachers."

are generally preached by him, were delivered in any pulpit in London, the church would be crowded to overflowing. Nor am I singular in this opinion, for several of my brother missionaries, after hearing him, have expressed themselves in terms of the highest admiration of his pulpit abilities. The people, also, everywhere, listen to him with great attention and delight."

In 1860, death deprived Mr. Thomas of this beloved native co-laborer, and the missionary thus testifies to his worth: "His affection, his simplicity, honesty, and straightforwardness, his amazing pulpit talents, and profound humility, endeared him to me more than I can describe. The last sermon I heard from him was, without exception, the greatest sermon I ever heard. The text was, 'Enduring the cross, despising the shame.' Never did I hear Christ so exalted by human tongue. The effect was perfectly overwhelming."

My third specimen is Bartimeus, an eloquent blind native preacher at the Sandwich Islands. From the lowest physical, intellectual, moral, and social degradation and wretchedness, in his state of heathenism, Bartimeus (so named at his baptism) gradually rose, under the new-creating power of the gospel, to be a devoted, active, eloquent, and successful minister of the Word. The late Dr. Armstrong, a judicious and able missionary, who was with him five years, speaks thus of him: "He is a short man, and rather corpulent, very inferior in appearance when sitting, but when he rises to speak he looks well, stands erect, gesticulates with freedom, and pours forth, as he becomes animated, words in torrents. He is perfectly familiar with the former as well as the present modes of thinking of the islanders, which gives him a power in comparisons, allusions, and direct appeals, which no foreigner will ever possess. Often, while listening with exquisite delight to his eloquent strains, have I thought of Wirt's description of the celebrated blind preacher of Virginia."

Bartimeus died in the autumn of 1843. "His funeral," says the Rev. E. W. Clark, one of the older members of the mission, "was attended by a large congregation of sincere mourners. The voice which had so often been heard among us in devout supplication, and in earnest entreaty, calling the sinner to repentance, was silent in death. His purified spirit, raised from the darkest heathenism, by the blessing of God on missionary labor, was at peace with the Saviour."

His calling to be a preacher was evidently of God. He had original endowments for that service. He had great strength of memory, and there has already been a reference to his eloquence. An illustration of both is given by Mr. Clark, writing from Wailuku soon after his decease.

"In January last, I met him at a protracted meeting, and was then more than ever impressed with the extent and accuracy of his knowledge of the Scriptures. He was called upon to preach at an evening meeting. His heart was glowing with love for souls. The overwhelming destruction of the impenitent seemed to be pressing with great weight upon his mind; and this he took for the subject of his discourse at the evening meeting. He chose for the foundation of his remarks, Jer. iv. 13: 'Behold, he shall come up as clouds, and his chariots shall be as a whirlwind.' The anger of the Lord against the wicked, and the terrible overthrow of all his enemies, were portrayed in vivid colors. He seized upon the terrific image of a whirlwind or tornado as an emblem of the ruin which God would bring upon his enemies. This image he presented in all its majestic and awful aspects, enforcing his remarks with such passages as Ps. lviii. 9: 'He shall take them away as with a whirlwind, both living, and in his wrath;' Prov. i. 27: 'And your destruction cometh as a whirlwind;' Isa. xl. 24: 'And the whirlwind shall take them away as stubble;' Jer. xxx. 23: 'Behold, the whirlwind of the Lord goeth forth with fury, a continuing whirlwind; it shall fall with pain upon the head of the wicked;' Hosea viii. 7: 'For they have sown the wind, and they shall reap the whirlwind;' Nahum i. 3, Zech. vii. 14, and other passages in which the same image is presented

—always quoting chapter and verse. I was surprised to find that this image is so often used by the sacred writers. And how this blind man, never having used a concordance or a reference Bible in his life, could, on the spur of the moment, refer to all these texts, was quite a mystery. But his mind was stored with the precious treasure, and in such order that he always had it at command. Never have I been so forcibly impressed, as while listening to this address, with the remark of the apostle, 'Knowing, therefore, the terror of the Lord, we persuade men;' and seldom have I witnessed a specimen of more genuine eloquence. Near the close he said, 'Who can withstand the fury of the Lord, when he comes in his chariots of whirlwind? You have heard of the cars in America, propelled by fire and steam, with what mighty speed they go, and how they crush all in their way; so will the swift chariots of Jehovah overwhelm all his enemies. Flee, then, to the ark of safety.'"

These three remarkable men were from the lowest grades of heathen life. What they became was the result of the grace of God, through the gospel, and I bring them forward that our hopes may be raised as to what God may be expected to do through a native ministry. We must not, however, expect such eloquent native preachers to bear a larger proportion among the ministers of their own respective countries, than such men do in our own. As in old Christian countries, so among preachers of heathen lands, they give a character to their profession. We thereby obtain a more exalted and just view of the capabilities of the profession; and they help to overcome the natural backwardness in missionaries to throw responsibilities on a ministry so recently rescued from the pollutions of idolatry.

My own estimate of the value of a native ministry has been rising for more than a score of years. A large number of the Christian islands in Central and Western Polynesia are properly reckoned among their trophies. They have been the fearless pioneers of the white missionary, facing dangers which to him would have been fatal, and which were sometimes fatal to themselves; and many a beautiful Christianized group in the broad Pacific is now manned solely by native missionaries and pastors.

The question naturally arises, and needs a brief reply, Whether mission churches may be expected to hold fast to their profession, in case the missionaries should withdraw, and leave them to themselves? There are some very interesting facts bearing on this question.

The churches of Tahiti, one of the Society Islands, were thus situated, for twenty years after the English missionaries had been excluded by the French. They were living under French rule, and fully exposed to French vices and to Roman Catholic influences; and were left by the missionaries, moreover, without native pastors. Yet, as is related elsewhere, they at once instituted pastors from among themselves, and more than held their ground. Tahiti and its dependencies are still under French rule; but it was stated last year by a London journal, that there are now thirty-seven native Protestant parishes and churches with only native pastors, containing three thousand communicants; and that Pomare, the queen, and nearly all her people, still adhere to the Protestant faith.[1]

And we have seen how it was in Madagascar, after the banishment of the English missionaries, and during five and twenty years of persecution. I know of no more remarkable firmness in the primitive churches. The blood of the martyrs in Madagascar, as in ancient times, was the seed of the church. We have seen, too, how it was with the native Christians in India, during the great rebellion; which had for its object not only the overthrow of the English power, but the utter destruction of Christianity, and when the native Christians were without the presence and support of their missionary fathers and brethren. Nowhere — never, was greater firmness shown by persecuted Christians than by those.

As the rebellion did not extend to Southern India,

[1] *London Patriot*, Aug. 16, 1866, p. 542.

the native Christians there did not pass through the fiery ordeal of their brethren at the north. Yet the Rev. Mr. Thomas, the venerable missionary already quoted, bears the most pleasing testimony concerning the native Christians under his missionary care. "I do not for a moment doubt," he says, "but that this people would retain their religion, if the English government in India, and all the missionaries, were providentially withdrawn from the country. Their stability arises very much, I think, from their knowledge of God's holy word, and the very great extent to which the power of reading that word has been afforded by means of our village vernacular schools."[1] Thus showing wherein lies the strength and glory of Protestant missions, as distinguished from those of the Romish Church.

It is natural also to inquire, Whether what are called revivals of religion are common in churches among the heathen? They appear to me to be not unfrequent, and to be evidently the work of the Holy Spirit. Indeed, revivals of religion do not seem peculiar to any age, or country, where there is vital religion. The reformation in the days of Hezekiah is declared to have occurred "suddenly."[2] It was both sudden and rapid. So was that in the time of Ezra. So was that in the time of John, the

[1] *Church Missionary Report*, 1864–5, p. 134.

[2] 2 Chron. xxix. 36.

forerunner. So was that of the Pentecost. Such must have been the character of much of the success of the Apostle Paul; else why was he represented, by his opposers, as creating so great a disturbance? Such was the reformation in the time of Luther, whose grand victory was achieved within ten years after he first raised the standard of reform. The "Great Awakening" in New England was also sudden and rapid. So was that at the Sandwich Islands. In a very few years, subsequent to 1836, more than thirty thousand hopeful converts were added to the church. Nor was the progress of the gospel less rapid in the Islands of the South Pacific. We have seen how it was in Sierra Leone, in Madagascar, and among the Karens of Burmah. In the missions of Western Asia there have been frequent revivals, though no one was very extensive. And we have reason to believe that this general law of progress in the kingdom of Christ will be more and more exemplified as the time for the world's conversion draws near.

In the Christian Church, which is yet but partially sanctified, the stream of gospel grace has not a continuous, even flow. It meets with obstructions; and when it rises above them and overflows them, we call the overflow a revival, a reformation.

The influences that modify revivals of religion are clearly seen in the heathen world. The really great awakenings hitherto, have all been among what may be called the aboriginal races, where the gospel encounters less of organized antagonism than in the conquering and dominant races. And by pressing the work among these more pliant races, the Evangelical Church has not only gained important positions and advantages, but has had the encouragement it so much needed at the outset of its great work, to labor hopefully and patiently in the fields of greater difficulty, where the harvest must needs be delayed, but will be more abundant when it comes.

CHAPTER IX.

MISSIONARY LIFE ILLUSTRATED.

Fundamental Principles. — The Missionary contemplated in his Relations — as a Son; as a Brother; as a Husband; as a Father — to his Missionary Board; to his Mission; to the People for whom he labors. — Influence of the Missionary Life on Mental Development; on Piety; on Happiness. — Cautionary Suggestions.

I PROPOSE to illustrate the Missionary Life in some of its more important relations, as that life has fallen under my personal observation. Of course on such a topic I must draw my facts from the experience of that Board of Missions, with which I have been officially connected. There will be an advantage in presenting this particular aspect of the missionary life; and should secretaries of other societies do the same with theirs, it would doubtless be found, that there is no great diversity in its general aspects.

It is a fundamental principle, that the missionary goes on his mission in the discharge of his own personal duty; not as a servant of the churches, and not as a servant of the missionary society. The churches and the missionary society are his helpers, to carry out his own benevolent purpose. The missionary is indebted to the churches just as the churches are indebted to him; and he does their work in the same sense in which they do his by supporting him. This is the view that best comports with the prosecution of missions on an extended scale.

Moreover, the missionary and the pastor both derive their authority from the same commission. Both are alike "called of God" to the ministry of the gospel. The notion that "evangelists," in the Scripture sense of that term, were restricted, as an order of ministers, to the apostolic age, and that pastors are now the only Scriptural ministry, — which bears too great a resemblance to the old Popish notion, that ministers may not be ordained *sine titulo*, — though countenanced by some of the Puritan Fathers, was disowned by the Presbyterians in 1764, and is not in keeping with the command of our Lord, as at present understood, to preach the gospel to every creature. If there be any class of gospel ministers, which is clearly recognized and enjoined in the New Testament, to endure until the world is converted, it is Christ's ambassadors to the benighted and the lost; it is those who devote their lives to the extension of his kingdom.

Should any one affirm, in opposition to this view, that we find directions in St. Paul's Epistles only for the office of presbyters, then what are the Epistles to Timothy and Titus?[1]

[1] See Appendix VI.— Looking from the author's stand-point, it seems

I now contemplate the missionary in some of his more important personal relations.

1. In his relations as a *son* and a *brother*. It is not uncommon for parents to make objections, at first, to the going of a son or daughter on a foreign mission. This is often the result of mere natural instinct; as in the mother of Samuel J. Mills, though she had dedicated him from his birth to the work of missions, and when it is so, as in her case, the objection soon yields to reflection. Sometimes

strange that the fathers of Congregationalism should have taken the limited view some of them did of the office and duties of the gospel ministry, and of the power and duty of the churches to provide a competent ministry for planting churches outside of Christendom, and supplying those churches with a competent pastorate. To instance only the excellent Dr. Owen, in his *Discourses of Spiritual Gifts*. [*Works*, iv. p. 275.] After declaring it to be the principal work of an evangelist, "to go up and down from one place and nation unto another, to preach the gospel unto Jews and Gentiles as yet unconverted," he asks: "Who shall now empower any one hereunto? What church, what persons, have received authority to ordain any one to be such an evangelist? It cannot be proved," he adds, "that any church or person has power or authority to ordain a person into this office!" That the eminent divine was writing with no reference to the claims and exigencies of the heathen world of his times, with the restricted idea of the church as a self-preserving, self-governing, and not a self-propagating body, and mainly with his eye on hierarchal assumptions so rampant in those times, is obvious from the general tenor of his reasoning. Had he lived in our day, he would on no account have shut up the preaching ministry of the church to the pastoral office, nor to lands already Christianized. Nor will the evangelical churches and ministry of any denomination, in these days, allow themselves to be restricted in their labors for the kingdom of their blessed Lord and Saviour.

it is the result of ignorance concerning missions, or of a lack of pious reflection, or of deficient self-consecration. In such cases it is not common, I believe, for parents to yield, until they clearly see that the mind of their son or daughter is made up on conscientious grounds. Supposing the parent to be in the wrong, there is the more call for calm persistence in the child, because such a state of mind must be injurious to the parent, and because the parent will be almost sure to yield at last (if a true disciple), and to find the sacrifice conducive to his growth in grace and religious enjoyment.

I recollect but one instance, and that many years since, in which a mother regarded the mission contemplated by her two sons with such nervous terror, as to threaten the overthrow of her reason. Both of the sons were members of the Andover Seminary, and the case was so marked, that I advised them, as a filial duty, to relinquish the idea of going abroad, and they are now highly useful pastors. Our Saviour's declaration, Mark vii. 11,[1] is obviously applicable to cases of this sort; as also, when the comfortable support of parents requires the young minister to remain near them. There is a tradition of Dr. Milné, the celebrated associate of Dr. Morrison, in China, which probably has some foundation in

[1] "But ye say, If a man shall say to his father or mother, It is Corban, that is to say, a gift, by whatsoever thou mightest be profited by me, he shall go free," etc.

fact; that before decidedly entering on his preparation for a foreign mission, he labored to secure a cottage, a cow, and a few other needful things for his Scottish mother, which placed her in comfortable circumstances. In so doing, he complied with the spirit of our Lord's injunction. I recollect one instance, and but one, of a missionary actually coming home, which he did with the approval of his society, to look after an impoverished and dependent mother. Very few cases have come within my knowledge, however, where parents have actually suffered for want of support, as a consequence of giving up their children to the gospel ministry among the heathen. Questions of this sort have more frequently had weight when the theological student was deciding upon his duty prospectively, and generally because of younger brothers or sisters requiring protection and aid. It is my belief, that the claims of kindred have exerted very little more legitimate influence in relation to foreign missions, than they have in determining where to settle in pastoral life at home.

2. I contemplate the missionary in the relations of a *husband* and *father*. That he should generally go as a married man, is beyond all reasonable question. With an intelligent, pious, well-educated wife, having good health and a devoted spirit, his value as a missionary is greatly enhanced. She faces danger and endures hardship as well as he. Her courage,

faith, and patience among barbarous heathens, fully equal her husband's, and her presence adds much to his safety, and the more if she have little children. When the wife proves unable to endure the exposures of a missionary life, if the medical opinion require a visit to this country, and the mission advise it, the executive committee seldom hesitates to afford the means for a return, and reasonable facilities, also, for a recovery of health. When a recovery, such as would warrant a return to the mission, is out of the question, an honorable release is granted, and the missionary exercises his ministry in his native land. Some of the most esteemed of our home ministers have been of this class.

How is it with the children of missionaries? I am probably as well informed on this subject as any other person, and I approach it with pleasure. I speak of the children after they have been separated from their parents, and brought to this country for education.

In continental tropical regions, there are reasons in the climate why children should be sent home; but generally they may be safely retained there until about the age of twelve years, in which time the very important result is secured, if it ever is, of impressing the parental relation strongly upon the mind and heart of the child. There are various reasons, besides the climate, for sending children home. By obtaining a part of their education here, they will be of far greater value as the probable successors of their parents in the missionary work. Indeed, a competent education for that service, or for any of the higher departments of a Christian life, cannot be well obtained either in India or China; and when the time comes for a transfer to the parental home, the parents, though weeping over the sacrifice, are ready, out of love to their offspring, to welcome it as a boon.

The time for sending the children home rests wholly with the parents, as also does the choice of a guardian; for it is expected that the parental authority will always be delegated by the parent to some one in this country. The expenses of the voyage are usually met by the missionary society, which also makes an annual grant to the child of about one hundred dollars until eighteen years of age, when applied for by the guardian. As the missionary society sustains an equal relation to all the returned children, and could not be at the expense of giving a liberal education to all, it is obviously precluded from making grants expressly for the education of any one at college. It aims to do just enough, as shown by experience, to secure a place for the returned children of missionaries in the great current of social life in this country, which bears along the children of Christian parents. It aims to do just enough to enable and induce relatives and friends to do the rest. More than this would tend to defeat the object of sending the children home. A permanent fund raised for this purpose, which some have urged, besides being unnecessary, would be detrimental in various respects to the best interests. of the children. A separate school for them, which some have strongly recommended, would be a calamity, since they ought by all means to be educated along with other boys and girls, along with the young men and women of their generation. Missionaries would generally, and with good reason, oppose such a separation and isolation of their children.

I have made considerable progress in obtaining positive information as to the results of this system. Answers have been received to one hundred and eighty-four printed circulars sent to returned children above twelve years of age, or to their guardians. The age of the oldest of these is now almost fifty years, and their places of residence of course it is not always easy to ascertain. The number of males was ninety-five, and of females eighty-nine. Of the ninety-five males, seventy-one were reported to be members of churches; and of the eighty-nine females, seventy-eight were thus reported. That is to say, one hundred and forty-nine of the one hundred and eighty-four were church-members. Although the Board has never made a single grant, so far as I recollect, expressly for a college education, for the reason just stated, yet as many as fifty-one of the ninety-five males have received such an education, or are now receiving it; and thirty-one others are in academies, and believed to be generally preparing for college. That is to say, eighty-two of the ninety-five males are reported as having received, or as now receiving a liberal education; and thirteen of them have been or are now in the gospel ministry. Of the eighty-nine females, seventy-eight are reported as having received, or as now receiving, an education in academies or high schools; and thirteen of them are, or have been wives of missionaries. Responses from those not heard from, would, I believe, vary but little from the reports already received.

These will probably be regarded as remarkable results, — superior, perhaps, to what we should find on a similar inquiry into the circumstances and history of any other class of children in our country; and they are directly referable to the providence and grace of God. How large a proportion of them we may number among the followers of the Lamb! How large a proportion receive the best education our country affords! And yet who is able to tell, in respect to most, in what manner all the expenses of their college or high school education have been met? We see clearly the hand of Him, who said, "Lo, I am with you always."

3. I next contemplate the missionary in his rela-

tions to his *Missionary Board.* The missionary has the same ecclesiastical liberty which pastors have at home; and he is, at the same time, as much under proper controlling influences. No body of ministers is more free, or under greater responsibility. I say this in view of the fundamental principle with which I started, that the missionary goes on his mission in the conscientious discharge of his personal duty to his Lord and Master. And I rejoice in being able to say, that, in this service, he is quite sure of what is or ought to be a comfortable support. The enterprise of the celebrated Müller, in England, is often spoken of as if it were peculiarly a work of faith. It does not seem to me to be so very peculiar in this respect. That of the American Board, in appropriating half a million of dollars and more for an expenditure a year before it is received, is not less a work of faith. The trust in God is the same in nature, the same in degree; and so, substantially, is the use of means. This is true as to the support of every missionary. The pledge given by the missionary society of a support to its missionaries, is nothing more than the expression of an assured faith, that the means will be provided. The Board can give no more than it receives. There is no firm footing for the society, or for its missionaries, except in the promise of the great Lord of all. If the missionary feels sure of a support, it is for precisely the reason that is said to animate the celebrated philanthropist just named.

I believe there has been no case in the experience of the American Board, where the missionary has failed to receive his full salary, nor do I believe there ever will be. The ground of this confidence is in faith; strengthened indeed by a long experience, and by the well-known fact in missions to foreign heathen lands, that such a support is essential to their existence. Nor do I believe it will ever be found more difficult than it has been heretofore, to provide for the returned disabled missionary, and for the missionary widow. As for the returned children of missionaries, I cannot doubt that a way will ere long be devised, with but little actual increase of expense, to enable every missionary, acting through his relatives and friends, or in coöperation with them, to take the whole arrangement for the education of his children in this country into his own hands, just as ministers do who are in the pastoral office at home.

I next inquire, how it is with the missionary when no longer able to labor in his field. The case differs from that of the pastor at home chiefly in this, that the Executive Committee of the Board, perhaps without having greater power than parishes generally have to do what is equitable in the case, has yet a stronger disposition so to do. Each case is treated on its own individual merits, with the intention always to do what is equitable. There is some times a difference of opinion between the missionary and his mission, and sometimes between the missionary and his committee; but in all cases, so far as I recollect, where an appeal was made to the public judgment, the final result has been, substantially, with the mission, and with the committee. I fear as much as this can hardly be said of parishes here at home as a general fact, nor even of churches, in relation to their dismissed pastors.

The case of returned widows is the most difficult to treat, because they so easily pass out from observation. This is specially true of the more meritorious among them. Nevertheless I believe, that as a class, they are, to say the least, as much favored as are the widows of pastors at home. Some persons have advocated the raising of a fund for their support; and such a fund could be raised. But it would injure the Board, without being of use to them. The possession, by the Missionary Board, of a greater amount of permanent funds than is actually needed for its credit in the world of commerce, would weaken that principle of faith, on which so much depends. And where it is a fact, that as much is allowed to widows, all things considered, as ought to be, to aid them in serving the Lord Jesus in their widowed state, then it would not be expected that they should receive a greater amount, were there a widow's fund. Nor would grants made to them from such a fund be any less a charity than they are under the present arrangement. Nor, in either case, would it be more a charity than our blessed Lord submitted to during his whole public ministry on earth. The servant is not above his Lord.

After carefully examining the experience of the American Board from the commencement of its operations, I have no hesitation in affirming, that the widows of missionaries have been as kindly cared for, as a class, as are the widows of pastors in this country; and I could use even stronger language, were it needful.

The result of my observation on this whole subject, during the past five and forty years, is, that the relation between the missionary and his Board is one of great mutual satisfaction; though of course not without its share of the misapprehensions and trials which are incident to every sphere of human life.

4. We come next to the relations sustained by the missionary to his *mission*. In the mission he belongs to a self-governing republic, where every man has an equal vote, and where the majority rules; with the right, however (which is very rarely exercised), of an appeal to the Prudential Committee, and ultimately to the Board. Years ago, a certain mission was much afflicted by divided counsels among its members, and the cause was not apparent.

It was at length ascertained, that this was the result of a want of a proper division of labor among the several missionaries. The missionaries had not a sufficient weight of responsibility resting upon them individually. This principle, in its relations to missions, was then somewhat of a discovery, and has since been acted on with the most happy results. When missionaries have been trained to feel fully the moral responsibility of a majority vote (as it has been found that Europeans, from a deficiency in their early education, seldom are), and when each has a sufficient pressure of duty, this method of organizing missions works exceedingly well.

The policy of the American Board is, to throw all possible responsibility upon the mission thus organized. That is not, however, in the technical sense, an ecclesiastical body. It is simply a mission acting under the commission of our blessed Lord, with liberty to do what is needful for its greatest success. Of course there is, as there ought to be, much room for the exercise of a wise discretion, and for the development of experience. We have been learning, during the fifty or sixty years past, in what manner a mission should be worked, but probably have yet more to learn. We have learned this: that particular forms of ecclesiastical machinery, because they work well at home, are not therefore to be regarded as exactly the thing to be set up in young Christian communities formed in heathen lands; and precisely what the modifications should be, is still an open question. We have learned, moreover, that matters of this sort should be mainly left to the discretion of missionaries in the field. They have liberty to form associations, or presbyteries, as they feel the need of them; yet since their financial questions all belong to the mission as such, and since most of the questions that arise have more or less connection with finance, their social life is very much in the meetings of the mission, or of its committees. Moreover, it is a fundamental principle, in the system of missions now under special contemplation, that ecclesiastical bodies for native churches and pastors, should be exclusively for them; the missionaries sustaining to them only the relation of advisers.

Of course the relations of missionaries to their missions in no degree affect their relations to their ecclesiastical bodies at home. The Board may dismiss a missionary for malpractice, but cannot depose him from the ministry; yet the ecclesiastical body at home may call upon the Board for the facts within its knowledge, when investigating the conduct of a missionary to learn whether he should be deposed from the ministry.

I should add, that missionary societies and the missions, though technically speaking not ecclesiastical bodies, have become (as has been elsewhere affirmed) a component part of the great modern structure of the Christian Church, as it is being organized under God's providence, for the conversion of the world; and they should be permitted to sustain the responsibilities and perform the duties, that are essential to the successful prosecution of the missionary work on the broad scale of the world.

5. We next contemplate the missionary in his relations to the *people for whom he labors.* He is an ambassador from the Sovereign Lord to benighted men in a state of rebellion, with a message of mercy. And it seems reasonable to suppose, after he has acquired the language of the people, that no elaborate process of education is needful to make the people understand his message. Many of the earlier missionaries thought otherwise; and it would be easy to find statements, by eminent men now in the "Better Land," showing how the heathen must be elaborately educated into the Christian import of the words God, sin, holiness, and other similar terms, before they will be able to comprehend the gospel message. There is something in this, if the gospel message is to be conveyed to the heathen simply through a process of education. But the heathen *know* that they are sinners; they have a conscience; and if boldly and affectionately approached by one whose own heart is full of the subject, and solemnly assured of their lost condition as sinners, and of the free salvation offered them through the

Lord Jesus Christ, experience has abundantly shown, that there is no way so effectual as this of securing the aid of the Holy Spirit for their conversion. The gospel may have direct access to the most debased heathen mind. Of this there is evidence in the abounding proofs of the success of missions. We see it in Sierra Leone, among the Karens and Shanars of India, in Madagascar, in South Africa, and on the Pacific Islands. The especial demand in missions for education and for books comes *after* the attention has been arrested, and more especially for converts, and for such as are being trained for the gospel ministry. Nothing necessarily precedes the simple declaration of salvation through the cross of Christ, when it comes from lips that have been touched with a coal from off the altar of God.

6. I now contemplate the missionary simply as a *man*. And, first, as to the influence of missionary life on his mental development. I believe there is as much of this development in missionaries, as there is in the home ministry; and the question I raise is only how this is possible in circumstances apparently so unfavorable. I account for it by the fact, that, with the more intelligent missionaries, the pressure is not less upon the mental faculties, than it is in the pastoral office at home; and this is as true in the more barbarous heathen countries, as it is in the more civilized. I even

think, that the mental pressure upon the intelligent and conscientious missionary is often greater than it is upon his brethren at home. For he finds that there is everything to be done, and that he is the only one to do it. He must be feet to the lame, eyes to the blind, ears to the deaf, and must almost reconstruct the intellect, and almost recreate the conscience. Did this responsibility come upon the missionary all at once, he could not bear it; but come it will, sooner or later, and the intelligent and faithful missionary need fear no loss of stimulus to his mind. It is the same that operated on the mind and heart of the apostle to the Gentiles; and it will increase with his years, especially in its demands upon the judging and administrative powers.

How is it with the influence of the missionary life upon the happiness of the missionary? Among the more than four hundred ordained missionaries, with whom I have sustained an intimate official relation, there have been cases of extreme sorrow; arising from early prostration of the health, from the predominance of morbid sensibilities, from failure to acquire the language, and other causes. But these have been the exceptions, not the rule. The missionaries as a body have been happy in the field and work of their choice. They have seemed to me, when among them at their several homes, both men and women, to be, as a whole, the happiest clerical families within my knowledge. There is no way of accounting for this, but in the fulfillment of the Saviour's promise. For it is a fact that missionaries, being far away from civilized Christian society, experience a certain degree of loss in the diminished pressure of a wholesome public opinion, which surrounds and sustains us in Christian lands like an atmosphere; thus creating a need of more grace to insure right feeling and living, than is required at home. Nor do I believe that any Protestant missionary, without this special grace, is likely to persevere in his mission. But the grace that is needed is usually imparted; and if sacrifices are demanded, there is a pleasure in making them for Christ which is proportioned to the sacrifice. That missionary mother, parting with her child on the Burman shore, when she raised her hand to heaven and exclaimed, "O Saviour, I do this for thee!" must have felt a joy at that moment, rising above her grief, akin to that of the martyr at the stake. And what joy had Sarah Lanman Smith, dying in Western Asia, when she declared that, for the world, she would not lay her remains anywhere but there on missionary ground.

And this leads me to speak, finally, of the influence of missionary life on the piety of the missionary. For the reason just now stated, more strength of piety is required to be a good missionary among the heathen, than to be a good pastor at home. I do not claim for missionaries a more perfect exhibition of the Christian life, than is seen in the home ministry; but since, in their exposed circumstances, they need a higher and firmer tone of the inward Christian life, I think that, through divine grace, they have it. I believe that is the impression made by them, as a class, in their visits to this country. At any rate, that is the impression they have made upon me.

I have long been impressed with the general character of missionary death-beds. The love of native land and of the friends in that land, is not diminished by distance or the lapse of time, and death sometimes comes early to the missionary, and unexpectedly, and in circumstances of great discomfort; yet I recall no case of regret expressed at meeting it, by the missionary, or his wife, under any circumstances on missionary ground. The sentiment expressed by Mrs. Smith, has been the common sentiment with missionaries; and the venerable Allen Graves, when he came from India, many years ago, for the benefit of his health, and found that he must die, proffered a request through me, that he might be allowed to return to India and die there, which request was granted. Harriet Newell, when told, on the Isle of France, that she was soon to leave the world, exclaimed, "Joyful news! I long to depart." The last audible words of Levi Parsons, dying in Egypt, were, "The angel of the Lord encampeth round about them that fear him." Mrs.

Poor's dying words in Ceylon were, "Glory to God the Father, to God the Son, to God the Holy Ghost"—words, it may be, among the first she uttered on reaching the heavenly world. And her venerated husband, dying many years after, whispered, as he closed his eyes on earth, "Joy! Joy! Hallelujah!" "If *this* be the *dark valley*," said the excellent Mrs. Hervey, dying soon after her arrival in India, "there is no darkness in it; all is light—light!"

And the cases might be easily multiplied of calm, peaceful trust in Christ in the dying hour, of a tranquil hope of immortality, and of gratitude for the privilege of living and dying in the work of missions.

I may not close without a few suggestions, which are needed to prevent misapprehension.

As I have stated the case, the support of the foreign missionary and his family is more nearly a uniform and adequate supply of their temporal wants, than is generally enjoyed by ministers and their families in this country. The final cause for this, in the ordering of Divine Providence, would seem to be, that the prosecution of missions among heathen nations by married missionaries, would not otherwise be a possibility. How could a missionary, with wife and children, as human nature is, possibly keep the field in a tropical region, surrounded by a half-civilized, unsympathizing, heathen people, with only a partial or uncertain support? Very different would it be, were he anywhere within the bounds of his native land, in a community homogeneous with himself, where only a few years are needed for the incoming of civilization to develop a congenial home for his family; and still more, were he laboring in an already matured and well-organized Christian community. A mission composed of married missionaries does indeed cost considerably more than would a mission composed of persons that are unmarried; yet such a mission is so much more effective abroad, and so much more interesting at home, that it is easier, in point of fact, to obtain the means of supporting it from the churches, than it would be to support a mission of unmarried missionaries. An adequate support is believed to be an essential thing in foreign Protestant missions, since on no other supposition would such missions be possible on an extended scale.

Yet it is by no means true, as is often asserted, and as is perhaps generally believed, that the trials of the home missionary life are greater than those to which the foreign missionary is subjected. I do not undervalue the trials of the home missionary. My habit for many years has been carefully to note them, as set forth, monthly, by the Home Missionary Society; and they are a noble testimony to the self-consecration and zeal of that enterprising, devoted, and most useful and essential body of Christian ministers. But the most painful trials of gospel ministers, whether pastors or missionaries, are those which appertain to their spiritual vocation; and here the foreign missionary must be the greater sufferer. I have long ceased to expect a foreign missionary to persevere in his work, who does not enter upon it as a life of faith, and with a certain amount of physical, mental, and moral adaptation. Mere philosophers will not go on such missions, and mere philanthropists would not remain long, should they happen to go. Impulsive, unreflecting piety will give out before the day of embarkation, or retire ere the language has been acquired, or the battle has fairly begun. Fine conceptions of the beautiful in social life, glowing apprehensions of pastoral duty, broad and elevated views of the nature and relations of theological truth, are not sufficient to give enduring life to the zeal of a missionary. Something more than all this is needed. There must be the grand aim, the living, undying purpose, of reconciling men to God, and thus extending the kingdom of the blessed Redeemer. There needs to be a real enthusiasm, sustained by a spiritualized doctrinal experience, and by the "powers of the world to come." Nothing short of this will keep the foreign missionary cheerfully and long in the field.

And even with such missionaries, — who are men

after all, — it would be disastrous for a mission, should a well-founded apprehension come over it of failure in the temporal support of their families. A great mercy it is to the heathen world, and to the churches as bound to publish the gospel through the whole extent of that world, that the providence and grace of God, in the experience of the past fifty years, afford a wonderful guarantee for the earthly support of the missionary and his wife and children. It is one of the significant facts of our times, for which we should ascribe glory to God.

CHAPTER X.

HINDRANCES AT HOME.

The Chief Hindrance. — Want of Information. — Pastors will find this. — The Facts stated. — How the Ignorance is to be removed. Causes that are purely Providential. — Human Agencies. — Pastoral. — Sabbath-schools. — Monthly Concert of Prayer. — Missionary Publications. — Ecclesiastical Bodies. — Benevolent Societies. Hindrances resulting from Misapprehensions and Objections. Skepticism. — Change in the Evidences of Piety. — Circumstances favoring the Pastor. — The Responsibility of Christian People. Ministers all stand related to the Whole Work.

My present object is not so much to specify the hindrances to the work of missions in the churches at home, which exist in the form of misapprehensions and objections, though they will receive a brief consideration, as what I conceive to be, in true Christians, the root and source of them all; namely, ignorance of the facts in missions. I am to speak, then, of this great obstacle in Christian churches to the progress of the missionary work, and how it is to be removed. No department of duty, at the present time, is more deserving than this of critical attention from ministers of the gospel, and from the churches.

I. I must first illustrate the fact of this ignorance. The deficiency is in what may be called appropriate information. Specific duties demand appropriate facts, and these are indispensable. It was seeing the wounded man who fell among thieves, which called forth the compassionate ministrations of the good Samaritan. It was beholding the sin and misery of mankind, that brought the Son of God from heaven on his mission to earth.

Pastors will be sure to find among the members of their churches a deficiency in that kind of information, which is productive, through the divine blessing, of a missionary spirit. Our age is indeed called, and very properly, a reading age. "The popular taste," as one has justly said, "is discursive; travelling over the fields of trade, agriculture, commerce, and all the productive industries of the times. It follows the diplomacy of cabinets, and the movements of armies, with the world's map constantly in hand. It is alive to the lessons of science, the attractions of literature, and especially the fascinations of fiction, in its dealings with life and religion. And yet here is a cause confessedly transcending every other, in the judgment of the Christian mind, which, if we were to estimate its importance by what the bulk of the people know about it, we should be forced to set it down as one of the most insignificant topics of the day."[1]

This is the strong testimony of a writer in our father-land; and it is applicable to our own country.

[1] *The Missionary News*, 1866, p. 110.

How little accurate information has the great body of church-members in our best churches, as to the moral and religious condition of the world! Perhaps there are no churches in Christendom, unless we except the Moravian, which have a better missionary development than the Congregational churches in the States of Massachusetts and Connecticut; and I draw my illustration specially from them because I have more certain information concerning them. I believe that nowhere does a larger proportion of Christians read about missions, and pray for them, and contribute for their support. Yet it is known that even in the best of those churches, nearly one fourth of the members really contribute nothing for sending the gospel to the heathen, and scarcely more than a fifth part give attendance at the monthly concert of prayer for the conversion of the world. It is believed, also, to be true of those churches, with few exceptions, that not more than one professedly Christian family in three or four takes, or even looks into the monthly journal, which contains a definite and intelligent account of the missions they are pledged to support. The want of missionary information in the Presbyterian Church would seem to be also great, if we judge by the fact, stated on high authority, that nearly one half of the four or five thousand churches, in the year 1865, made no contribution whatever in support of the foreign missionary cause.

I will not presume to say how far missionary publications are actually read by those who take them, nor what amount of missionary information is actually imparted at the monthly concert. But I believe the interest which truly Christian people take in the missionary work, is equal to their correct knowledge of it. For we must charitably suppose, that the apparent insensibility of so many real Christians to the enlargement and glory of their Redeemer's kingdom on earth, is not because their hearts are really cold and dead to the interests of that kingdom, but because they know so little about it.

The great hindrance to the development of a missionary spirit in the evangelical churches, is in this lack of appropriate information. Its removal will, of course, require labor and time.

II. What are the means and agencies, by which this desirable, and even necessary end is to be attained?

1. I am happy to say, in the first place, by causes that are purely providential. The Providence, which has so marvelously opened the heathen world for the messengers of the gospel, as already described, is operating constantly in the churches, with a steadiness and force like that of the laws of nature. We are really part of a great progressive system of social religious life, and are moving on together. There

is inherent power in facts and ideas. Our social religious life is subject to the great laws of Providence. The stupendous changes already noticed as going forward in the heathen world and in Christendom, as the result of God's providence, should lead us to expect corresponding changes in what may be called the religious world, and especially in the evangelical churches. As an illustration of this onward movement, I refer to the early fathers of New England. Their writings show, that training the churches, intelligent and pious as they were, for the work of converting the heathen world, scarcely formed any part of their conceptions of pastoral duty. And the general tone of the very best informed ecclesiastical literature down to a late period, tells the same story. It was so, also, in pastoral life. The author's father was pastor of a church for nearly a score of years, and joyfully greeted the first developments of the missionary spirit in our own country. Yet he did not realize the duty of enlisting his church in missions to heathen nations, until about the time of the forming of the American Board. He was not blameworthy in this. There had been no perceptible call for it. The idea of that specific pastoral duty had not at that time a place in the public mind. It was a new idea; the introduction of a new power into the churches of our land.

But then commenced a remarkable inflow of facts, lights, and influences from the outer world upon the ministry and upon the churches of our land; forming one of the religious characteristics of our age. And these influences have never ceased their inflow, like tidal waves, with a constantly increasing power. It was with the church of God, in this respect, as it is with the sleeping world as day approaches. The stars are shining, and the breaking day reaches only a few. But the morn advances, and, with the rising sun, hamlet, village, and city awake, and go forth to the duties of life. The evangelical spirit of our churches has been coming, and is coming, more and more, under this providential influence; nor may we believe there will be an arrest of its progress, until the condition and claims of the heathen world are generally recognized by the really pious, and stand out in the light of a glorious day.

This providential inflow of missionary information and influence upon the churches, and the consequent development and growth of the missionary spirit among pastors and people, should encourage us. It is a blessed thing, and the wise and faithful pastor will favor it by every proper means.

2. Among the human agencies for the removal of this paralyzing evil, the first place is to be given to the pastoral. What should pastors do to remove the ignorance, and consequent indifference, of their people?

Their attention should be early given to the children of their charge, who need to be educated to a knowledge of what will be their future duty as Christians. There is doubtless a great deficiency here. Children are believed to have a less specific training for benevolent giving, especially giving for foreign missions, now, than they had when such missions were a new thing, forty or fifty years ago; though, in many other respects, there has doubtless been a progress. Our Sabbath-schools, so far as I have been able to learn, while they distinctly inculcate missions to the heathen as among the duties prescribed by the gospel, and while many of the schools give for the education of heathen youth, do yet allow to modern missions no prominent place in their system of instruction. So far as I have yet been able to learn, they give it, with here and there an exception, no place at all, excepting an occasional address from a returned missionary, which is of course an excellent usage. The text-books, in this respect, seem to me not to be up to the demands of the times. I find no distinct reference to modern missions in any of the text-books I have consulted. Nor have I yet heard of any, which treat at all of the missions in our day. I see not how the text-books in common use would be constructed differently, or the teaching be materially changed, were there no missions in existence, and were there no heathen world accessible to the churches. In a late Sabbath-school convention, no reference was made to this class of duties, nor to the development of Christian character in the rising generation, as having anything to do with the conversion of the unevangelized world.

Yet certainly no Christian duties are more really important, and none, in this age, more fundamental in the development of Christian character, and as a test of its genuineness. The foundations for a broad and elevated Christian character need to be laid in youth. Then is the time to inculcate the duty, to awaken an interest in the work, and to cultivate the habit of giving for its advancement. If this be not done then, it never will be done effectually. If additional text-books are needed for this purpose, let them be prepared, and judiciously introduced into the Sabbath-school instruction.

Of course the Sabbath-school library will need attention. Such libraries are very greatly deficient in this department. The reading has too much of fiction, is too sensational, and creates in the minds of the children a positive distaste for the plain matter-of-fact connected with the extension of Christ's kingdom. This is a calamitous result in the religious education of the rising generation, and is a dark omen for the future. Indeed, there is probably no department of influence in the Christian Church of our times, that needs more prompt and thorough attention, than do these libraries.[1]

[1] There are signs of improvement. Mr. Warren's *Twelve Years*

Missionary societies are sometimes formed in Sabbath-schools. Quite recently my attention has been called to a successful experiment of this kind in a town of Connecticut, extended through a score of years. The principal agent in the case was the superintendent of the school.[1] A missionary association was formed of the pupils, and became a popular institution. Once in a quarter, the Sabbath-school monthly concert was converted into a missionary concert; when the children were encouraged to bring in written resolutions, or sentiments, and lay them on the table, from whence they were taken and read in the course of the meeting. They were also invited to select and write out texts from the Scriptures, fitted to stimulate the missionary spirit of the school, and these were also read. From samples of these resolutions and Scripture extracts, I judge that their influence must have been good. Reports were occasionally read by the president; and he availed himself of every opportunity to secure addresses from returned missionaries, and often succeeded; and some of those speakers, no longer among the living, whose memory is cherished by the

among the Children, is a valuable contribution to the literature for the young. So is Mr. Parmelee's *Life Scenes among the Mountains of Ararat.* So, also, is Mr. Wheeler's *Letters from Eden, or, Reminiscences of Missionary Life in the East.* Mr. Wheeler's *Ten Years on the Euphrates, or, Primitive Missionary Policy Illustrated,* though written for adults, should be in libraries for the young, as well as the old.

[1] J. H. Stickney, Esq., Rockville, Ct.

churches, must have left a salutary impression on those youthful minds.

In another Sabbath-school, the missionary field was divided among the children of the advanced classes, and, once a quarter, the Sabbath-school monthly concert was devoted to missions. Each of the children was expected then to bring in some fact, or facts, concerning his own field. In this way missionary information was constantly coming into the school, and a missionary spirit was promoted.

As Sabbath-school societies are educational, it should be their aim to train the youth for the great Christian work of their future lives, and their attention should be directed to the missionary work at home, as well as abroad. The destitute of our own lands, the degenerate churches of the East, the Jews, the pagan nations, and the missions among them, should each receive their share of attention; of course, with the help of maps, and other appropriate illustrations. All they will need is a presiding spirit, well informed and interested on the subject of missions.

Another department of pastoral duty is the monthly concert of prayer for the conversion of the world. That should be what its name imports, — a prayer-meeting for missions, foreign and domestic; literally, for the conversion of the world. The information and prayers should not be restricted to the missions of one society, nor of one denomination, nor to one class of missions, nor to the missions from our own country. Moreover, the pastor should guard against feeling himself, or allowing his people to feel, that the meeting is unimportant, much less a failure, because only a few attend it. Those few, even should they happen to be chiefly females, are really, in respect to the missionary cause, what the "three hundred" were to the "ten thousand," in Gideon's army.

Experience teaches that we must not expect even good people to take a very lively interest in the information given at the monthly concert, while they know little of the geography and history of missions. We remember how the newspapers, in the late war, accompanied their accounts of battles and sieges with maps and illustrations. While the only effectual remedy for ignorance in missionary geography is early training, much can be done in the missionary prayer-meeting itself, by pastor and others, through a judicious use of maps and other illustrations.

The churches in some parts of our land seem, just now, to be somewhat in a transition state as to their religious habits. In many places, the afternoon preaching service is giving place to the Sabbath-school; and if the second preaching service be not relinquished altogether, it is transferred to the evening, to the no small peril of the monthly concert, where that meeting has been held on Sabbath evening. What shall be done in this case? This monthly missionary prayer-meeting was the outgrowth of the missionary spirit, and is believed to be quite necessary to the life and vigor of that spirit. It has been asked, whether the weekly church prayer-meeting may not be converted, once a month, into a missionary prayer-meeting. That has been tried, but in many cases it has been a short-lived experiment. The first Sabbath in the month is the best time for the concert; and might not the Sabbath evening preaching service, once a month, where it exists, be so modified as to meet the exigency? This, also, has in some cases been tried, and it only needs that pastor and people enter heartily into the arrangement. Take the broad view, just now intimated, of the field as occupied by the various societies at home and abroad, of the whole active efforts of the church, and let the people be at the expense of providing their minister with the needful sources of information, and the needful illustrations, and there would be no serious difficulty.

Much will of course depend on the manner of conducting the monthly concert. It is the result of my own experience and observation, that there is no more safety in going into this meeting without previous preparation, than there is into the pulpit on the Sabbath. Indeed, permanent success in that meeting requires that this department of pastoral duty should by no means be forgotten in the habits of study, which are cultivated in the seminary course. Men, who go through the seminary in habitual neglect of the intelligence concerning which I now speak, will be likely to go through their ministerial life in the same manner. But with the established habit of keeping the monthly prayer-meeting in view in the miscellaneous reading of the month, and with a hearty interest in the subject, an adequate preparation for the monthly concert will not be found to interfere with the weekly preparation for the Sabbath pulpit.

I am not in favor of reading much at that meeting, and what reading there is should, for the most part, be avowedly illustrative of some point or points that have been distinctly stated. The object is to awaken an interest, rather than fully to satisfy it, and thus lead the people to read for themselves. And there should be so much of intelligent and appropriate remark by the pastor, as will make the reading of the people at home more interesting and profitable, and also induce those who thus read to value the prayer-meeting. Pastors may have the world before them, with the whole range of efforts to evangelize it, as also the opened books of providence and grace, from which to draw materials. It is often the case that lay members of the church might materially aid in giving the intelligence. But in this meeting there is and can be no adequate substitute for the pastor. You might even bring in secretaries of the great missionary societies, with autograph letters of missionaries in their hands; yet if ordinarily there be uncertainty as to the pastor's attendance, or doubt as to the reality of his interest, the meeting will not be a success.

The use of maps and other illustrations is so important in the monthly concert, that, if they cannot be otherwise obtained, it would be well to employ for this purpose some part of the contributions on that occasion. The well-known missionary maps of Mr. Bidwell are invaluable. Those prepared by Professor Guyot are not missionary maps, yet, having some special excellences, a pastor, conversant with the geography and history of missions, may use them to advantage.

It might be well, occasionally, to employ the skill of young amateur artists in the parish to furnish rough drawings of the more interesting illustrations of the pagan world, to be used at the missionary prayer-meeting. The young artists themselves will at any rate be interested.

Another department of pastoral duty has respect to the various missionary publications of the day. In this important department, many a pastor, not having made up his mind what he ought to do, does nothing, and the whole is left to chance, that most irresponsible and inefficient of agents. It is not recommended that the pastor become an agent for any of the publications. All he needs to do is, by a legitimate pastoral influence to create a desire, a feeling of necessity for the knowledge, and then let it be distinctly known how that knowledge may be obtained, and his end is gained. The religious newspaper, though important in its place, does not and cannot supersede the necessity for the missionary monthly; and the missionary monthly will be more likely to be valued and read, if paid for, than if received as a gratuity; but is better as a gratuity, than not at all.

3. It is proper to say a word concerning the meetings of ecclesiastical bodies. In some portions of New England they seem not to be just what they should be in relation to the benevolent movements of the church, since they cling so tenaciously to traditional usages. Time is given grudgingly to the benevolent operations of the church, as if they had no right to it. It is much as if the grand object of Christian churches was self-defense, self-preservation, self-edification. This is the old feeling and habit, transmitted from former generations. The remedy is with the pastors. The Christian Church is not a fortress, nor a garrison; it is an army in the field, intent upon the enemy. I know not whether a similar lack of practical interest exists in ecclesiastical meetings elsewhere. But if the great

Christian work providentially devolved on the church, finds only a reluctant place in the large ecclesiastical bodies, how can it be otherwise in the local churches?

4. A word concerning the relations of pastors to benevolent societies. These relations are very direct and simple. The benevolent societies, whether existing in the form of ecclesiastical boards, as in the Presbyterian Church, or as voluntary boards or societies, as in the Congregational body, are indispensable auxiliaries to the churches, and the pastor avails himself of their aid, so far as he deems it expedient, for increasing the knowledge and developing the benevolence of his people. The churches have now so long acted through them, and in every possible way recognized their agency, that, for the purposes for which these organizations exist, they have come really to form a part of our ecclesiastical system. They are, as has been already affirmed, an integral part of it. This is alike true of all the larger institutions. The Board of Missions of the Old School Presbyterian General Assembly, and the American Board of Commissioners for Foreign Missions, are both, in this respect, on the same footing. Each of them, in their respective and appropriate spheres, performs services, which neither of the large ecclesiastical bodies of the land can possibly perform; and thus the churches, acting through them, accomplish the great evangelical duties of the

day. And it is a sign of progress that the nature, relations, and duties of these benevolent agencies are better understood, and more highly appreciated now, than they once were.

III. I now state briefly some of the more important misapprehensions and objections, growing out of a want of correct information, which hinder the development of the missionary life in our churches.

The first I shall mention is this — that the heathen are so very degraded and wicked, as to be unworthy of the great effort that is necessary to give them the gospel.

Another, not so often raised as formerly, is, that the expense of money and life in the foreign missions is more than we can afford.

Another, heard less frequently than it once was, but frequently operating as a silent influence, is, that missions have had but little success.

It is sometimes objected, that but a small part of the contributions actually reaches the heathen.

Another objection has a lodgment in many a mind, that would hesitate to give it utterance; that the heathen will not be lost without the gospel, and therefore it is unkind to send the gospel to them.

It is further objected, that charity begins at home; that it were better to bestow the money and labor on home missions; that we must take care of our own great country, where we have as much as we can do; that our country is worth a score of heathen nations, etc. The objection assumes a protean form; but the amount of it is, that we shall be more in the way of our duty, and be doing more for our own growth in grace, for the spiritual interests of our own nation, and for the building up of the Redeemer's kingdom, by restricting our evangelical labors within the bounds of our own country, and neglecting the world at large.

Some people believe that the conversion of the world is not to be looked for in the present dispensation, nor to be accomplished by the present agencies; that Christ's advent is to be pre-millennial; that the world will grow worse, instead of better, till his coming; which is to be sudden, and attended by convulsions; that the wicked are then to be destroyed; and that the Jews are to be miraculously converted, and made the favored people under this new Messianic reign, with Jerusalem for the capital. All I shall say in respect to this is, that it absurdly makes certain earnestly contested interpretations of prophecy as to Christ's second coming, and not his express command to "preach the gospel to every creature," the rule of action in this great matter.

Upon the other objections I shall make a few general remarks.

As to the degraded and wicked condition of the heathen, it will suffice to say — that Christ certainly commands his gospel to be preached to the heathen; that, for the most part, they are no more degraded and wicked than were our own wild and ferocious ancestors of Druidical times; and that, in point of fact, the gospel does elevate them.

As to the cost of life and of money in missions, it may be replied — that the cost of life, on the whole, has been scarcely greater in the missions abroad, than in the ministry at home. The average missionary life in India, fifteen years ago, was sixteen years and a half, and it is longer now. In 1858, the more than sixty ordained foreign missionaries from the Andover Seminary, then living, had been prosecuting their work on an average of seventeen years.

As to the pecuniary cost of missions, it is easy to show, that the country is in no danger of being impoverished by them. The expenditure of the American Board for fifty-six years, did not exceed the cost of a hundred and fifty miles of railroad in Massachusetts; and was nearly three millions less than the average expense of a single week in the late war. The cost of an iron-clad man-of-war was double the yearly expenditure of the American Board. The cost of the Sandwich Islands mission, for the whole forty-six years of its existence, was less than that of an exploring expedition of about three years, under Commodore Wilkes, sent by the United States government into the Pacific Ocean.

The objection, that but a small part of the money

contributed reaches the missions, is founded on sheer ignorance. In one of our Western States, a banker when called upon by the collector for a subscription for foreign missions, gave him ten dollars as his annual contribution, and then gave him fifteen dollars more — to aid, as he said, in sending it to them. He meant, that it cost more to send his donation to the mission, than the donation was worth. This was wholly a misapprehension. The cost for everything in the administration of one of our large Missionary Boards, including every species of agency, is only about eight per cent. of its receipts. Of every dollar contributed, therefore, ninety-two cents find their way to the missions. The banker already mentioned is said once to have remitted his donation directly to the mission in Turkey, but he gained nothing by the operation. Indeed, it is not possible for this objection to be entertained by one who reads the well authenticated treasury reports of the missionary societies.

The proof that the heathen are not saved without the gospel, is in the explicit command of Christ to preach the gospel to them; in the argument of the Apostle Paul in the first chapter of his Epistle to the Romans; in his own labors among the heathen; and in the uniform testimony of missionaries to the unholy lives and characters of the heathen of our day, and to their acknowledged consciousness of sin and guilt. The assumed unkindness in sending the gospel to the heathen, is on the assumption that many of them, by rejecting it, will incur a deeper condemnation. This must be admitted; but then if the heathen perish without the gospel, and may be saved by it, there is obviously the same reason for preaching the gospel to them, as there is for preaching it to the ungodly in Christian lands.

What can a pastor say to objections founded on the exclusive claims of our own great country? An eminent clergyman residing in Missouri once said, that the religion they needed for the West, is one "strong enough for the conversion of the world." And we might well ask, whether our home missions would really be prosecuted with their present vigor, had we not, at the same time, missions in Asia, Africa, and the Islands of the sea? The principle underlying this objection, were it to govern the churches throughout our land, would be a monstrous national selfishness, destructive of every generous Christian feeling. It is important to remark, that this objection is generally made under an erroneous impression as to the proportion actually contributed to these two branches of the same great work. Dr. Mullens says that, in one hundred and fourteen London churches in 1865, not more than one fourth of the benevolent contributions were for foreign missions; and that in 1866, out of every £100 contributed by eighty Congregational churches in London and the country, only £15, or less than one sixth, were for foreign missions. In the Free Church of

Scotland, during ten years, only six per cent. of the sum contributed for religious objects went for foreign missions. I am not prepared to say what is the proportion in our own country. But it should be remembered, that every foreign missionary society combines a number of objects, while what is actually the home missionary work is divided among several societies, as the Home Missionary, Church-building, Sabbath-school, Education, etc. We are glad to feel assured, in the existing relations of the unevangelized world to the church, that the true church of Christ cannot have an exclusive regard for either home or foreign missions, since the spirit of the true church, so far as informed on the subject, will necessarily be responsive to the all-embracing command of its Redeemer and King. I shall be excused for the utterance of my own belief, that the subversion of foreign missions would be destroying the great wheel, in the vast machine of many wheels, of which our benevolent system is composed.

Such are some of the causes, which keep the churches from putting forth their energies for the extension of the Redeemer's kingdom. It is thus that skepticism, in one form or another, paralyzes the arm of the church. Let a man doubt whether the heathen deserve our sympathy, whether they are in perishing need of the gospel, or whether they will be really benefited by it, and you cannot interest him in sending them the gospel. Let a man doubt whether God really intends to accomplish the conversion of the world, whether the time has really come for engaging in the work, or the efficacy of the means employed, and, until these doubts are removed, you cannot have his hearty coöperation.[1]

I need not take time to prove, that upon pastors of the churches rests especially the duty of removing these obstacles. This they can do by seeing that their people are properly informed as to the facts, which bear so strongly on their personal duty in this peculiar age of the world. We are to aim at two things; correct information, and its bearing upon the development of Christian character. The evidences of personal piety need now to be reinvestigated and reconstructed. In former ages, the tests of Christian character were persecution, imprisonment, the rack, the stake; they were suffering in some form. Piety and the profession of it stood connected, in God's providence, with losses and privations. But times have changed. Piety and the profession of it are now respected. The grand test of piety now, is the life of faith, benevolence, giving for the cause of Christ, self-denying efforts.

The treatises on this subject need to have an additional chapter. Few Christian people yet realize the vast change there has been in their position and relations, as regards the world perishing for lack of

[1] See Dr J. P. Thompson's *Introduction to Foster's Essay*, p. 58.

the gospel, nor the effect of this change upon the evidences of their own personal piety. Many a church-member has a comfortable hope of heaven, while doing almost nothing for extending Christ's kingdom and the blessedness of his reign, and feeling no interest in the cause. This might have been safe for the soul in the days of Richard Baxter, or even in the days of our grandparents. But God has brought a mighty change over our situation, and our relations; and if any choose to be ignorant of the fact, it is a willful ignorance, that will not avail in the great day. In any view, it is disloyalty to the Lord of Glory. Just here is the grand defect in the practical Christianity of our age. It responds not, as it should do, to the call of God's providence. Nothing can be more certain, than that the vast changes in the unevangelized world do immensely concern us as Christians. And it is time that God's ministers should speak out plainly on this subject. Satan hath great wrath, because of the shortness of his time. By infidel philosophy he is seeking to gain possession of the human understanding, and to fortify it against all approaches of the truth to the hearts of men, and his emissaries are going into all the world. Moreover, the Roman hierarchy is prepared and determined everywhere to oppose the extension of Christ's spiritual kingdom, and will be the grand opponent of the true church in its effort to extend Messiah's reign; and if successful in that, it will be almost sure to recover once more its lost dominion in Christendom.

Pastors have much encouragement, then, in view of those providential tidal waves of influence from the unevangelized world already spoken of, which are flowing in upon the churches, and now more than ever. In most churches they will find there has been a favorable beginning, and some progress in the right direction; that there is no longer the profound indifference or the early opposition to missions. Perhaps they will find that one half, or even more, of their church-members already contribute something for the cause. Perhaps as many as a third of them, and those the best, assemble at the monthly missionary prayer-meeting. Perhaps even a larger number are more or less in the habit of reading missionary intelligence. Possibly a member of the church is a missionary, or among the honored dead fallen in the service.

If all pastors of the churches could be induced to take the decided stand with their people, which many have taken, — educating them for the work of missions, and urging them forward in it, — we should soon have the men and the funds that are needed, and great would be the joy among the people of God.

CHAPTER XI.

DIFFUSION OF MISSIONS.

Human and Divine Agency. — Import of the Divine Command. Important Facilities. — Progress in Missionary Explorations. — Progress in Missionary Occupation; in Western Asia; in India. Vast System of Railways in India. — Their Bearing on Missions in India. — Progress in Eastern Asia; in the Pacific Ocean; in Africa. Great Reduction in the Cost of Occupation. — Progress in giving the Bible, and a Religious Literature. — Advance in Contributions. Recent Date of the Missions. — The Forces now in the Field. Portions of the Unevangelized World not yet reached. — General Conclusion.

Two things in missions are perfectly distinct, and yet are intimately connected. These are the human agency, enjoined by the command of our Lord to "preach the gospel to every creature;" and the divine agency, or God's blessing on the missions, involved in the promise, "Lo, I am with you." The latter includes the providential opening of the unevangelized world to the gospel, the preparation of Christendom for the work, and the uprising of the Evangelical Church, which were the themes that first claimed our attention.

I propose now to show what progress has been made in obeying the Saviour's command, to "go into all the world." This command, as recorded by the different Evangelists, reads thus: "Teach all nations;" "Preach repentance and remission of sins in my name among all nations;" "Go into all the world;" "Preach the gospel to every creature." The duty therefore prescribed for the people of God, is a proclamation of the gospel, as far as may be, to all the inhabitants of the world.

As has been already remarked, we have a practical illustration of the duty devolved on Christians in the mission of the Apostle Paul, as it was set forth in the fourth chapter. He labored in the great centres of influence, planting in them self-propagating churches, and he and his associates did what more they could in the regions adjacent.

As auxiliary to the progress of the Evangelical Church in planting its missions, I mention two important facilities, which have been providentially secured.

One is a recognition of the claim of missionaries to the protection of their own governments. This protection even the nominally Protestant Christian governments were at first backward to give. The earliest formal and official recognition of it in this country known to me was in the year 1842. Daniel Webster was then Secretary of State, and in consequence of a representation made to the government in that year, he thus wrote to the Minister resident at Constantinople: —

"It has been represented to this department," says Mr. Webster, "that the American missionaries, residing in the Ottoman dominions, do not receive from your Legation that aid and protection, to which, as citizens of the United States, they feel themselves entitled; and I have been directed by the President, who is profoundly interested in the matter, to call your immediate attention to the subject, and to instruct you to omit no occasion, where your interference in behalf of such persons may become necessary or useful, to extend to them all proper succor and attentions, of which they may stand in need, in the same manner that you would to other citizens of the United States, who, as merchants, visit or dwell in Turkey."

This claim of the foreign missionary for protection in the lawful prosecution of his mission, was afterwards distinctly recognized by successive Secretaries of State, and the usage may be regarded as now settled.

Years after this, the four great powers of Christendom negotiated the memorable treaty with China, noticed at the outset of our discussion, and made express provision for the protection of both missionaries and their converts.[1]

While we should rely for protection in the work of missions mainly on the Lord of missions, it shows an important advance in our work, when the "Roman

[1] See Chapter I.

citizenship" of the missionary is recognized by Christian governments.

I also notice a remarkable change in the secular newspapers, as regards the benevolent operations of the church, and missions in particular. Mr. Sydney E. Morse states, in his "Memorabilia" of his father, that the institution of the "Boston Recorder," in the year 1816, induced as many as twenty country newspapers to go into the publication of religious intelligence. According to my recollection, this practice afterwards declined, and the more influential newspapers in the cities did not come into it for many years afterwards. There ought to be a more specific record of the manner in which this was effected, than I am able to make from personal recollection. I think it was in the year 1844, that the late Rev. Austin Dickinson began his judicious and successful efforts to enlist the commercial newspapers in the publication of religious intelligence. Believing that this would be advantageous to them, as well as to the cause of religion, he made an engagement with certain leading journals to prepare for them brief articles of religious news, such as he deemed suitable for their columns, with a promise of their insertion. The way being thus opened, the same promise was obtained from editors of other papers; and he at length sent around more extended summaries in printed slips. The editors became at length convinced of the propriety and policy of obtaining the intelligence through paid reporters sent for the purpose to attend the meetings of benevolent societies. It was by efforts such as these, that the secular newspapers were gradually led to open their columns for religious news. The marvelous progress since made in this direction is evinced by the fact, that the newspapers in the city of Chicago, in 1865, made full and accurate reports, from day to day, of the proceedings and speeches at the annual meeting of the American Board in that city. It is easy to see what a prodigious gain this access to the secular newspapers is, for the cause of religion and of missions.[1]

In proceeding to state the progress of the Evangelical Church in measures for obeying the Saviour's command, I notice, —

1. The progress made in special missionary explorations. These have been found indispensable to the advantageous occupation of an unevangelized country by missions. A mercantile house sends a man to explore for it who is skilled in trade; the warrior sends a soldier; the missionary society sends a missionary. There is a great deal in the point of view. Our traveller must have the eye, the ear, the heart of a missionary. Lion-hunters would not answer our purpose in Africa; nor would the members of the London Anthropological Society. Nor can

[1] See Appendix II.

we implicitly rely, in such a country as China, so far as vital points in missions are concerned, upon the reports of unmarried Jesuits, with their unscrupulous concealment of their own character and objects, and the half-Christianized Buddhism of their religion.

We must make our own surveys. We do it geographically, that we may know where to find the people, and what physical causes affect their pursuits and characters, and will facilitate or obstruct our operations. We do it statistically, to know the number of youth to be gathered into schools; of families to be supplied with the Bible; of cities and villages to be furnished with the stated preaching of the gospel; and of souls to whom a Saviour's love must be proclaimed. We investigate the social relations of the people, in order to know the ties of family, neighborhood, business, pleasure, government, and religion, which bind them together; and also, what repellant influences there are to produce "hatred, variance, emulation, wrath, strife, envyings, and such like;" of which we are assured, that "they which do such things shall not inherit the kingdom of God."

That to which I would call special attention is, the extent to which this work of MISSIONARY EXPLORATION has been carried. I can give only a brief illustration. Somewhat more than forty years ago, the late Dr. John C. Brigham, afterwards Secretary of the American Bible Society, was sent by the American Board to Buenos Ayres, in South America, with instructions to cross the Southern continent, and visit the republics along the Western slopes, as far north as Mexico; which occupied him about two years. Dr. Brigham's report, published in the "Missionary Herald," was adverse to an occupation at that time, mainly on the ground of the predominant influence of the Popish priesthood in the several governments. The world has moved forward since then, and recent missionary explorations in several of these countries have reached a more favorable result. Ten years later, the Rev. Samuel Parker was sent, by the American Board, with some others, across the continent of North America, to see what could be done for the Indian tribes on either side of the Rocky Mountains. The investigation was pushed to the shores of the Pacific, and was the first step in the demonstration, afterwards made by a missionary of the same Board, of a practicable wagon-road through the Rocky Mountains; which demonstration history will testify to have saved Oregon, the Washington Territory, the Columbia River, and perhaps even the golden mines of California, to the United States. In 1829, the Rev. Eli Smith and myself traversed the Peloponnesus and Greek Islands. Out of the exploration just mentioned grew directly the more important one of Messrs. Smith and Dwight through Asia Minor, Armenia, and Georgia, as far as to the region inhabited by the Nestorian

Christians of Persia; who before that time were scarcely known to the modern Christian Church. The whole of Palestine, and a large portion of Asia Minor and Syria, had previously been surveyed by missionaries of the American Board, and of the Church Missionary Society, as were also several districts of Northern Africa. There has since been a missionary survey to some extent, by German missionaries, of Abyssinia and the interior of Eastern Africa; also, by English missionaries, of a part of the island of Madagascar. The missionary exploration of a large part of Southern Africa by Campbell, Moffatt, Livingstone, and others, furnish chapters of surpassing interest in the history of missions. Of the Western coast of Africa there has been a missionary survey along at least two thousand miles, and also for a considerable distance up the river Niger. But in Africa there is yet much unknown land.

The whole great country occupied by the two hundred millions of India, is now sufficiently known for missionary purposes. So are Assam, Burmah, and Siam. And a process of missionary exploration is now advancing somewhat rapidly in China, with its four hundred and fourteen millions of inhabitants, and its thirteen hundred thousand square miles. Some parts of the Indian Archipelago are not well known in a missionary point of view; neither is Corea, nor Japan, nor Chinese Tartary, nor Central Asia. But the Isles of the Pacific Ocean are known to a very great extent, and so are the Indian tribes of our Western wilderness.

Indeed it may be truthfully said, that the missionary survey of the world has now been carried so far forward, that scarcely anything more needs to be done in that way at present. As a preliminary work this exploration was necessary, and it has been in great measure accomplished, and by missionaries under the supervision of missionary societies; and it will not need to be repeated.

In the year 1812, as is generally known, it was not possible for the American Board to determine upon a field for a small band of five or six missionaries, and those missionaries were actually sent to India without any very positive instructions as to where they should labor. And for many years after this, as I can testify, the needful information as regards the heathen world at large, was gained with considerable difficulty. But now, we should scarcely be at a loss in designating hundreds of missionaries, and in giving them specific instructions.

2. It will be natural for us to consider the progress which has been made in the MISSIONARY OCCUPATION of the unevangelized world. Regarding the smallness of the invading force, the number of important centres occupied is truly marvelous. The single point we have now in view is, the occupancy of cen-

tral and influential posts. We commence in the countries of the Mediterranean.

The English Church Missionary Society was the first to move towards this part of the world, which it did in 1815; sending Mr. Jowett, an enlightened scholar, whose published "Researches," as I thankfully remember, were a valuable guide and incentive forty years ago. He was followed by Mr. Lowndes, of the London Missionary Society. In 1819, Messrs. Fisk and Parsons, of the American Board, went forth to occupy Jerusalem, then believed to be an important centre in that part of Western Asia. Beirût, the capital of Syria, was next occupied, by Messrs. Goodell and Bird. This was in 1823; and it was the beginning of that great movement of our American churches, which has since extended through Turkey, and into Persia; and gained a footing in most of the more important influential posts among the races speaking the Arabic, Turkish, Syriac, Armenian, and Bulgarian languages. The churches have taken possession, moreover, of what may be regarded as the religious centres of the Greek, Armenian, Bulgarian, and Syriac churches; and there are but few places in Western Asia, north of Arabia, not now occupied by foreign missionaries, which we should desire to see occupied for any length of time by other than native laborers.

Passing over the countries of Central Asia, all yet destitute of evangelical missionaries, we step from among the bigoted Moslems of Afghanistan into British India; and there, in its northwest corner, we find missionaries. Going from thence, down through the hundred and twenty millions in the great valley of the Ganges to Calcutta, we find a large number of the more important posts in possession of different missionary societies; though as yet, for the most part, with an altogether inadequate missionary force. The valley of the Indus is also beginning to be occupied by missionary stations; and so is Rajpootana.

From Calcutta towards the southwest, and from Surat and Bombay towards the east and southeast, and over the great populous peninsula of India, missionaries are found at very many of the more influential centres; and the same is true of Ceylon. A late number of the "Friend of India," published in Calcutta, affirms, that thirty societies in Great Britain, the United States, and Germany are at work in India, with five hundred and forty white and two hundred and twenty native clergy, and eighteen hundred native catechists; working in four hundred central stations, with two thousand three hundred branches; and that they have eighty thousand boys and thirty thousand girls in their schools. The annual cost is reckoned at £300,000, or $1,500,000; of which $250,000 are given by people in India who are conversant with the facts; and $100,000 by the native converts themselves.

India is of great extent, and travelling has heretofore been exceedingly laborious and expensive. It has been hard to see in what manner missions could permeate the country. It is therefore important to mention, that durable railways are now considerably advanced through its whole extent, under the patronage of government, which guarantees an income of at least five per cent. to the several English companies building the roads.

The railway system embraces an extent of about five thousand miles, and the larger part of it has been completed. What is called the "East India Railway," running up the valley of the Ganges, connects Calcutta with Delhi, a distance of a thousand miles. The "Great India Peninsular Railway" connects with the one in the Ganges valley, at Allahabad, about five hundred miles above Calcutta, crosses the Deccan plateau, and descends thence to the Concan and Bombay, and from Bombay it proceeds to Madras; the whole length of the line being twelve hundred and sixty-six miles. The ascent of the Ghauts on this line from Bombay to Madras, was a work requiring upwards of seven years, during which as many as forty thousand laborers were occasionally employed upon it at one time. "Beginning its ascent along a spur thrown out from the main range, this incline continues its upward winding way through long tunnels piercing the hardest basalt, across viaducts spanning ravines of great width and depth, often along what is simply a large notch cut in the face of a precipice."[1] The "Madras Railway" crosses from Madras to a port on the Malabar coast, eight hundred and twenty-five miles. The "Bombay, Baroda, and Central India Railway" goes northward from Bombay into the fertile province of Guzerat, three hundred and twelve miles; and may yet be extended through Rajpootana to Delhi. The "Punjaub Railway" extends from Delhi through Lahore, the capital of the Punjaub, and thence westward to Mooltan; from whence there will be a connection by steamers, and by the "Scinde Railway," with Kurrachee, a seaport near the mouth of that river. The extent of the "Punjaub Railway" is five hundred and sixty-six miles, and of the "Scinde Railway" one hundred and nine miles. From Calcutta, the "Eastern Bengal Railway" runs northeasterly one hundred and fifty-nine miles, and may yet be extended to the borders of China; and the "Southeastern Railway" twenty-nine miles, to a point on the neighboring coast.. The "Southern India Railway," one hundred and sixty-eight miles, connects Madras with Negapatam, a seaport on the eastern coast of the continent; and will probably be extended through the Madura and Tinnevelly provinces to Travancore.

On the 1st of May, 1868, nearly four thousand miles on these railways were open to travel and traffic,

[1] *North British Review,* 1868, p. 177.

and an additional thousand miles were under construction. Bombay is therefore to become "the sea-gate, through which the postal communications of Europe and India are henceforth to flow."

The estimated cost of these five thousand miles of railway is four hundred and fifty millions of dollars; and, under the orderings of Divine Providence, the whole is built as really for the church, as for the world, *and wholly at the expense of the latter.* These railways are not less important in a missionary point of view, than they are in their relation to the social, civil, political, and commercial interests of India. The saving to the church, in its work of converting India, will be immense in travel, labor, time, exposure, health, life, and expenditure. Bombay, and not Calcutta nor Madras, must henceforward be the great landing place and point of departure for missionaries to India. And how easy, how comparatively inexpensive and safe will be access to every part of the country. In how short a time will the lines radiating from that great commercial entrepôt transport the missionary to the valleys of the Ganges and the Indus, to the northern provinces, and far down into the Peninsula.

The more influential posts in Burmah, Assam, and Siam eastward of India, are occupied by missionaries. There are also missionary stations on the great island of Borneo, and on the Molluccas and Celebes. In the maritime provinces of China, nearly every important port has missionaries; and there are missionaries some hundreds of miles up the Yangtszkiang, the great river of China, others half-way from the sea to the capital, others in Pekin, and there is a missionary post beyond the famous Chinese wall. Japan has also been entered by Protestant missionary societies, and so are different portions of Papal Europe, and of Spanish and Portuguese America.

In the Pacific Ocean, a large portion of the more important groups of islands are occupied, and so extensively that the chances of shipwreck among savage pagans have been greatly reduced — as I presume the rates of insurance would show.

Nearly the whole of Southern Africa has, for many years, been under religious culture by missionaries. So is a small portion of the eastern coast, and a part of Madagascar. So is the coast of Western Africa from the equator a long distance westward, and there are missionaries on the Niger, and also in Egypt.

This will suffice for an illustration of the extent, to which the more important regions of the unevangelized world have been occupied.

3. There has been great progress in reducing the cost of missionary occupation. For this we are largely indebted to the business enterprise of men of the world, as seen in steamships, railways, and other

signs of progress in civilization too numerous to specify; all of which are doubtless providentially intended to aid the church in its great work of evangelizing the world of mankind. These are economies on a grand scale. But what I have now specially in view, are economies in the working of the missions themselves. This I can best illustrate from the experience of the institution with which I have been intimately connected. The number of stations and out-stations connected with the American Board has increased, since the year 1852, from one hundred and forty-nine to five hundred and eighty-six; and its laborers, foreign and native, from six hundred and twenty to twelve hundred and sixty-four, and its churches, from ninety-four to two hundred and five. Yet the expenditure rose only from $310,000 to $442,000, which, considering the comparative value of gold at the two periods, was really almost no increase at all. The number of foreign laborers decreased somewhat in this time, but the increase of native laborers was more than threefold; and thus it was that the number of occupied posts could be nearly quadrupled, as they were, with very little actual increase of expenditure. Native laborers cost far less than foreign laborers. Then there was, as already described, an increase in spiritual agencies, which are less expensive than secular agencies. The native churches, moreover, were more than doubled; and sixty-two of these churches received native pastors for the first time, with the understanding that they would support them wholly, or in part. It is important to add, that in associated, self-governing missions there is necessarily a growth of experience, and of superintending and executive power, and new discoveries of the relations and capabilities of the missionary enterprise, and new arrangements and combinations for increasing the economy and efficacy of its spiritual agencies.

This progress of economy in the working of missions might be illustrated at great length, but I content myself with instancing the saving in houses for public worship. Each of the churches of course needs one such house. It is the misfortune of some of the older missions of which I am now speaking, that their first houses for worship were not erected for Christian congregations, — for such congregations were then scarcely existing, — but for large gatherings of heathen children in schools, taught by heathen masters. Those schools no longer exist; but the church buildings erected for them do, and each of these, built after our Western models, cost so much that, being naturally looked upon by the natives as proper models for houses of worship, they necessarily stand somewhat in the way of the native Christians themselves erecting appropriate houses in their several villages. The India missions, in 1854-55, decided, in view of their own experience, that the style of houses for worship ought to have a general correspondence with the dwellings of the people. In the same year the missions in Western Asia resolved that, extraordinary cases excepted, the houses for public worship should be cheap and plain, and should be built only when there were congregations to render them necessary; and this for the reason, that such houses should correspond to the size of the congregations, and should be built, in good part, by the people themselves.[1]

The past fifty years especially have been the time for gaining experience; and the experience, though sometimes expensive, we have for use in all future time.

4. In nothing have the Protestant churches been so agreed in the working of missions among the heathen, as the duty of giving them the Bible. This surely is obedience to Christ's command, and I am to state briefly what has been done in this department.

Often one of the first things missionaries had to do among a savage people was to catch the fleeting sounds in their utterances, and express them in a written form. There being thousands of these in every language not easily distinguishable, we may imagine the labor and patience that were required. The missionaries of the American Board have, to a greater or less extent, reduced twenty languages to

[1] *Annual Report of the American Board,* for 1865, pp. 23, 25.

writing, all of them, except the Modern Syriac, barbarous languages. I have not the means of determining how many rude languages, on the whole, have been subjected to this process. But we know, that, within the last half century, the entire Bible has been translated into thirty-nine languages, outside of Christendom, embracing nearly all the more important languages; the New Testament into thirty-five others; and portions of Scripture into forty-eight others — making one hundred and twenty-two languages in the great field of Christian missions, that have been enriched and ennobled within fifty years past, by having at least portions of God's Word transfused into them. And it is a wonderful fact, that by far the largest part of the necessary work of translating the Scriptures has been already accomplished.

Scarcely less than a hundred million copies of the Scriptures have been issued, in whole or in part, since the formation of the British and Foreign Bible Society in 1804; and not less than ten millions of these have gone into nations beyond the bounds of Christendom. And we are impressed with the comparative magnitude of this branch of the enterprise, when we reflect that these ten millions of Bibles are more than double the number of copies believed to have existed within the bounds of Christendom, during the three centuries and a half from the printing of the first Bible, in 1460, down to the era of Bible societies, and a far greater number of copies than were in the hands of mankind through all the ages of the world, from Moses to the Reformation. What an advance is this in obedience to Christ's most beneficent command!

The number of other books, and of tracts, that have been printed in the languages of the unevangelized nations, in this era of modern missions, it is impossible to estimate with certainty. I know that the American Board has published them in forty-two languages, and to the extent of more than a thousand millions of pages; and that the American Baptist Missionary Union has published in thirty-three languages, and to the extent of more than two hundred millions of pages. These two American societies alone have published in not less than sixty-eight different languages of the unevangelized world; and the number of titles to their works, and of course the number of separate works, does not fall far short of three thousand. The amount of printing by the General Assembly's Board, I cannot state with certainty, but it is believed not to fall short of three hundred and sixty millions of pages. Though other societies may not have operated through the press to the same extent, we yet see how immense, on the whole, must have been the product of the missionary press, and the addition to the means of knowledge, and especially of religious knowledge, in the heathen world.

5. There has been an encouraging progress in the contributions for the support of foreign missions. The American Board began with one thousand dollars in its first year, and has since received more than half a million in one year; and the sum total of its receipts is about twelve millions of dollars. The Presbyterian Board of Missions has a sum total of four millions five hundred thousand dollars; and the American Baptist Union of more than four millions. These are given merely as illustrations. There has been a corresponding growth in the receipts of the great missionary societies generally, both in this country, and in Great Britain. The combined receipts of twenty-four British foreign missionary societies for the propagation of the gospel among the heathen and the Jews, in the year 1867, exceeded two millions of dollars. That of twelve American missionary societies, for the same object, in the year 1868, exceeded one million five hundred thousand.

It is a remarkable and very encouraging feature in the financial history of the larger missionary societies, that dividing their existence into periods of a few years each, there has generally been an increase of receipts in each of these periods. The law is one of growth and progress; and the continuance of this progress seems more probable now than ever.

It should be borne in mind, that what I am now seeking to develop, is not the success of missions in the way of converting the heathen. It is rather the great preparation for success. It is the progress in learning the precise nature of our work; in securing influential positions in the unevangelized world; in improving our methods of employing native forces; and in substituting the more potential spiritual agencies for such as are less potential.

We should reflect on the shortness of the time since the oldest of the foreign missions began to operate. I myself well remember when there was no missionary in Turkey; when missionaries were debarred from the greater part of India; when none were in Burmah, none in China, none in the Indian Archipelago; when there were none in Africa, excepting Sierra Leone, and the southern extremity of the continent; and none in the great island-world of the Pacific Ocean, except some small groups in the south.

But how is it now? The number of ordained missionaries in the field falls but little short of two thousand. There are nearly a thousand missionary stations, occupied by missionaries; and nearly three thousand out-stations, occupied by a native ministry of some sort. The native helpers in the missions, of all kinds, cannot be less than five thousand; and perhaps half of these are preachers of the gospel, and more than three hundred are pastors of native churches.

Thus much as to the missionary force already in the

field. Of converts, churches, and nominal Christians I shall speak hereafter.

It is proper that we should take some notice of those portions of the unevangelized world, which have not yet been reached by Christian missions.

In respect to Africa, my thoughts go back to the evening of September 22, 1833, and to the first Presbyterian church in Philadelphia, where was then assembled one of the finest audiences I ever beheld. Then and there the two first missionaries of the American Board to Africa received their instructions as missionaries to the Western coast; and I never performed that service with a feeling so nearly approaching enthusiasm. To my then unchastened imagination, it seemed easy to cross the Kong Mountains, and to ascend the Niger and Tshadda to the supposed pastoral highlands of the interior; and there, meeting the missionary forces from the East and Southeast, to unite with them in lofty praise over Africa's redemption. The remarkable mission of Mr. Johnson at Sierra Leone, already described, was prior to that time, and fresh in my memory, and so was that of Dr. Vanderkemp and others among the Hottentots of South Africa. But it seems not to be the divine purpose that Equatorial Africa shall be evangelized by the white man, or that it should be effected by any means until slavery had been abolished in Protestant Christendom. It was reserved, as I now love to believe, for the descendants of Africans to carry the gospel to the lands of their forefathers. And we may expect them to be forward so to do, when once their own Christian privileges have become assured. No white man should join their missions; and men from their own race will in due time be their agents for raising funds from among themselves, and perhaps, too, their secretaries for correspondence with the African missions.

The Mohammedans number one hundred and forty millions, and, as a race, have heretofore not been accessible to the gospel. The abolition of the death-penalty for renouncing Mohammedanism by the Sultan in the year 1843, is probably without effect in provinces remote from Constantinople. But the progress of Christian empire, whether Russia, France, or England be the triumphing power, will go far to abolish this fundamental law of Moslemism. And experience encourages the hope, that where this is done, large numbers of Moslems, — descendants, it may be, of ancient Christians, — will embrace the gospel. At present there is no distinct call to plant missions among the Moslems of Northern Africa, or Central Asia.

Of Thibet we know almost nothing, and therefore I may not speak of it.

The Roman Catholic world is shut against us, so far as the Romish priesthood have the power of so doing. Such power they had, until within a single year, in Spain and Austria; and now have in Portugal, and several of the smaller Roman Catholic States of Europe. They wield it more or less in most of the Roman Catholic American States. In France they are yet able greatly to embarrass the Protestant press and ministry. In Italy, and even in Spain, their power seems to be considerably broken.

I come to this general conclusion; that the Evangelical Church is now fast occupying the central and influential points in all countries that are really open to the heralds of the cross; not thoroughly and effectually, but in part, and with the intent and expectation of enlargement, until the end is accomplished, and these countries become the Lord's.

CHAPTER XII.

SUCCESS OF MISSIONS.

The Missions yet in the Infancy of their Experience. — Success among the North American Indians; in the Isles of the Pacific; in China; among the Karens of Burmah; in India; in Madagascar; in Africa; in Western Asia. — Extent of the Invasion. — Strength of the Invading Army. — Summary. — The Hope of the Church.

I COME to a most interesting portion of my great theme, namely, the fulfillment of Christ's promise to be with his missionary servants. The fulfillment has been commensurate with the obedience.

In illustrating the success granted by the Head of the Church to modern missions, I adduce, as heretofore, the more striking proofs, and these will generally be found in the older missions. Many of the more important missions are of recent date; as, for instance, the missions in Northern China and Japan, several in Northern India, and several in Northern and Western Polynesia. It is also to be remembered, how few are the years since the discovery was made of the vital importance of native pastors to the development of self-reliant, enterprising native churches. I begin with the nearest field.

1. Missions have been crowned with success, all

things considered, among our North American Indians. This is contrary, I believe, to the general opinion. The missions to the Cherokee and Choctaw Indians, tribes numbering together about forty thousand souls, were begun in the years 1816 and 1818. In 1860, these Indians were pronounced a Christian people. They were then as accessible to Christian preachers, and listened to them with as much deference, to say the least, as their white neighbors in the adjoining States. The professors of the Christian religion among them were in as large a proportion, as in any part of our country, and Christianity was their only religion. They recognized the Sabbath as a divine institution, and transacted no public business on that day. Among the Cherokees, the Bible was required by law to be read in the schools, and no person denying the being of God, or a future state of rewards and punishments, could hold a civil office. In addition to sixteen white preachers of different denominations, the Cherokees had more than forty licensed native preachers.[1]

Surrounded by slaveholders, and being such to some extent themselves, those Indians suffered much in their religious condition during the late war. Nevertheless, they are a monument and proof of what might have been accomplished among the Indians of North America, through the grace of God, but

[1] See *Report of American Board* for 1860, p. 137.

for the pernicious influences of white neighbors and traders.

A more remarkable triumph of the gospel was among the Dakota Indians in Minnesota, within the past six or seven years. There had been missionary labors among them before, but without much apparent success. In 1862, the pagan Dakotas resolved upon exterminating, in true Indian style, the whites who had encroached on their hunting-grounds, and they actually commenced a general massacre. The missionaries and their families escaped only by a painful flight, in which they were aided by Christian Indians. It was a renewal of the old King Philip war, and the exasperated whites, as aforetime, when the Indians had been subdued, made little distinction between the innocent and guilty. Two thousand Dakotas were held in military custody, of whom more than three hundred were sentenced to death by a military commission, though less than forty were executed, in consequence of an appeal to President Lincoln.

The missionaries were allowed free access to the Indians under this military restraint, and then commenced their harvest. Within three years, more than five hundred Dakotas were admitted to the church on giving credible evidence of piety. Two thirds of these soon learned to read and write their own language, and several were licensed as preachers of the gospel.

Just think of a scene like the following, which occurred during the first of those three years. It is in a company of some hundreds of Dakotas, just embarked on the Mississippi River for a residence — to them a banishment — far up the Missouri River. The missionary who accompanied them, writes thus: —

"As darkness shut in the skies, the Indians looked out upon their native hills, as they said, for the last time. We were hardly under way, however, when from all the different parts of the boat where the Indians were collected, we heard hymns of praise ascending to Jehovah; not loud, but soft and sweet, like the gentle murmuring of waters. Then one of them led in prayer, after which another hymn was sung, and so they continued till all were composed, and, drawing their blankets over them, each fell asleep. The next morning, before sunrise, they were again at their devotions. So they continued, evening and morning; and these services were commenced without any suggestion from us."

Think, too, of another scene, near the centre of Minnesota, on the brow of what is called the "Mountain of the Prairie," looking out upon a wide and beautiful prospect. Here the missionary writes in October, 1867: —

"Our first public meeting was on Friday, a little before sunset, when we preached to nearly one hundred persons, seated on the grass in the open air, most of whom had come that day from five to ten miles. Not half a dozen were within three miles in the morning, and the nearest house was more than fifteen miles away. Most of the day we were occupied in examining candidates for church fellowship. In the afternoon we found our audience considerably increased by such as had come in during the day, notwithstanding the unpleasant weather. Two women had walked more than twenty miles, and, lest they might be late, came most of the lonesome road in the chilly air of the night. One of these, more than fifty years old, came to Mr. Riggs, and handed him five dollars, which she and her daughter gave for the support of the gospel among their people.

"Most of the Lord's day was spent in public religious exercises. I can find no words to express my feelings of joy and wonder, as on that day I contemplated God's mighty doings among these Dakotas. They were more than sufficient to compensate for a weary journey of several hundred miles over the trackless prairie. When the candidates for baptism were called for, more than fifty presented themselves, including parents and children, of whom twenty were about to partake of the Lord's Supper for the first time."[1]

In the year 1852, ten American missionary societies had missions among the Indian tribes; with

[1] *Missionary Herald*, 1863, p. 205; 1867, p. 387.

ninety-four ordained missionaries, thirty-eight native preachers (of whom I think few had received ordination), nine thousand nine hundred and sixty-four church-members, nine hundred and thirty-six in boarding-schools, and about fifteen hundred in day-schools. The decline in these missions, since that time, is attributable mainly to national causes, into which it is not needful that I now enter.

2. My next illustration is from the Islands of the Pacific Ocean. These islands have awakened an extraordinary interest during the past half century. I have the titles of more than sixty volumes concerning them, in the English language, which are chiefly occupied with the Christian missions; not to speak of the contents of missionary periodicals, reports, and pamphlets, which, if printed in volumes, would largely increase the number. I can only glance at this great field; but even a glance will reveal to us missionary triumphs, exceeded by nothing since the apostolic age.

The Sandwich Islands come first in the geographical order. The system of idolatry there, such as it was, had its overthrow before the arrival of the American mission in 1820. This singular occurrence is traceable to no Christian cause. It was a revolt, under God's providence, from the oppressive restrictions of the *tabu*. Yet the timing of the two events, is what no believer in the divine government will overlook. The missionaries anticipated no such thing when they sailed from their native land; nor did the natives overthrow their bloody altars with any expectation of the coming missionaries. Nor is it by any means certain, that this occurrence materially hastened the triumphs of Christianity. Seventeen years after the commencement of the mission, and when the primary truths of the gospel had been generally diffused, there commenced throughout the Islands, as the evident result of an outpouring of the Holy Spirit, a wonderful religious movement affecting the entire native mind; and more than a fourth part of the adult population was then added to the church.

The generation in which this remarkable triumph of grace occurred, has nearly passed away. Yet almost a third part of the inhabitants are, at this time, members of the church, of whom more than eight hundred were received as communicants in the year 1868. There are now thirty native churches on those Islands, with native pastors supported by themselves; which churches also support thirteen native foreign missionaries in the Marquesas Islands and Micronesia. And they contributed more than $29,000 in gold, the past year, for various Christian objects, including the publication of nearly three million pages of Christian literature. Having myself traversed all the Sandwich Islands, five years ago, I do not hesitate to declare the United States to be no more entitled, as a whole, to the appellation of Christian, than are those Islands.

Let us turn to islands in the South Pacific. Twenty-three years before the gospel was brought to the Sandwich Islands, a company of English missionaries landed on Tahiti, in Eastern Polynesia, and after laboring in great discouragement almost a score of years, they rejoiced over their first convert. Then began a religious revolution on that island, the evident work of the Holy Spirit, which will always deserve a place in the Christian history. Island after island, group after group of islands, in quick succession threw away their idols, and embraced the gospel. In some cases, the mere tidings of what had occurred on Tahiti, though carried only by a native convert, was enough to produce this result. Indeed, it may almost be said, that the chief instruments in this propagation of the gospel, were native evangelists. In less than twenty years, Christianity had become the only religion in most of the numerous islands westward, through the space of nearly three thousand miles. Never was there seen an overthrow of idolatry more extensive, or more rapid and complete.

The chief foreign agency in Eastern and Central Polynesia, was that of missionaries of the London Missionary Society, and the reader will be interested in the following recent testimony given by that society: —

"Sixty years ago, there was not a solitary native Christian in Polynesia; now, it would be difficult to find a professed idolater in the islands of Eastern or Central Polynesia, where Christian missionaries have been established. The hideous rites of their forefathers have ceased to be practiced. Their heathen legends and war-songs are forgotten. Their cruel and desolating tribal wars, which were rapidly destroying the population, appear to be at an end. They are gathered together in peaceful village communities. They live under recognized codes of laws. They are constructing roads, cultivating their fertile lands, and engaging in commerce. On the return of the Sabbath, a very large proportion of the population attend the worship of God, and in some instances more than half the adult population are recognized members of Christian churches. They educate their children, endeavoring to train them for usefulness in after life. They sustain their native ministers, and send their noblest sons as missionaries to the heathen lands which lie farther west. There may not be the culture, the wealth, the refinement of the older lands of Christendom. These things are the slow growth of ages. But these lands must no longer be regarded as a part of heathendom. In God's faithfulness and mercy, they have been won from the domains of heathendom, and have been added to the domains of Christendom."[1]

[1] *Report of London Missionary Society* for 1866, p. 7.

But the most remarkable results are in the Feejee Islands, about eighty in number, with a population of two hundred thousand. Thirty years ago the people were all cannibals, and delighted in their horrid feasts. If a hundred white men had been cast upon their shores before the entrance of the gospel, they would all have been immediately killed and eaten. Seamen dreaded them. An American vessel from Vancouver's Island, not long ago, was wrecked at sea. The crew took to their boat, and after drifting some hundreds of miles, struck at length on a coral reef. Reaching the shore, they found themselves on one of the Feejee Islands, and gave themselves up for lost. But one of them picking up a book from the sand, exclaimed: "Jack, I say, all's right; here is a Bible! Thank God, Christianity is here, and we shall be saved!" And so it proved. There is no record of more remarkable courage, self-denial, and success in missions, than that of the English Wesleyan missionaries on those islands. The mission was commenced in the year 1835, and within thirty years of its commencement, one hundred thousand, or about one half, of the inhabitants, were in possession of the Scriptures in their own language; and, according to the latest intelligence, ninety thousand attended public worship, including the Sabbath-school children; and there were twenty-two thousand church-members. The Feejeean preachers numbered six hundred and sixty-three. Forty-five of the native preachers had received ordination, or were candidates for it; while the number of teachers exceeded one thousand, and there were thirty-six thousand in the schools. The people, thus brought under the power of the gospel, have of course ceased from their cannibalism, while polygamy and infanticide are fast passing away. Value is now set upon human life. No more do the avengers of blood come as savage warriors, or as stealthy assassins, but make their peaceful appeal to laws, founded on the Word of God. An English naval officer, speaking lately of a religious service he attended on one of these islands, says: "I was very much impressed by the scene before me. Only fifteen years before, every man I saw was a cannibal. Close to me sat the old chief, Bible in hand, and spectacles on forehead, who was, twenty years back, one of the most sanguinary and ferocious of this terrible land; and within twenty yards of me was the sight of the fatal oven, with the tree still standing, covered with the notches that marked each new victim."

An affecting contrast to all this is seen in islands and districts which have not yet been reached by the gospel. There the natives continue to devour one another; to bury their sick alive; to strangle their widows, murder their infants, and prosecute their treacherous and cruel wars. The newspapers gave recently an account of the murder of a missionary and his assistants, while venturing across the largest of the pagan islands.

A few years more, and all this will have passed forever away. We need only to estimate with some care the causes now in operation in that part of the world, in order to be assured that missionaries, native or foreign, will erelong be found on every island of that great ocean, with the certainty of reclaiming the inhabitants to the worship of the true God.

3. In China, a world of heathenism, there has been scarcely time yet for more than the first harvest fruits. It is not forty years since a missionary was safe only within the trading factories of Canton; and not even there, if his profession were publicly avowed. But now, the missionary may traverse nearly the whole of that mighty empire. Missionaries labor openly and freely at all the chief marts of trade along the coast, and one of the strongest missions is in the great metropolis. The success we can yet speak of in that vast domain of paganism, is chiefly of discovery, of accessibility, of peaceful occupancy, and of some promising first fruits.

4. Our progress westward brings us next among the Karens of Burmah. I had occasion, in a former chapter, to state the remarkable success of a Karen evangelist, named Quala; who, in the space of three

years, was the means of hopefully converting more than two thousand of his countrymen.

It is forty years since the mission was commenced among the Karens, and the success of that native evangelist was five and twenty years after that time. Contemporary with that remarkable man were the labors and successes of the missionary, Mr. Vinton. After some years successfully spent in Maulmain and the surrounding country, Mr. Vinton removed into the province of Rangoon, where his Christian ardor found ample scope in unoccupied districts among the Karens. This was in 1852, and in six years he died. In the first of these years, Mr. Vinton received five hundred Karens into the church. His labors were apostolical. The country over which he travelled was destitute of roads, and the people were poor and ignorant. His last tour was in districts not before traversed, and was the immediate cause of his death. The heat was fearful. Several nights he slept in bamboo jungles, and one day he rode forty miles on an elephant across burning rice-fields. In these six years, Mr. Vinton planted forty churches, opened forty-two houses of worship, and thirty-two school-houses, and between eight and nine thousand Karens were raised to the level of Christian worshippers. In the rainy season, when he could not travel, he employed himself in bringing forward a native ministry, and about one hundred native pastors, evangelists, and school-teachers were thus trained.[1]

[1] *Gospel in Burmah.*

The mission, to which Mr. Vinton belonged, contained, in the year 1868, sixty-six native ordained pastors and evangelists, three hundred and forty-six native preachers unordained, three hundred and sixty native churches, nineteen thousand two hundred and thirty-one church-members, and nearly sixty thousand native Christians of all ages.[1] This surely is success; this is the blessing of God.[2]

The Karens, the Santhals, the Coles of Nagpore, the Mahars of Western India, the Shanars of Southern India, the Hottentots and Kaffirs of Africa, the islanders of the Pacific Ocean, and the American Indians, are nearly all in the same stratum of society; and their low social position makes a change of religion comparatively easy. To the poor, the gospel comes with its most alluring power; and, in the early stages of the missionary enterprise, it was necessary, owing to the weakness of faith in the churches of England and America, to give a disproportionate attention to aboriginal races. By the speedier

[1] *Report of Amer. Bapt. Miss. Union*, for 1868.

[2] The *Madras Observer* states that a gentleman, not in sympathy with the Baptists, but a great traveller, performing his journeys on foot, said, that on one occasion he found himself for seventeen successive nights at the end of his days' journeys through the forest, in a native Christian village. He also bore a high testimony to the religiousness of the people, more particularly to their strict observance of the Sabbath, and their abstinence from the use of intoxicating liquors. *Bombay Guardian*, Oct. 31, 1868.

results thus obtained, the churches at home were prepared to enter upon more costly and protracted efforts in the more populous and difficult regions.

5. The Santhals inhabit a country through which the railway of the Ganges valley passes, not very far to the northwest of Calcutta. In 1865, three years ago, there were only three Santhal Christians; now there are four hundred.

The Coles inhabit a fine table-land, three hundred miles west of Calcutta, and are devil-worshippers, and exceedingly debased in morals. The Germans commenced a mission among them in 1845. Their first convert was not till after five years. Since then, the progress has been constant; and the native converts have done far more to spread the gospel, than the missionaries. "Who taught you about Jesus Christ?" asked a missionary of an intelligent native woman. "Who?" was her reply; "why this teaching is all over the country." She had in view the propagating spirit of the native converts. The number of communicants, at the latest date, was fifteen hundred, and that of the nominal Christians was much larger.

The most remarkable success in India, as regards numbers, has been among the Shanars, a great tribe of devil-worshippers, within one hundred and fifty miles of Cape Comorin. Thirteen years ago, it was my privilege to pass, with the Rev. Dr. Thompson, through their country, and to witness many interesting scenes. Dr. Mullens, who preceded us, characterizes the Shanars, in their heathen condition, as "an oppressed race; living on palm sugar; climbing trees, with hard, daily toil; untaught; with scarcely an idea about God; fearing only the powers that work in the sky, air, and earth, close around them; their only recreations the wild dances of devil priests, with the loud drumming and rude feasts that ever accompanied the dances." "They have been easy to win," he says, "but hard to raise.' Yet we may remember what Mr. Thomas, the able missionary among this people, said concerning the ten thousand converted Shanars under his care. The missionaries employed in this field during the last twenty years, though generally able men, were backward, until of late, to ordain native pastors. But the native preachers among this people number over five hundred, and the nominal Christians are estimated at one hundred thousand; all separated from heathenism, formed into congregations for regular Christian worship, with their names all on the mission rolls. These native Christians contributed $20,000 (in gold) for religious purposes, in the year 1866. The Rev. John Thomas Tucker died in that year. He was connected with the Church Missionary Society in Southern India, and, during a mission of twenty years among this people, baptized three thousand five hundred Christian converts. And these converts he saw destroy, with their own hands, fifty-four devil temples, and build sixty-four houses for Christian worship. He had also the satisfaction of seeing thirteen of his native converts ordained to the work of the gospel ministry.

6. The successes among the more degraded and accessible classes of India, seem to me not to compare, in importance and value, with results already attained in the vast East India empire of Brahminism. In this Brahminic empire, there are now missionary laborers at more than a thousand stations and out-stations; and nowhere do they appear to labor in vain. Dr. Mullens declares, that "the greatest fruit of all missionary labor in India, is in the mighty changes produced in the knowledge and convictions of the people at large." He assures us, that "the Hindus are learning, everywhere, that an idol is nothing, and that bathing in the Ganges cannot cleanse away sin." He declares his belief that, while the vested interests of idolatry are of enormous value, while Brahmin families may be counted by millions, while the Hindu system dates back long before the coming of Christ, and is a most formidable antagonist; "yet even Hinduism, so powerful, so rich, so ancient, is giving way at every point."[1]

[1] Dr. Mullens, at the Conference of the Evangelical Alliance in Amsterdam.

The same distinguished missionary also says, that knowledge of gospel truth is spreading more widely every year, that it is moulding the opinions of native society, and is the only power that has increasing influence. He says, that everywhere in India, in Ceylon, in Burmah, in the great cities, in the open country, in the seats of commerce and of government, and in the centres of native opinion, "it is Christianity alone, which makes real advance;" and that the Christian agency "was never more compact, more judiciously located, more steady in its working, more calm and quiet in its tone."[1]

I am now speaking of the Hindus. Considerable time must be allowed for a general religious and social change to take place among a hundred millions of people, whose religious and social habits date back three thousand years. But they are human beings, with minds like our own, capable of being influenced and moulded by the gospel; and they are tenacious of their convictions, when once on the side of the gospel, as we saw marvelously demonstrated in the great rebellion.

A recent India statement places the number of communicants in the churches at fifty thousand, and the number of nominal Christians at two hundred and fifty thousand; and puts their annual contributions for religious objects as high as $100,000.[2] Dr.

[1] *Ten Years' Missionary Labor in India,* p. 196.

[2] *Friend of India.*

Mullens states the number of missionaries in India to be five hundred and eighty, and estimates the number of native helpers at more than two thousand.[1]

An extract from the "Church Missionary Intelligencer," for October, 1868, gives a striking view of the existing condition of the India mind. "In India, the present time is a season of disruption, not of ice and frost, but of prejudices and popular superstitions which have long fettered the energies of the natives. The sullen reign of Brahminical idolatry has been invaded by influences, at first despised, but which have gathered strength, and are manifesting their power; and the native mind, breaking forth from the old prescriptive bonds, is coming widely into action. The unquestioning servility wherewith dense masses of population had submitted themselves to the degrading superstitions submitted to them by former generations, is at an end. Men no longer consider themselves as shut up in the religious opinions of their fathers, and bound to think only as they thought. They have discovered what it is to be intellectually free; and as the old prejudices, no longer able to endure the strain, yield and break, the human mind, rushing forth with a wild impetuosity of movement, not only casts off what is false, but, confounding all distinctions of right and wrong, liberty and license, antagonizes against that truth of God which

[1] *London and Calcutta*, p. 137. See Appendix VI.

would exercise over it a just control, and preserve it from extravagance. There is a conflict of opinions: there is therefore cause for anxiety, and a pressing necessity for wise and arduous efforts on the part of all who desire the true happiness and prosperity of India, lest the educated Hindus, the first fruits of India's emancipation, in ceasing to be idolatrous, become stereotyped in skepticism."

7. The remarkable triumphs of grace in the island of Madagascar, inhabited by the negro race, were stated in a former chapter, and need not be repeated.[1] It will be remembered that, not long after the gospel had been planted, the English missionaries were driven away by a pagan queen, and that the native converts, left to themselves, and subjected to a terrible persecution for twenty-five years, yet grew in numbers; so that, only seven years after the return of the missionaries, there were ninety churches and one hundred and one pastors, within and around the metropolis; and the church-members were five thousand two hundred and fifty-five, and the nominal Christians twenty thousand. I think nothing more remarkable than this is found in the history of missions. In five years, subsequent to 1861, the people erected a hundred simple houses for worship at their own cost. And only two years later, we have authentic information, that a new

[1] See Chapter VIII.

queen and her government have publicly renounced idolatry, sent away the great idol, and stopped the government works on the Lord's day, and that the places of Christian worship are crowded to excess. At one large church erected by the missionaries, more than two thousand were counted in one church on the Sabbath.[1]

8. Equatorial Africa, it would seem, must be evangelized by her own sable sons; and our lately emancipated millions should do the work. The loss of life among white missionaries from the climate, demonstrates this, but their labors have also demonstrated the feasibility of the work. I may not repeat the marvelous but well authenticated story already related concerning the labors and successes of Mr. Johnson at Sierra Leone.[2] The most promising mission now in Western Africa, is perhaps the purely African mission of the Church Missionary Society on the river Niger, under the guiding influence of that highly respectable negro bishop, the Rev. Dr. Crowther, who was taken from the hold of a slave-ship when a boy, brought to Sierra Leone, and educated there and in England. The missions along the West African coast, are estimated to contain a nominally Christian population of more than fifty thousand; thus forming an excellent base for future missionary operations in the interior.

1 *Christian World.*

2 See Chapter VIII.

In respect to South Africa, it should perhaps be said that the grand result of the missions there has been to save the Hottentot, Kaffir, and other tribes, from being utterly destroyed by the Dutch and English colonists, who would fain have seized their lands, and either massacred the people, or reduced them to slavery. Were it not for the blessing of God on the missions, such would doubtless have been the result over the whole country, from Cape Town to Natal, and far interior.

The first missionary was a Moravian, who commenced his labors in 1736. Visiting Europe after a few years, the heartless Dutch India Company forbade his return, and a half century passed away, with a benighted generation, ere the mission was resumed.

Soon after the return of the Moravians, the celebrated Dr. Vanderkemp, sent by the London Missionary Society, arrived. He has been followed by many other missionaries from various societies; and South Africa is now occupied through fourteen degrees of latitude, and nearly as many of longitude, and the number of church-members connected with the various missionary societies exceeds twenty thousand. In a qualified sense, it may be regarded as a Christian country.

In the early history of the missions in this part of Africa, there is much to awaken both a painful and a pleasing interest. The bloody raids, or "commandoes," as they were called, sent forth by the colonial governments for the avowed purpose of exterminating the Bushmen, may well excite our horror. A missionary once knew a Dutch farmer, who said he had been on nearly fifty commandoes, and claimed to have himself killed hundreds of the natives. Sometimes villages were surprised, the men murdered, the cattle captured, and women and children carried away to be bond-slaves of the murderers of their husbands and fathers. The career of those wicked men was arrested many years since by the bold appeals of the Rev. Dr. Philip, of the London Missionary Society, to the Christian public of England.

On the other hand, some noted instances of the transforming power of the gospel are furnished by the South African missions. Who has not heard, for instance, of Africaner, a Hottentot chief on the western side of the continent? His native hills were within a hundred miles of Cape Town. These becoming occupied by Dutch invaders, Africaner and his brothers were driven north. At length, taking refuge beyond the Orange River, he became a daring robber chief, and spread the terror of his name over a wide region. The colonial governments offered rewards for his capture, or death, and commandoes were sent against him, but in vain. Berend, a Griqua chief in his neighborhood, was hired to make war upon him, and between them there were many bloody conflicts. Tribes fled at Africaner's approach. The desert was afraid of him, and he was a terror even to the English colony. In 1818, the well-known missionary, Mr. Moffat, ventured to take up his abode with Africaner, and from that time the robber was a man of peace. He was a new man. His temper, deportment, habits were changed. He was the missionary's friend and helper, his nurse in sickness, an indefatigable reader of the New Testament, and zealous for the propagation of the gospel. Next year he accompanied Mr. Moffat to Cape Town, but such was the dread of his name along the route, and the incredulity as to his conversion, that it was difficult to know how to convey him safely. When at the Cape, men wondered at the mildness of the outlaw, on whose head a price had been set, and the good people were delighted with his piety and knowledge of the Scriptures.

On his return homeward, Africaner met with Berend, the Griqua chief, with whom he had had so many deadly encounters. Both were now converts, and they sat down together in the tent of the missionary, and united in hymns of praise, and in prayers to a common Father in heaven. Two years later, Africaner entered into the joy of his Lord.[1]

9. The triumphs of grace, contemplated thus far,

[1] Moffat's *Missionary Labors*, etc., p. 182.

have all been among pagans. Coming into Western Asia, we should find ourselves among the degenerate churches of the East, and what we are now to contemplate, so far as space will allow, is the progress of a reform among a people nominally Christian.

I must pass by the Arabs of Syria, the Turks, the Bulgarians, and the Nestorians; though of the Nestorians I ought to say, that more than six hundred are recognized by the missionaries as worthy communicants, and nearly seventy of the Nestorian ecclesiastics are evangelical preachers of the gospel.

I can only state some of the leading facts illustrating the blessing of God on the mission to the Armenians, who number about two millions.

How much that people needed a republication of the gospel, and a religious reformation, is evident from their calling on the Virgin Mary as their mediator, and not upon the Lord Jesus, and that they hold to auricular confession, to absolution by the priest, to penance, transubstantiation, baptismal regeneration, intercession of saints and angels, to the worship of the cross, relics, and pictures, and to prayers for the dead.[1]

The Bible Society was in the field as early as 1813, with the version of the Bible in the ancient but unspoken language of the Armenian people. Editions were afterwards circulated in the spoken languages, and then it was that the priesthood commenced their

[1] Dwight's *Christianity in Turkey*.

opposition. The native Protestants were calumniated, imprisoned, plundered, exiled, and all with the concurrence of the Sultan Mahmoud. But God interposed. The army of the Sultan was overthrown by the Egyptians, on the plains of Nezib, and Mahmoud's death in his own palace followed after a few days. The exiles were then recalled, and the reform gained in notoriety and public sympathy more than it had lost. This was in 1839.

Four years later, the execution in Constantinople of an Armenian, who had embraced Mohammedanism and afterwards renounced it, led the Christian powers of Europe to demand a pledge from the Sultan, that no such insult to the religion of Christian Europe should be repeated, and the pledge was given.

At that time, some thousands in Constantinople were intellectually convinced of the truth of evangelical doctrines, and there were many such in the provinces. The first evangelical church was organized at Constantinople in 1846, and the holy influence extending across the Taurus Mountains, a church was gathered at Aintab in Central Turkey, and one of the largest Protestant congregations in the empire.

In 1847, the English ambassador procured an imperial decree constituting the native Protestants a separate and independent community. And this was soon placed beyond the possibility of a change, by what is called a *Hatti-Sherif*, having the imperial autograph, which was placed in the hands of the Protestants.

I have already illustrated the remarkable progress of the gospel at Aintab and Marash, in Central Turkey, and also at Harpoot, in the eastern section of the empire.[1] Suffice it now to say, concerning the mission to the Armenians, that it numbers sixty-three Protestant or evangelical churches, containing two thousand seven hundred and sixty-six members. Of native pastors there are thirty-six, nearly all supported by the people; forty licensed preachers, nearly three hundred native helpers, of pupils in the schools six thousand; and of acknowledged Protestants about fourteen thousand, but the number of those who are really Protestant in opinion and feeling must be far greater.

Behold now the camp-fires of Immanuel's army, — extending over a large proportion of the Pacific Islands; along the Chinese coast and into its interior; over the greater part of India; over Western Asia; on the great island of Madagascar; over almost the whole of South Africa, and along its western coast for two thousand miles; in the frozen regions of Labrador and Greenland; and among the Indians of our own West and the British Northwest.

Does any one think that these fires will be suf-

[1] See Chapter VIII.

fered to die out? that this army of Immanuel, giving up in shameful defeat, will retire before the powers of darkness? Will He, who gave his life to ransom the world from sin, under whose banner and in obedience to whose command this army has gone forth, ever forsake it while loyal to his cause?

Should the army of invasion seem to any to be a little flock, still it is that "little flock" to which the Lord Jesus declares it is the Father's good pleasure to give the kingdom. It is an army, of which it is foretold, that "one shall chase a thousand, and two put ten thousand to flight." It is further to be considered, that every true convert becomes of course a loyal soldier for life, and these loyal soldiers are increasing by thousands every year.

The number of mission churches at present in the unevangelized regions, is two thousand and five hundred; of church-members, more than two hundred and fifty thousand; and the nominal Christians may be reckoned at not less than a million. The ordained missionaries, nearly two thousand in number, are already greatly outnumbered by the native preachers, and the gospel is taking root in at least four thousand places beyond the bounds of Christendom.[1]

Persecution cannot arrest this work; it would rather facilitate its progress. The Romish Church cannot greatly retard it; but will rather serve as an

[1] See Appendix VIII.

incitement to Protestant Churches. Nor will the wars of Christendom. Missions had their rise when Christendom was in arms. In no way can the progress of these missions be arrested, except by a general decline in the evangelical churches; and it is undoubtedly a fact that foreign missions, vigorously prosecuted, will themselves almost ensure against the possibility of such decline.

CHAPTER XIII.

CLAIMS OF MISSIONS ON YOUNG MINISTERS.

Excessive Claims of the Churches. — Unsafe to decide the Question of Duty before Inquiry. — How many Missionaries the Churches will support. — How many are needed. — The Sort of Men needed. From whence they are to come. — How early the Question of Duty should be decided. — Reflex Influence of Missionaries. — The Call for Pastors to become Missionaries. — The Pastoral Office now, and in Apostolic Times. — A Common Responsibility.

I PROPOSE to inquire what are the claims of foreign missions upon young ministers of the gospel. But before doing this, I must ask attention to two preliminary inquiries.

The first is, Whether the claims asserted by churches at home upon the personal services of the gospel ministry, are excessive. It is a well-known fact, that every local church feels itself entitled to the best minister it can get. I hardly need illustrate the force and extent of this sentiment in the churches. It is the same in every denomination. In a population not exceeding fifteen hundred souls, with as many as three evangelical churches of different denominations, each having a competent pastor, with seats in the houses of worship enough to accommodate every family, and with a Sabbath-school for every child; yet if there be a number of evangelical residents, who belong to neither of these denominations, they will feel it right to organize a fourth church, and to bring a fourth evangelical minister into the place, if they can, even though obliged to ask aid from the Home Missionary Society; and perhaps they would not be restrained should the consequence of this be, that one of the other churches will also feel the need of asking home missionary aid.

The question I raise is this, — and I do it in the interest of a perishing world, — Whether the fundamental law of benevolence in Christ's kingdom does not make this an excessive and unauthorized demand upon the ministry; and whether, in all such cases, the question of a right so to do, ought not to be seriously entertained by the churches, and by candidates, councils, presbyteries, and home missionary committees and societies.

My second preliminary inquiry is this: May a candidate for the gospel ministry safely assume, before inquiry, that his appointed field of labor is in his native land? I do not think that he can. The Head of the Church has certainly a specific work, and a specific post, for each of us, for which he has given us some special fitness, and which he will make known to us, if we are willing to do his will, and institute the proper inquiries. The kingdom of our blessed Lord evidently has no national boundaries.

"The field is the world;" and the Redeemer will not be satisfied with "the travail of his soul," until his kingdom become coextensive with the earth. The time has now evidently arrived, when the churches and ministers of Christ are bound to aim directly at that result. Were universal conquest the leading object of our nation, then every student in our military and naval schools would regard the field of his duty as in some sense coextensive with the world. In the naval service, indeed, it is scarcely otherwise now. And are not candidates for the gospel ministry in training for the world? Can any man, preparing to act under Christ's commission, say, before inquiry, where will be his post of duty? When this is done, I have always felt that it is at great peril. It is a self-evident truth, that we are nowhere so likely to enjoy the presence of Christ, and success to our labors consequent on the influences of the Holy Spirit, as in the path of our duty. Is it not so? Where else can we be assured of the promise, "Lo, I am with you?" I see not how to escape from this conviction; nor is it an unpleasant one to entertain. Allow me to refer to my own experience. Few ministers of the gospel have been providentially called to travel more over the world than I have been, or have been placed where they have more felt the need of the divine presence and aid; and there is no telling the sweet influence, at such times, of an assurance, that we are in the very place and the very work God has assigned us. Young ministers will feel this hereafter, as they cannot now, especially in the great emergencies of life. For a young minister to decide upon his post of duty before a conscientious inquiry, is like an officer in the army acting without having read the instructions of his commander.

I now enter upon my main inquiry, namely —

The extent of the claim of foreign missions upon young ministers of the gospel. The subject resolves itself into several distinct inquiries.

1. How many missionaries may it be presumed the churches will support? Missionaries receive support from the churches at home; there being the same objection to receiving it from the churches gathered among the heathen, as there was in the days of the Apostle Paul. There are indeed few well defined facts, on which to base a precise answer to this inquiry. The American Board, for instance, as I can bear testimony, has never, in a single instance, deemed it wise to decline the proffered services of a missionary for want of funds; nor am I aware that the thought was ever really entertained of recalling a missionary from the field for that reason. We have no more certain means of knowing how far the churches may be induced to go in supporting missionaries, than our government had, in the year 1861, of knowing how far the nation

would go in supporting an army for putting down the great rebellion. The enthusiasm of young men to enlist as soldiers, had everywhere the effect to stimulate the patriotism and call forth the energies of the country. So it is in missions. I have often felt, that the pecuniary embarrassments of the American Board were owing more to the tardy accessions of new missionaries, than to any other cause. The declaration, "Here are we, send us," when heard by the churches, has a wonderfully animating influence. Nor would the ascertained disbelief of the churches in their own ability to support double or quadruple the number of missionaries now in the field, however positive that disbelief might be, any more prove their actual inability, than was their well-known want of faith in their ability to support the six missionaries, who came forward in the year 1810.

I have long believed, and do now as confidently as ever, that no man, fitted for the missionary service, is justified in declining a mission from the apprehension that he will not be supported in the field; and I should be greatly surprised if the man is living, who will ever know of a well informed missionary society declining, for that reason alone, the services of a competent missionary candidate.

2. My second question is: How many missionaries are needed? Recruits are in constant demand to keep the number of missionaries good. But mis-

sionary conquests cannot be made, or even held, by simply doing this. In missions we must advance, or we shall lose ground. And with such preparations as now exist for diffusing Christianity, the idea of an arrest of progress ought never to be entertained. The existing system of missionary societies is competent to superintend and carry forward a vastly enlarged system of missions. In the business of the world, large trading or manufacturing establishments are found more economical than small ones, and it is so in missions. It is not necessary to increase the existing number of missionary societies. Suppose the missions all to be organized for self-government (as most of the American missions are), then it is obvious, that an increase in the number of well educated missionaries will add to the self-directing power of the missions, and so diminish the responsibility resting upon committees at home. Again, suppose that the churches among the heathen are all formed on the self-governing, self-supporting, self-propagating plan, as the churches founded by St. Paul evidently were, then I see not why existing missionary societies, enlarging their operations by a regular progression, would not suffice for superintending missions all over the heathen world; embracing thousands of missionaries, and tens of thousands of native pastors and preachers. There would not necessarily be any insupportable weight of responsibility resting on committees and executive officers. Permit me again to illustrate by the missions, with which I have long been connected. With five hundred missionaries, instead of one hundred and fifty, as at present, the weekly meetings of the executive committee would only need to be somewhat more prolonged occasionally, but I think not to be multiplied. The home department might require an additional secretary, and the foreign department an assistant secretary, and the treasurer would need an assistant and some additional clerks. But the increase of labor and cost, and the increase of difficulty in the administration, would bear no proportion to the increase in the magnitude and working power of the system. Indeed, the percentage of cost would diminish with the increase of business. The official correspondence would not keep pace with the increase in the number of missionaries; for the larger the missions, the more will they be self-reliant, and the less need will there be of writing often to individuals. Nor am I able to perceive a limit to possible discoveries in respect to the relations of things, and the settling of principles and usages, and the systematizing of labors. There has been an immense advance in experience during the past fifty years. Problems and processes of thought, that oppressed the minds of the early secretaries, have long been embodied in maxims and usages; and though numerous problems remain to be resolved, and new ones are constantly arising, the solutions are going on, and the chaos of facts is coming into something like order and beauty. This progress is constant, under the laws of Christ's kingdom, nor is there any apparent end to it; while the effect is continually to enlarge the ability of the executive officers to attend to the increasing business of their several departments.

Though this reasoning does not give a definite reply to the question, "How many missionaries are needed?" it shows that very many more would find ample employment, than there is any present prospect of obtaining.

3. What sort of men are needed? It is a well-known fact that the military academy at West Point furnished leaders for both of the contending armies in the late war. And leaders of a similar grade are required in the foreign missions, and for similar reasons. The incipient work of planting, organizing, and training churches, composed of converts from heathenism, even in the most barbarous countries, requires more talent, as I have already said, than is ordinarily demanded for the pastoral office at home. For you have to deal with a strange people, and a strange language, with strange manners and customs, with consciences dead or altogether perverted, with religions more depraved than human nature itself, and with social life that is rotten to the core. With anything but the gospel and the grace of God,

one would despair in such a field. Yet experience shows that, with the gospel and the grace of God, there is useful and ample scope here for sanctified talent of the highest grade. Taking the average of labors and results in the heathen world, I do not believe that the pastoral life of our own favored country can show more abundant fruits. The eloquent preacher, when once he has acquired the language, finds his talent not less effective there, than here. And the demand for varied and cultivated talent is nearly the same in all the fields, as well in Polynesia and Africa, as in India and China. As the mission advances, giving rise to churches, schools, a native ministry, and a Christian community, there arises also a demand for what is called the organizing and administrative talent, more varied and more imperative than can often occur in our home pastoral life. In my own intimate acquaintance with missionaries, I recollect no case where there was fitness for the work, and time for development, where it seemed probable there would have been a greater usefulness at home. Passing by the immortal pioneers, I advert to two or three representative men, whom it has been my happiness to know intimately.

My first is the late Dr. William Goodell, of blessed memory, so long a missionary at Constantinople. You may go to the utmost stretch of probable supposition of what would have been his usefulness as a pastor anywhere in his native land, and you will see ample reason to believe, that at home he would have missed the sphere for which he was made, and to which he was called of God.

It was so with Dr. Eli Smith, who died in Syria in the year 1857. As a scholar, he excelled most of his brethren; as an accurate observer, he equaled the late Dr. Edward Robinson; as a translator of the Scriptures, he had no superior. He found his field by yielding early to the impulses of grace on his heart, and by following the leadings of Providence; and the peculiar adaptedness of the field to his tastes and talents, was an after-discovery. I knew him while in the seminary, and had ample opportunities to know him before entering on his mission, and through all his missionary life, and I never doubted that his usefulness was greater as a missionary, than it could have been anywhere in his native land.

It would be easy to draw other illustrations from missions in Western Asia. But to my own mind, there are cases quite as striking in the pagan world. The late Henry Ballantine, of the Mahratta mission, had a more fruitful record in India, — in the native churches, in the native ministry, in the hymns and songs of the native worship, than he could have had at home. And suppose the late Dr. Miron Winslow had settled as a pastor in Connecticut, or Dr. Daniel Poor, in Massachusetts, or Dr. David Abeel in the city of New York, or Dr. Culbertson, in one of the choicest stations at home in the gift of the Presbyterian Church; would they have been as useful as they were in heathen lands? I cannot believe it. And I believe the same might be affirmed, with even more evident truth, concerning many of their associates of less fame, both living and dead.

With such scope for talent of all kinds, and with such demand for it, the answer to the question, "What sort of men are needed?" is obvious: We need the ablest and the best.

4. From whence are they to come? My first answer is, from the churches. The churches have a responsibility here. In very many of them there are young men of talents and character, who need only the advantages of education to go forth as heralds of the cross. But few of them have the means for obtaining an education, and, as a body, they are therefore turning their attention to farming, trade, the mechanic arts, or scientific pursuits. Ought not every church and every pastor to see, that Christ's appointed ministry for the world's conversion does not thus suffer loss? Not that any one church need assume the whole expense, except in extraordinary cases; but the young men should be liberated from the thralldom of the world, and put in the way of seeking an education, and a bountiful Providence will do the rest. Were one fourth or one sixth of the three thousand Congregational

churches, and one fourth or one sixth of the four or five thousand Presbyterian churches to do this, a few years would suffice to startle and electrify the world.

But whatever the churches may see fit to do, we shall have to look to the theological seminaries. Missionaries, more than home pastors, as a class need the training and discipline of the seminary. We have no institutions in this country for the exclusive training of missionaries, as they have in England, and on continental Europe, nor do we need or desire them. We require for our missionaries, with occasional exceptions, an extended and thorough education, and we expect them generally to make equal attainments with the ministry at home, and, at the same time, secure the great advantage of being fellow-students and companions of those who are to become pastors of the churches which must furnish the means of their support and usefulness among the heathen.

There must be some way of approximating the number of missionaries, which a theological institution may be expected to afford. Until within a few years past, it has been my duty to visit the Seminary at Andover officially, in quest of missionaries. I distinctly remember one of these visits, made in the year 1856, in which I had private interviews with as many as thirty-four of the students from the different classes, who called on me, separately, to confer in respect to their duty. My aim was, as usual, simply to aid them in deciding the question of duty for themselves. I made a private memorandum of each case, which I preserved, and from which I learn, that at least fifteen of those brethren then appeared to me to have a clear providential call to the missionary work. The whole number then in the Seminary was one hundred and fourteen; and I was thus assured that I had conferred with nearly a third part of the students, and saw evidence in them of serious thought on the subject; and that they would become missionaries, or, if providentially hindered, would be good missionary pastors. I did not see those who had devoted themselves to the home missionary work, because it was ever a set purpose with me not to interfere with home missions; but I felt assured that they too would at least be missionary pastors. I also thought it right to assume, that others of the two thirds whom I did not see, had already considered and decided the question, and did not feel called upon to reconsider it. In point of fact, seven of those whom I did not see, afterwards became foreign missionaries.

From my personal knowledge of individual experiences then and subsequently, I came to the conclusion, that as many as twenty-two members of the Seminary, at that time, were called of God to publish the gospel beyond the bounds of Christendom. And I feel confident, that it would have been beneficial to that institution, to New England, and to the West, had each of the three classes sent forth as many as seven of their number into the unevangelized world. The number of those who actually went on foreign missions, was ten, or about one in eleven. Of all who have been connected with that institution from the beginning, only one in sixteen has become a foreign missionary. Yet there are few theological institutions, from which the heathen world is authorized to expect so large an annual contribution of well educated, devoted missionaries, as from that Seminary. From the semi-centennial catalogue of Princeton Seminary, published in 1862, I learn that, up to that time, its foreign missionaries were as one to seventeen. From the Hartford Seminary I am informed that fifteen, out of three hundred and fifteen, have gone as foreign missionaries. Of the proportion from other seminaries, I have not the means of speaking confidently.

5. How early should the question of duty be decided? The earlier the better, if it be with the Scriptural condition, "If the Lord will." There will be a better training for the work. The decision can be reconsidered upon any considerable providential change in circumstances. A delay until near the close of the preparatory studies, is almost sure to prevent a thorough and impartial examination, and so to keep the man at home. The reasons

need not be specified.[1] The best time for an offer of service to a Missionary Board (as I view the matter), is at the commencement of the senior year. The theological studies are then generally completed, the case is ripe for consideration, and the senior year will give time enough for the needful mental and social adjustments.

The effect on a seminary of having none in it who are resolved and active in relation to missions, both home and foreign, is unfavorable to the spiritual interests of the institution. Such missionary students as might easily be named, were great spiritual blessings to their institutions. They raised the tone of piety, and their influence upon those who remained at home as pastors must have been good.

6. What is the influence of foreign missionaries on the churches at home? — I mean the reflex influence of their mission. The question is not as to their usefulness on the whole, nor as to their usefulness in the foreign field, but as to their usefulness in the churches of their native country, as a consequence of their going abroad. This should have its weight in deciding the question of duty. Missionaries exert this reflex influence by their example, by their personal influence on the pastors of their acquaintance, by their letters through the channels

[1] See *Quart. Register* of the American Education Society for 1831, pp. 245–253.

of their Missionary Boards, by their private correspondence, by their visits to their native land, and as being a constituent part of the great foreign missionary organization that is constantly reacting upon their native land. Tell me if Aldin Grout, of the Zulu mission in South Africa, could have exerted so great and beneficial an influence as pastor of a church at home, as he has done and is now doing, — I say not among the Zulus of Africa, — but upon our American churches. It may be that even his visit home, in the year 1858, alone exerted a greater influence on our churches, than he could himself have exerted upon them by a life-work as a home pastor. Tell me, if Titus Coan, who for five and twenty years has been, under God, the renovating, organizing, governing power along a hundred miles of the Hawaiian shore, — whether he could have found such a scope and reward for his labors in his own country? This great comparative usefulness he could not indeed have foreseen, and it does not itself prove that any other one would have been as useful abroad as he has been, even if as enterprising and laborious. But it shows what a field of usefulness he himself would have missed, had he not listened to the call of God when in the Auburn Seminary.

And in what ministerial field of usefulness, here at home, could you have placed the late Dr. H. G. O. Dwight, where he could have exerted half the influence for good in the United States, that resulted in his native land from his missionary career in Turkey?

How many beloved names crowd upon our recollection! We think of Swartz, of Zieganbalg, of Brainerd, of Henry Martyn, of Judson, of Gordon Hall, of John Williams, of Lowrie, and scores of others whom I would gladly name. At the call of God, they went forth to proclaim salvation to the heathen; and, by so doing, they not only accomplished more good abroad, than it is probable they could have accomplished at home; but in so doing they seem to have duplicated their lives, by the good they effected in their beloved native land.

7. Is there a call on pastors to become missionaries? It must be obvious, that if any, under mistaken impressions of duty, have settled as pastors, who were really called of God to be missionaries, they cannot be wholly at ease in that position; for they are not in that path of duty, where they are most assured of the Saviour's presence, and of the consolations and aids of the Holy Spirit. Such pastors, when seasonably convinced of their error, will seek to correct it; and some such, relinquishing their pastorates, have already gone into the foreign field, and are happy in "doing their first works." One, formerly a pastor, has lately written thus on the subject from his distant field of labor: "Let a pas-

tor," he says, "whose attachments to his people are very strong, and who has the confidence of his associates in the ministry, and some acquaintance with all the churches in the country, leave his people, and, guided, as he believes, by the Spirit and providence of God, enter heartily upon the work of foreign missions; and he carries with him the sympathies and prayers, not only of his parish, but of his associates in the ministry, and to some extent of their parishes. Now they will look upon the missionary work with a new interest. They know at least one missionary, and they will watch for intelligence from him. They will *read* concerning missions as they have not read before; and as the people read their interest will increase, and with an increase of interest will come an increase of prayer, and the more they pray, the more they will give. The children will catch something of this new interest; the Sabbath-school will feel it; and no wonder if, in future years, others come forward and offer themselves to the same blessed work, tracing their convictions of duty to impressions made in childhood by that pastor's consecration to the cause of missions."

The time is coming, I believe, when there will be a special demand on pastors; and the demand will be on the more experienced and eminent ministers, men of commanding presence and eloquence, skillful organizers, and conversant with ecclesiastical principles and usages. When churches have become very numerous in heathen lands, the visits of such men to the missions for one, two or more years, will be needed, to assist the missionaries by their counsels, and to assure the community at home by their reports; and the usefulness of such services will be ample compensation for the sacrifice they will involve.

I close with a few general remarks.

The pastoral office in Christendom is differently related to foreign missions, from what it was in the apostolic age. Then, pastors were all connected with what we now call mission churches; that is, they were pastors of churches gathered among the heathen as the result of apostolic missionary labor. But pastors, in this country and in Great Britain, are now the spiritual leaders of the evangelical churches, which have assumed the responsibility of sending forth and supporting Christian missionaries. The responsibility of these Christian pastors is, therefore, of the same nature with that of the missionaries. It is the common responsibility resting on both the senders and the sent. All are acting under the same commission, in obedience to the same command, in view of the same promise, and for the same great and glorious end; namely, the proclamation of the heaven-born salvation of the gospel, and the establishment of the Redeemer's reign, in all parts of the world. And the same responsibility rests equally upon the churches. We are not of those who look upon the clergy as a body distinct and separate from the churches. Nor do we look upon the churches as principals in this work of the world's spiritual illumination. Pastors, missionaries, churches, all are mere agents, mere instruments of the Almighty Redeemer, and together form his great army for the subjugation of our rebellious race.

But my present concern is with the gospel ministry. To me it is a self-evident truth, that ministers at home are as much bound to do what they can, in their circumstances, for the vigorous extension of Christ's kingdom, as are those brother ministers, whose sense of personal duty calls them to go abroad. The ministers of Jesus Christ, wherever their post of duty, stand related to the whole work on the broad scale of the earth. Foreign missions have, therefore, a claim upon all Christian ministers, according to their means of affording aid. Not the pastoral work alone, not home missions alone, not foreign missions alone, but laboring to make the gospel known "to every creature," at home and abroad, is our proper business as the ministers of Christ.

Every minister must of course use his discretion in determining the proportionate attention he shall give to the several departments of his calling; and there will be no harm, on the whole, should there be a diversity of views on this subject. Only let the fact be admitted of a common responsibility for the world's spiritual illumination, and, looking from that stand-point, we shall fall into no material error as regards our personal duty.

CHAPTER XIV.

THE ROMISH MISSIONS AS AN OPPOSING POWER.

Leading Object of the Romish Church. — The Theme for Discussion. Romish Missions since the Reformation. — Had the Heathen World all to themselves, and reported Vast Successes. — Their Missions a Failure. — The Statement not weakened by Recent Developments. — Principles underlying Protestant and Romish Missions contrasted. — Superiority of Protestant Missions as a Converting Power. — Romish Missions nevertheless formidable. — Best Manner of working Protestant Missions in their Presence. — Grounds of Hope for the Future.

THE leading object of the Romish Church at the present day, is probably the conquest of England and the United States. To a secret, cunning, ambitious, and unscrupulous society, like the Jesuit order, the all but universal suffrage of our country, and the amount of popular education controlled by that suffrage, must be specially attractive. They will need much looking after, and should be met with every proper effort to fortify the Protestant community against them, and to acquaint the Roman Catholic people with the knowledge of salvation through Christ alone.

But papal missions in Protestant Christendom, however important and interesting, come not within the proper range of this work.

My theme is the Romish Missions in Heathen Lands, as opposed to Protestant Missions. I shall not question their propagating power, as a consequence of their acknowledged zeal, activity, and enterprise. That power they have in common with Protestant missionaries. My object is rather to show the inherent weakness of Romish missions to the heathen, as compared with Protestant missions, in their lack of a transforming power upon the heart and life of man, converting him from sin to holiness.

I shall first enumerate the principal Romish missions to the heathen, from the time of the Reformation to the opening of the present century, and shall note the great success claimed for them, and also their signal failure as they appeared at the opening of the century. I propose then to contrast the principles underlying the Protestant and Romish missions, in order to show the inefficiency of the latter as a converting agency. Nevertheless Rome being a formidable antagonist as a self-propagating body, I shall briefly illustrate that fact; and then offer some practical suggestions as to the best manner of working Protestant missions in the presence of those from the Romish Church. The extent and variety of my subject-matter will require great conciseness of statement.

I. I am to enumerate the principal Romish missions to the heathen, from the time of the Reformation to the opening of the present century.

The most remarkable period of these missions was from the institution of the order of Jesuits, about the middle of the sixteenth century, to the end of the seventeenth. The foreign missions of the Romish Church were, in some sense, a result of the Reformation. Their leading object was to oppose and counteract the Reformation. In this period, besides the order of Jesuits, there were founded at Rome, the Congregation for the Propagation of the Faith, and the Seminary for the Education of Missionaries, both well endowed, which still exist. Several institutions for foreign missions were also formed in France, embodying a large amount of enterprise. Speaking of those institutions, Mosheim says: "From these colleges and societies issued those swarms of missionaries, who travelled over much of the known world, and from among the most ferocious nations gathered congregations that were, if not in reality, yet in name, and in some of their usages, Christians." "Among these missionaries," he says, "the Jesuits, Dominicans, Franciscans, and Capuchins, obtained the greater glory. Yet they mutually assailed and accused each other, publicly, of disregarding and dishonoring the cause of Christ, and even of corrupting his holy doctrines. The Jesuits, in particular, were the most spoken against, by the others, who labored with them in the glorious cause of enlarging the Saviour's empire, and by the great body of their own church."[1] The testimony of Mosheim is

[1] Mosheim's *Hist.*, vol. iii. p. 245.

corroborated by other testimony. How exceedingly corrupt and mischievous the Jesuits were as casuists, is set forth with marvelous wit and power, by Paschal in his "Provincial Letters," written about the middle of the seventeenth century.

The order of Jesuits was suppressed by Pope Clement XIV. in 1773, two hundred and thirty-three years after its establishment. This was done in compliance with the demands of the papal kingdoms, which could no longer endure its abuses. Yet the Jesuit order was not thereby annihilated. The suppression involved the confiscation of their immense possessions, and the necessity of their assuming the citizen's dress; yet the spirit of the order remained, and probably its organization, and they gradually attained to influential employments in seminaries for education, in governments, and in the church. In 1814, after Napoleon had abdicated the imperial throne, and when the nations of Europe were beginning to rejoice in their freedom, Pius VII. reconstituted the order.

The Jesuit order is reported now to contain somewhat over eight thousand members; which is a large number of such missionaries to be scattered over the world.[1] They confess, however, to a much smaller number.[2]

As they are believed to constitute the chief mis-

[1] Boston *Daily Advertiser*, March, 1868.

[2] See Appendix IX.

sionary power of the Romish Church, and have been the principal means of the revival of its missions, I must say somewhat more concerning them.

The General of the order resides at Rome, and no Roman emperor, no despot of any age, had a more absolute sway. Legislative, judicial, and executive functions all are vested in him. He is to every Jesuit the ruler of thought, conscience, and volition, and from him there is no appeal. Every dignity and emolument is at his disposal, and he holds his office for life.

It is difficult to ascertain what was the actual Roman Catholic missionary force in the heathen world, at any one period. The historian of the Dutch missions in India estimated the number of Romish missionaries in the East, in the year 1706, at two thousand. Rome gives very little account of her proceedings to the world, or even to her own people. Cardinal Wiseman says "the Propaganda publishes nothing." "No appeal," he adds, "is ever made by it to the public. The Congregation meets privately, and although persons who take pains may procure information, there is nothing like an official document put forth, to bring what is done by its missionaries before the world."[1] This concealment has ever characterized the missions of the Propaganda.[2] The Jesuits have had a somewhat different

[1] *Lectures*, 1836, p. 219.

[2] Venn's *Life of Xavier*, Preface and p. 267.

policy, especially as regards their favorite Xavier, but it is not easy to know how much to believe.

There can be no reasonable doubt that during the sixteenth, seventeenth, and some part of the eighteenth centuries, the Church of Rome prosecuted missions in the pagan world beyond anything yet witnessed in the Protestant Church. Their more important missions I will now enumerate.

They had one in India for three hundred years, commencing with the sixteenth century. They had one in Japan for the greater part of a hundred years, commencing with 1549. They had one in China without any serious obstruction, for one hundred and forty-four years, commencing in 1579. They had one in Paraguay, in South America, for one hundred and seventeen years, which began soon after the close of the mission in Japan. They had one in South Africa, in the kingdom of Kongo, for more than two hundred years, until about the middle of the eighteenth century.

These great fields the Romish missionaries had all to themselves. They had the sole occupation of them during the space of from one to three centuries. Not a Protestant came near them; excepting a few Danes in a small section of their India field, near the close of their third century. Never had missionaries a fairer opportunity to Christianize whole nations.

II. They reported great successes; though my impression of their magnitude is considerably modified, when I take into account the duration and extent of the several missions. In Japan, the religion they proposed was adopted by great numbers of all ranks and qualities. In China, the Tartar Emperor, Kang-he, was educated by a Jesuit, and proclaimed the Christian religion (meaning the Romish) to be good and salutary, and that all his subjects were at liberty to embrace it; and his reign of more than fifty years gave the Romish missionaries every possible advantage. Their Chinese converts were reckoned by hundreds of thousands. In Paraguay, the Jesuits estimated their baptized Indians at one hundred and twenty thousand. In Africa, the kingdom of Kongo, according to the showing of the missionaries themselves, was, for more than two centuries, completely under the influence of Rome; so that if the inhabitants are not all in civilization and Christianity, that a pagan people are capable of being made under the training of Romish missions, the fault was their own. The facilities they there enjoyed were such as Rome can scarcely ever expect to have again.[1] "Nor was the papacy established in Kongo," says the historian, "in a hasty or superficial manner. It was a work, at which successive companies of missionaries labored with untiring assiduity for two centuries. Among

[1] Wilson's *Western Africa*, p. 134.

these were some of the most learned and able men that Rome ever sent forth to the pagan world. It was a cause, too, that always lay near the heart of the King of Portugal, when that nation was at the climax of its power and wealth. The royal sword was ever ready to be unsheathed for its defense, and her treasures were poured out without stint for its support." [1]

III. Yet every one of these protracted missions, as they appeared at the opening of the present century, was a failure.[2] And I do not know how it can be proved, that any one of them was a permanent blessing to the nation in which it labored.

The Kongo mission perished entirely on the withdrawal of Portuguese protection, and "left the unfortunate inhabitants of that country," as the historian declares, "in as deep ignorance and superstition, and perhaps in greater poverty and degradation, than they would have been, if Roman Catholicism had never been proclaimed among them." [3]

After the expulsion of the Jesuits from Paraguay, in 1767, "the greater number of the inhabitants relapsed into a state of barbarism." [4]

As regards China, Father Ripa, a missionary from

[1] Wilson, p. 329.

[2] On the general subject of the failure of Romish missions, see Venn's *Life of Xavier*, p. 262 and onward.

[3] Wilson, p. 329.

[4] Venn, p. 315.

the Propaganda, residing at Peking, and writing after the Chinese mission ceased to exist as a public and tolerated institution, makes the remarkable declaration, that of the five hundred missionaries sent from Europe to China during the hundred and forty years of the mission, none of them so mastered the language, as to be able to preach intelligibly to the people at large.[1] He could not mean to say, that some of them were not skilled in the written language, but that they were not able to preach intelligibly in the common spoken language of the people. We credit, therefore, the testimony of Dr. Williams, in his history of the Chinese Empire. "It is probable," he says, "that there may have been true converts among the myriads of adherents to Romanism; but what salutary effects has this large body of Christians wrought in the vast population of China, during the two hundred and fifty years since Ricci established himself at Nanking? None, absolutely none, that attract attention." After candidly admitting, that "many of their converts exhibited the greatest constancy in their profession, suffering persecution, torture, imprisonment, banishment, and death, rather than deny their faith," he adds: "but the mass of Romish converts in China can hardly be considered to have been much better than baptized pagans."[2]

The Abbe Dubois, after having spent twenty-five

[1] Venn, p. 301. Williams' *Middle Kingdom,* 4th ed., vol. ii. p. 314.

[2] Williams' *Middle Kingdom*, vol. ii. p. 324.

years in Southern India as a Jesuit missionary, affirms, that the renowned Francis Xavier, who is now attaining the rank of a patron saint to Romish missions, "being disheartened by the invincible obstacles he everywhere met in his apostolic career, and by the apparent impossibility of making real converts, left India in disgust." And this fully appears in Xavier's correspondence.[1]

The course pursued by the Jesuits in their Madura mission, and its results, should not be suffered to fade from public recollection. It is thus described by Dr. Mullens, in his excellent work on "Missions in South India," published fourteen years since. After stating what glowing accounts were given by the Jesuits of their success, he says: "Such is their own account; but there is evidence of the clearest kind, from their own pens and from papal records, that the whole plan of their mission was a lie; that it began in lies and perjury, and was so maintained, and by lying and deception was utterly ruined in the end." This language is severe, but no more so than the truth. "From the outset," Dr. Mullens says, "Robert de Nobili and the others denied with oaths that they were Europeans, asserting boldly that they were real Brahmins. They dressed, bathed, and ate like real Brahmins, wore the sacred thread, put ashes on their breasts and foreheads, wore the native wooden shoes, and slept upon a tiger's skin. Them-

[1] Venn, p. 165 and elsewhere.

selves assert that their whole attention was given to concealing the fact that they were Europeans, since they augured the complete destruction of the mission from its discovery. Yet after all they failed with the Brahmin class, which it was their special object to win." Thousands on thousands of the Pariah class were baptized, but these Pariah adherents were never elevated. They also baptized, by stealth, thousands of dying heathen children. In this way they were able to boast of immense numbers of converts. "In managing their converts, they kept up the same system of deception and compromise. They allowed them the same cars and idolatrous processions as before, the Virgin Mary taking the place of the Hindu god. In their marriages, the heathen emblems, the heathen rites and customs as to food, were all kept up still. In their bathing, they still repeated the same formulas as before, uttering the name of some god as they touched each successive limb." "In fact," he adds, "their converts, except as to name, were exactly and in every respect the same heathen Pariahs, as they were before."[1]

The Jesuit mission to Abyssinia should be mentioned. It was commenced about the middle of the sixteenth century, and its object was to bring the country under the dominion of the Pope. For a

[1] *Missions in South India*, p. 134. For ample illustrations, see *Calcutta Review*, 1844, vol. ii. pp. 73–120.

time they had great success. In 1726, the emperor acknowledged fealty to the "successor of St. Peter." The Jesuits were received with favor, and had all possible facilities granted them. But they lost all prudence. The liturgy of Rome was introduced. The doctrine of Christ's person, as held by that people, was made an offense punishable with death, and the Inquisition was introduced to carry out this atrocious enactment. Five consecutive rebellions, with fearful bloodshed, were the consequence. The king finally relented, and in 1634 granted liberty of conscience; and the whole Roman structure fell instantly to the ground. In the next reign, the Jesuits were banished, and when more came, they were put to death.[1]

In the Philippine Islands, which have been held by the Spaniards, the Romish missionaries have maintained their supremacy for about three centuries. But the papal author of the "Voyage of the Novara Frigate," sent out by the Austrian government not long since on an exploring expedition, states, that "little, if anything, has been done for the prosperity and development of the country, or for the intellectual and moral advancement of the people;" and that "there, apparently, as in the other earlier dependencies of Spain, the Roman Catholic ritual has become mingled, in the most extraordinary manner, with ceremonies borrowed from paganism."[2]

[1] Venn's *Life of Xavier*, p. 312.

[2] Venn, p. 316.

I hope the reader is not wearied by this statement of the efforts of the Romish Church to secure a footing in the heathen world, and of their failure to exert a transforming religious influence upon the benighted nations.

The force of this statement will not be materially affected, should the dying out of the Romish missions be mainly attributed by Romish authors to the suppression of the Jesuit order, nearly a hundred years since, and to the paralyzing influence of the revolutions and wars on continental Europe. If a mission, after the lapse of a century, with all the facilities they enjoyed, cannot retain its conquests without keeping an army in the field, it is a failure. And thus it was with the Romish missions. No radical and permanent change has been effected in the religious sentiments and habits of the people among whom they had so long labored. Foreign bishops and priests were—and they are to this day—an essential condition of prosperity to the native papal communities.

Nor would the case be materially altered, should it appear, that some thousands and even many thousands of adherents to the Papal Church have secretly retained their allegiance to the Pope, both in China and Japan, since the missions were forcibly suppressed, and are now declaring themselves, upon an assurance of safety under French protection. For it has long been more than surmised, that Romish missionaries continued to enter China, after the suppression of the missions, under disguises such as Protestant missionaries would not deem allowable; and the same may yet prove to be true in Japan. I do not deny the sincere and eminent devotion of the Romish missionary to his church, and of the Jesuit to his order, nor their activity and enterprise. Self-righteousness may labor and suffer as remarkably, perhaps, as the religion of the cross. In ancient times, we know, it "compassed sea and land to make one proselyte," even though the proselyte became (if I may use the emphatic language of our Lord) "two-fold more the child of hell."[1] Pharisee, Stylite, Jesuit, Fakir, we see in each the power of the self-righteous principle, and we admit it. But on this singular phenomenon in our human nature, I need not enlarge.

The question before us is one of great interest. We are to remember, that the Romish Church and its missions are substantially the same to-day, in their nature and objects, and the means they employ, as they were two or three hundred years ago. The Jesuits may have learned more prudence, but they are the same.

IV. I am now to illustrate the inefficiency of the Romish missions as a converting agency, and this I

[1] Matt. xxiii. 15.

do by contrasting the principles underlying the Protestant and Romish missions.

1. It is a settled principle, in Protestant missions of the present day, not to call in the aid of the civil government, except merely for personal protection where they have a legal right to be and to labor. Whereas the Romish missions, from the Pope and Francis Xavier down, have advanced their interests by every possible use of the civil arm. Even since the commencement of the present century, there is said to have been no less than fifteen interventions of the French army in Italy, at the instigation of the Pope; and since the year 734, there have been forty-one such interventions at his call.[1] This reliance on the secular power is inherent in the Romish Church, and was one of Xavier's most mischievous practical errors. In Africa, so heavily did the Romish mission lean upon the king of Portugal, that the Kongo mission declined with the decline of Portuguese power.[2] In China, they so leaned upon the Emperor Kang-he, that their overthrow, so far as their tolerated existence in the empire was concerned, followed speedily on his decease.[3] Their subsequent hold, until the late treaties with France, as already intimated, has been through a concealed operation, that would not be deemed allowable by Protestant missionaries. The destruction of the Japan-

[1] See this illustrated in Venn's *Life of Francis Xavier*, pp. 277–316

[2] Wilson, p. 346.

[3] Venn, p. 306.

ese mission was owing, as its immediate cause, to the discovery of a political intrigue traceable to the missionaries.[1] In Paraguay, the fruits of the Jesuit mission perished as soon as the Spaniards had overthrown their army of converts. And the reader will remember how it was in Abyssinia.[2]

2. The Holy Scriptures lie at the foundation of every Protestant mission. But, whatever Romanists may say as to their Scripture translations in former ages, the Inspired Word has not been, and is not now, a recognized agency in their missions. While they freely expended money in erecting churches, colleges, and convents in India, they made no versions of the Scriptures in any of the vernacular languages.[3] Let any one read the lectures of Cardinal Wiseman on the Catholic Church, or almost any Romish accounts of Protestant missions, and he will have no doubt that papal missions are designed

[1] Venn, pp. 210, 300.

[2] "The Jesuits," says Dr. Geddes, in his *Church History of Ethiopia*, "were all to a man of the same opinion with that great apostle of the Indies, Francis Xavier, whose maxim, as Ravaretta informs us, was, that missionaries without muskets do never make converts to any purpose. The truth of which maxim John Bolunte, a missionary Jesuit, tells us is confirmed by universal experience; for neither in the Brazils, Peru, Mexico, Florida, the Philippines, or Molucca, have any conversions been made without the help of the secular power." — Quoted in Venn's *Life of Xavier*, p. 528. Dr. Geddes was for many years British Chaplain at Lisbon, and there studied the Portuguese history of missions.

[3] Dr. Allen's *India*, p. 559.

to be prosecuted with the least possible use of the Inspired Volume.[1]

3. The Protestant missions make great use of preaching, and of course expect every missionary to be able to proclaim the gospel in the language of the people. But the Romish missions, as a general thing, can scarcely be said to do either. It should be borne in mind that I am speaking only of their missions among the heathen. If there are now what may seem to be exceptions to this, it is because of their immediate proximity to Protestant missionaries. I have already adduced testimony of the incompetency of the former papal missionaries to preach intelligibly to the Chinese people. Father Ripa also affirms, that they made no attempt to introduce an educated native ministry, and that his own efforts in that direction at Peking, led only to scandal and discord.[2]

Dr. Wilson says, that but few of the missionaries

[1] See Marshall's *Christian Missions, their Agents and Results*, vol. i. pp. 1–59. The opposition of the Romish Church to allowing the use of the Scriptures by the people, is very ably set forth by Dr. William Barrows, in the *Bibliotheca Sacra and Biblical Repository* for 1860, vol. xvii. pp. 323–355. Cardinal Wiseman, in his tract entitled *The Catholic Doctrine on the Use of the Bible*, affirms of the principles held on this subject by Romanists and Protestants: "They are antagonistic, and we glory in avowing it." He says: "We answer, therefore, boldly, that we give not the word of God indiscriminately to all, because God himself has not so given it. We further say, that we do not permit the indiscriminate and undirected use of the Bible, because God has not given to his church the instinct to do so."

[2] Venn, p. 301.

in the African kingdom of Kongo made themselves acquainted with the language of the people. Even Francis Xavier, the most noted of the Romish missionaries, was never able to preach to the people in the East except through interpreters, and these often very imperfect. "Conceive," said he, in writing at one time to a friend, "what kind of sermons I am able to preach, when they who should repeat my address to the people, do not understand me, nor I them."[1]

4. Protestant missions are making more and more use of an educated native ministry; and, in the progress of experience, they are, to a certain extent, acting on the conviction, that native pastors are essential to the full development of native churches, and this conviction will be sure to gain ground hereafter in the evangelical missions. Whereas, a theologically educated native ministry, in our sense of the phrase, is not an element in the Romish mis-

[1] Venn, p. 37; also, pp. 197, 208, 258. Pope Gregory VII. thus states the sentiment of the Romish Church in favor of conducting its worship, as far as possible, in an unknown tongue. "In our frequent meditations upon the Holy Scriptures," he says, "we have discovered, that it has been and still is pleasing to Almighty God, that his sacred worship should be performed in an unknown language, in order that the whole world, and especially the most simple, may not be able to understand it. In a known language, the service would soon excite contempt and disgust, or it would happen that the common people, by repeating so often that which they could not comprehend, would fall into many great errors, from which it would be difficult to withdraw the heart of man." — *Bibliotheca Sacra*, 1860, p. 352.

sions; and of the native pastorate, educated on the ground, they know nothing.[1]

5. The local, self-governed church, is an indispensable element in Protestant missions. But the Romish missions have nothing of the kind. They have no local, self-governed churches. The Romish Church claims to be itself one and indivisible; but its unity, so far as it is real, is a terrible reality. It is a vast ecclesiastical despotism, numbering only those among its members, who submit implicitly to its authority. This is a chief reason of the well-known perpetual pupilage of the Romish missions, and of their decline as soon as their missionaries are withdrawn. Then there cannot but be everywhere a paralyzing influence in the generally prevailing belief in the dogma of baptismal regeneration, as being the only thing requisite to make a heathen a member of the church of Christ. The practice of baptizing dying children of heathens, would seem to be scarcely less prevalent in the Romish missions now, than it was in the sixteenth century. The "Annals of the Propagation of the Faith," published by authority, contained, only a few years since, the following statement by an apostolic vicar in one of the China missions. "The mission," he says, "continues its work of baptizing children in danger of death, and the Lord continues to bless it. Each

[1] I am aware that they now report some hundreds of native priests and divinity students in China. Nevertheless, I leave the text as it is.

year the number of those whom they regenerate, goes on increasing. In 1839, it was 12,483; in 1840, 15,766; in 1841, 17,825; in 1842, 20,068; in 1843, 22,292; and in 1844, 24,381." Native Christians of both sexes were employed and paid to seek out and baptize dying infants. The poor heathen parents willingly allowed these agents to spill drops of water on the forehead, declaring it to be good for the child, pronouncing, at the same time, the sacramental words. This was their baptism. According to the statistics (which bear evident marks of no small exaggeration), more than one hundred and twelve thousand infants were thus "regenerated" (to use their term) in this one mission, and "prepared for heaven," as they would say, in the space of six years.[1] Dr. Wilson, in his history of the Kongo mission, illustrates the same usage. "Father Garli states," he says, "that in two years he baptized 2,700 children. Another missionary is reported to have baptized 5,000 children in a few days. Another baptized 12,000 in less than a year. Father Merolla claims, in less than five years to have baptized more than 13,000, and he mentions the case of a brother missionary, who baptized 50,000, and of another, who, in twenty years, baptized more than 100,000."[2] Even Xavier was in the full belief of this doctrine, and claimed to have baptized a thousand infants in Ceylon, who died (as he says) before

[1] Venn, p. 42. [2] Wilson's *West Africa*, p. 337.

they could commit sin, and consequently (as he believed) had gone to heaven to intercede on his behalf. He regarded baptismal innocence as extending to the age of fourteen.[1]

6. Protestant missions have in them the spiritual life and power contained in the doctrines of regeneration by the Holy Spirit, justification by faith, and sanctification through the truth. Instead of which, the Romish missions have the doctrine of baptismal regeneration, which they regard as a saving ordinance, and they require of the baptized adult only an outward profession, without insisting on a change of heart, and often scarcely a reformation of life.[2]

Once more, —

7. The Romanists are justly accused of compromising with paganism in their modes of worship; and no earnest objection was made to this in the high places of the Romish Church, until the Jesuits in India had well nigh substituted paganism for Christianity. But such an accusation against a Protestant mission, if sustained, would at once deprive it of the confidence and support of the churches.

I think I have said enough to illustrate the immense superiority of the Protestant missions over those of the Romish Church, in their power to exert an influence on the heart and life of the pagan world. Whatever amount of true doctrine there

[1] Venn, p. 156. [2] Dr. Medhurst, as quoted by Dr. Venn, p. 308.

may be in the creeds of the Romish Church, for all the purposes of our present discussion it is a religion of forms, and rites, and ceremonies, which easily assimilate to the religious formalism of pagan nations. Such is the concurrent testimony of Protestant missionaries. The Romish missions withhold the Bible. Their school teaching rouses not, nor is it intended to arouse, the intellectual and moral powers. A select few are educated to govern, but the great masses are educated to obey; and we see what is the education for the masses, in the seventeen millions out of twenty-five in Italy, and the nine tenths of the population in Spain, who can neither read or write. Romish missionaries (at least those remote from Protestant missions) seldom preach; and are believed rarely to inculcate the doctrine of atonement through the blood of Christ alone, or sanctification through the Holy Spirit; and the preparation they would make for death and the judgment, is by means of baptismal regeneration, aided by lifeless ceremonies, and priestly absolutions.

Surely the Lord Jesus Christ did not promise his presence, nor the gift of his Spirit, to such missions as these.

V. Neverthless, Rome is a formidable opponent, and this I must briefly illustrate. Its numerical force cannot be less now, than it was in the sixteenth and seventeenth centuries, and its intellectual and pecuniary resources must be greater. It shares also with Protestants in whatever advantage results from the immense increase of facilities afforded by the progress of civilization.

Moreover, the Propagandist spirit of the Romish Church is reviving once more. The Society for Missions at Lyons acknowledges the annual receipt from the faithful of more than a million of dollars. Several of the old missions have been revived, and Romish missionaries are now widely scattered in heathen lands. The Reformation awoke the Papal Church to those vast missionary efforts we have just now passed in review; and the missionary spirit and effort now in the Protestant churches are rousing the Romish Church to a second grand effort, and will doubtless, for some time to come, exert that influence more and more. Romish missionaries will everywhere be our uncompromising antagonists. I am far from thinking, however, that this will be an unmitigated evil. Our Protestant churches and missions need to have a watchful and determined foe in the field. Our missionaries will be more wakeful and active for having the Roman legions encamped in their vicinity, always ready for an assault. It has seemed to me, from observing the working of the two systems at the Sandwich Islands, that the Romish missions, taking human nature as it is, have been hitherto an advantage to the cause there, on the whole.[1]

[1] I should not make this remark concerning the "Reformed Catholic Mission" at those Islands.

Again, subservient as the Romish missionaries are to the civil power, making use of it whenever they can, and paying back in the same coin, we must expect the Catholic governments, and especially Catholic France, to aid them wherever it has ambitious ends to accomplish; as it appears to have in China, Corea, Japan, Madagascar, Northern Africa, and the Isles of the Pacific, not to speak of Turkey and Italy.

VI. I now offer some practical suggestions, though with diffidence, as to the best manner of working Protestant missions among the heathen, in the presence of missions from the Romish Church.

1. Not by using their weapons. If we do, we shall be beaten in the use of them. A good while since, missionaries at Constantinople wrote that the Jesuits had attractive schools, teaching the modern languages, the fine arts, and the accomplishments; and that they would be likely to draw away the best youth, if the Protestant missionaries had no such schools. The reply was, that Protestants cannot go into that line of operation. Such schools are the forte of the Jesuits, and, do what we may, they would outdo us in that direction. A similar appeal was also made in the matter of church edifices. The reply was of the same import: if we undertake to compete in those things, we shall be beaten. We should not attempt it, either abroad, or at home.

Many persons seem to think that Romanists have the advantage of Protestants among the heathen, by a show and witchery in their forms of worship. It may be so, after heathen men or women have once been brought fully under the drill of their ceremonies. But I have seen nothing, in my visits to the missions, and learned nothing from my protracted and extended correspondence, to awaken a suspicion, that the simplicity of our worship is not far better for us, than all or any part of their parade and show would be; it being our peculiar object to make real, spiritual converts.

2. We should do just what the Romish missions do not do, and what they will not do. They will do nothing, intentionally, to rouse the intellect, and the moral sense, nothing to create a thinking, inquiring, reasoning habit of mind among their pupils and the people at large. We have everything to hope from this negative habit of theirs; and our grand aim should be to impart to our people a mental, moral, Christian discipline, such as results from doctrinal, practical, and experimental preaching, in plain, intelligent language. Mere conversation, even eloquent conversation, is not preaching, nor a substitute for it. Plain, direct gospel preaching is better for us than all the pretentious education and church edifices of the Jesuits would be. In fact, costly church buildings are a great drawback and hindrance in evangelical missions among the heathen.

It is so even in the Oriental churches. The fewer costly edifices we erect and have in missions to the unevangelized, the better. The world is not to be conquered or held by splendid church buildings, nor by a gorgeous ceremonial, but by the plain, simple preaching of Christ crucified, and by a worship which recognizes God as a Spirit, to be worshipped in spirit and in truth.

We should give the people the Scriptures, and organize our converts into churches — native throughout, self-governed, self-supported, self-propagating; with such a confederation of churches, in due time, as their multiplication and their advance in Christian civilization shall demand.

All this will be doing just what the Romish missions never do, and what they never will do. It is a method of operating, that differs radically from theirs. It is the apostolic method, and will have the divine blessing.

3. The Romish missions being so diverse from our own, both in their object and methods, our wise course is, to proceed in their presence very much as we should do if they were not in the field. How wonderfully, one would think, does their religion meet the spirit and aspirations of the world, — by its baptismal regeneration, its confessions and absolutions, its opus operatum, its priesthood, its easy conformity to the world, its saintly intercessors, and its queen of heaven. It being a grand compromise, it

would seem that its missions, viewed apart from the teachings of their history, would carry all before them. But they do not, even where no evangelical missions are in the field to oppose them. And where the gospel is present, with the appeal to the conscience made by its doctrines of sin, ruin, and redemption, we may expect these weapons of the Spirit to exert a converting influence on as many as are "ordained to eternal life." Therefore we should not anywhere be greatly disquieted by the presence of Romish missions. In China, we might treat them as a sect of Buddhists, in India, as we do the followers of Brahma, and in Western Asia, as we do the followers of Mohammed.

4. The strong feeling of many, that native pastors, if left alone among heathen, even after proper training, will be unable to withstand the Romish missionaries, is not sustained by facts. I have already stated how it was at Tahiti, for more than a score of years. And how nobly did native converts and pastors stand for a longer time, amid the terrible persecutions in Madagascar; and what a record have we of the firmness of Christian converts in the face of the India rebellion.

Let us, then, repose confidence in native churches and pastors, or rather in the grace of God to be manifested in their support, even under the trial of Jesuit casuistry and art.

5. Let us keep in mind the two grand peculiari-

ties of Protestant missions, namely: (1) That our object is the conversion and regeneration of sinners, their holiness in heart and life; and (2) That our hope of effecting this is through the gospel and the agency of the Holy Spirit. In these is our strength; and the want of these is the weakness of our adversaries. Even the earlier Jesuits, whatever may be truthfully said of the purity of their characters, of their sincerity, and their earnest desire for the salvation of souls, did not proclaim the Scriptural method of salvation. They were opposed to the true doctrine, sincerely, heartily so, as the grand heresy of the Reformation. They were, therefore, blind leaders of the blind. A regard for historical truth obliges me to say this even of Francis Xavier, notwithstanding his deserved reputation for personal piety in a dark age, and his marvelous zeal and enterprise in extending what seemed to him the kingdom of Christ.[1]

[1] "It is melancholy to find throughout Xavier's writings, amidst many noble religious sentiments, little which tends to exalt Christ, or to honor the work of the Holy Spirit. The Virgin Mary and the saints are obtruded into an idolatrous position. The religion which he attempted to propagate, was not according to the gospel of Christ. He has left on record his *Manual of Instruction,* and it proves to be a mixture of legends with the truth of God. Hence the elements of a great character were dwarfed and crippled by inferior motives, and anti-Christian principles. Great natural endowments and precious opportunities were wasted in the vain attempts to extend the kingdom of Christ by unauthorized expedients, and by 'will-worship.' Hence the contradiction between Xavier's natural force of character and his

VII. I close this chapter with a few hints at some of our grounds for encouragement. We have a vast advantage over the Romish Church, in not being obliged to keep an army in the field in order to hold it, when once the field has been conquered. History amply proves that this necessity exists in the Romish missions. With us there should be no hesitation, after liberating from their thralldom the slaves of sin, in clothing them with responsibilities. The more free they are, and the more able and disposed they are to think, feel, and act for themselves, the better for us; but it is not so with the papal missions. I fully believe that the Protestant churches are able to effect the conquest of the heathen world against all the opposing force of Romanism, if they will put forth determined efforts, with a due reliance on Him, who has graciously promised his presence. Rome, with all her numerical strength, and with all her wealth, will be no match for Protestant churches, when the latter are fully aroused to the use of their spiritual weapons.

There is more of active, reliable piety in the Protestant Christian Church now, than there ever was. But then, as we have already seen, it is yet but par-

spiritual inefficiency; between the expectation which would be formed of his success in any secular pursuit, and his utter failure in the missionary enterprise." — Venn's *Life of Xavier*, p. 259. Valuable extracts from this Life of Xavier will be found in the Appendix.

tially enlisted in the work of missions. Therefore it would seem that, until the arrival of the blessed day when the Spirit shall be poured more abundantly upon our churches, Romanism, in some of its forms, will divide the heathen world with the evangelical religion. And how small the change required of a Buddhist to be accepted as a true son of the Romish Church; how small in a Brahminist; how small in the wild African, and in the American Indian.

It would be presumptuous to predict what the future will be in the struggle of the Evangelical Church for the conquest of the heathen world, except as regards the grand result. Much must depend on the course of political events in Christendom, but inconceivably more on the vigor, wisdom, and piety with which the Evangelical Church shall prosecute the missions. Portugal, once the grand patron of Romish missions, has now scarcely a name and place in the world. Spain is in the process of what may prove, in the end, an anti-papal revolution. Hungary stands once more, apparently, on the verge of a Protestant reformation; and Austria is no longer, as heretofore, the obedient son of the Romish Church. The main dependence of the papal missions is now upon France; not so much because of a spirit of subserviency in that empire, as for the promotion of its own ambitious ends. What France stands ready to do, we see exemplified at Tahiti and the Loyalty Islands of the South Sea, and at the

Sandwich Islands. We see it exemplified in China, where the French not only demanded the free admission of papal missionaries into the country, but a restoration of the property which in former ages was held by the Jesuits. And we shall doubtless see the same thing done in Japan.

The Pope may not much longer be able to sustain his rank as a temporal sovereign; but whether he would be weakened or strengthened by the loss of that, is what I think no one can tell. His diplomatic relations would of course be changed, and he might not continue to receive the customary secular support from the papal nations; and his confidence in the Jesuits, and their subserviency to him, might be diminished. But his strongest hold upon his followers, after all, is spiritual; and one cannot be assured that he would not gain, if he were deprived of his temporalities, and even if cut loose from Rome, that sink of iniquity.

Either way, the Evangelical Church must expect to have the "Man of Sin" to contend with in the form of Romanism, for a long time to come, and we must make up our minds to it.

I regard the Papacy as an enemy of the Church of God, and to be opposed by all proper means. But so is the great wicked world, of which the Papacy is a part; and this particular form of the world's opposition is perhaps the very best for arousing the energies of the Evangelical Church. Even should every species of wickedness and enmity in the world combine at length under this form, it might ultimately prove to be a good thing for the true Church. Suppose that Church were to meet it everywhere in formidable phalanx, ready for a desperate conflict. That is perhaps the very warfare, which will soonest call forth the requisite Christian effort for subduing the world to Christ; not indeed without losses and crosses, probably not without fire and the sword, perhaps not without terrible exigencies which shall compel the Church to look to that Almighty Arm, in which alone is her strength.

When the conflict between the two great moral powers reaches its height, and the noise thereof becomes great, and men's hearts fail them for fear, then may be expected that divine, all-powerful intervention, foretold by prophets and apostles, and now the hope of the Church, which will give the victory to truth and righteousness.

CHAPTER XV.

RÉSUMÉ AND CONCLUSION.

Before closing the volume, it may be well briefly to review the ground we have gone over. Attention was first called to the remarkable opening of the heathen world to the gospel, such as was never seen before; and in the light of history we surveyed the grand operations of Divine Providence, by which this opening had been effected. We saw the leading nations of Christendom moved, as in Old Testament times, by the hand of the Almighty, all working together for this result; though they meant not so, neither did their heart think so. Hundreds of millions were expended by them for their own power and aggrandizement, but the results, or a large portion of them, were just as needful for the extension of the Redeemer's kingdom; and thus was accomplished, under a wonder-working Providence, what the Christian Church had not now, and perhaps never would have, the wealth and physical power to do.

The world becoming thus accessible to the gospel, we beheld the drowsy churches of Christendom slowly awaking to a consciousness of their duty.

Moravian and Danish Christians were the first to move; then a few English brethren; then a few in our country: and now there is scarcely a section of the Evangelical Church, in which there is not a response, and more or less of organized effort.

Seeing the heathen world so marvelously opening to the gospel, and the Evangelical Church awaking so extensively to the duty of Christian missions, we inquired into the nature of the apostolic missions, as set forth in the Inspired Volume. We there saw, with submissive wonder, how the apostles were left, somewhat as we are, to grapple with the difficult problems of their day, and how hard it was for them to disencumber their minds from long-standing Jewish prejudices. This being accomplished, and the spiritual nature of the churches they were to form among the heathen being settled, we followed the Apostle to the Gentiles in his mission, and saw him relying for success on the cross of Christ and the agency of the Holy Spirit. We saw him hastening through the different provinces of the Roman Empire, planting churches at central stations, and leaving them when fully organized, in the belief that the grace of God was sufficient to guard, multiply, and clothe them with power and glory, until the gospel should be everywhere triumphant. We beheld the leaven thus cast into the lump of heathenism gradually diffusing itself, until the whole was so far leavened, that imperial Rome was constrained to bow to the supremacy of the gospel, and assume the Christian name.

Looking for developments of the spirit of missions in subsequent ages, our attention was drawn unexpectedly to Ireland. In that remotest of the European islands, safe from Huns and Goths, and with Britain for a barrier against sea-roving Northmen, we found what proved to be a refuge for the Church in the disordered and dangerous period of the nominally Christian world following the downfall of the Roman Empire. From thence, in successive ages, we beheld evangelical missionaries going forth into Scotland, England, and especially into Germany, sowing the seeds, as it long afterwards appeared, of the great Reformation which blessed Europe and the world in the sixteenth century.

We next inquired into the nature of the modern warfare incumbent on the churches for subduing the world to Christ. We found it was spiritual; just such a warfare as the apostles waged, with precisely their object, with precisely their weapons, and with their dependence on divine aid. We found that the churches of Christendom, and the missionaries sent forth by them, had really the same responsibility in respect to the nature of the work, as that which rested on the apostles; namely, to establish churches in all places of influence, and to see that those churches had competent native pastors, and were trained to the three grand necessities of a Christian church, — self-government, self-support, and self-propagation.

Having assumed it to be the leading object of missions among the heathen to plant and multiply local churches composed of native converts, with a native ministry of the same race, we brought forward proofs, in the eighth chapter, of the value of such churches. This we did by adducing some of the more striking illustrations to be found among the native converts, and in the native ministry; and we saw reason to believe, that the spirit of Christ is in them, and that no better army is needed for the conquest of the world, than can be enlisted on the ground; provided there be a sufficient number of competent leaders from our training institutions at home, and that these be continued until the native army is sufficiently enlarged and disciplined for the exigencies of the war.

We then described the missionary life, as it had fallen under our personal observation. After asserting the high calling of the missionary as a minister of the gospel and an ambassador of Christ, we contemplated him in the various relations of his life, and then the influence of that life upon his mental development and his religious character and happiness.

Our next inquiry was, how far the modern Evangelical Church has actually obeyed the Saviour's command, to go into all the world. Knowing that the number of ordained ministers of the gospel sent into the field does not exceed two thousand, it was with some surprise and no small pleasure that we saw the extent to which the unevangelized world had been explored, with a view to its occupation by missionaries; and still more, how many of the more important and influential posts have been at least partially occupied; and that the work of translating the Scriptures has been effected in nearly all the more important languages of the heathen world.

Our attention was then directed to the fulfillment of the promise, "Lo, I am with you;" and we saw, almost everywhere in the missions, convincing evidence of the faithfulness of the Great Captain, and of his divine presence and blessing. We saw it among the Cherokees, the Choctaws, the Dacotahs, and still more on the Island-groups in the vast extent of the Pacific Ocean. We saw it among the Karens of Burmah, and the devil-worshippers of the Santhal, Cole, and Shanar races of India. We saw it in the mighty changes, that are being wrought in the knowledge and convictions of the millions in that country devoted to the worship of Brahma. We saw it wonderfully illustrated on the island of Madagascar. We saw proofs of it over a large portion of Southern Africa, and most signally displayed in the apostolic successes of the admirable missionary Johnson at Sierra Leone. We saw it in different portions of Western Asia.

It was natural to inquire, what it is that hinders a more rapid advance; and the chief hindrance seemed to be in the want of appropriate information and training in the churches at home. The methods of removing this, both providential and human, were indicated. It was also shown what are the demands of the cause of missions on the personal services of young ministers of the gospel.

An inquiry was then instituted, how far there is power in the Romish missions to exert a renovating influence on the heart and life of the pagan world. We found little proof of the exercise of such power in the history of those missions, or in the principles underlying them; and contrasting these principles with those of Protestant missions, we saw the immense superiority of the latter as a converting agency. Suggestions were then made, in the light of this discussion, as to the best manner of working the Protestant missions among the heathen, in the presence of missions from the Romish Church. Our first position was, that we should not use their weapons; and our second, that we should do just what they do not do, and what they will not do. For the world is not to be converted by costly churches, nor by a gorgeous ritual, nor by a religion of rites and forms, but by the plain, simple preaching of Christ crucified, and a worship which recognizes God as a Spirit, to be worshipped in spirit and in truth. Nor should we be disquieted by the presence of Romish missionaries, since that particular form of the world's opposition is perhaps the very best for arousing the energies of the true Church of God in the discharge of its great duty to the heathen world.

CONCLUSION.

There is no political movement in the world, that is commensurate with the missionary movement; none that embraces so many nations, none covering so large a portion of the globe. It is the Christian Church going forth, under its Great Captain, for the subjugation of the world.

The imperial warrior, who not many years since convulsed the civilized world with his ambitious schemes, used to make himself intimately acquainted with the nations he designed to conquer. As a means to his end, he studied their geography, numbers, government, and history, with the characteristic ardor of his great mind. Facts were the lights in which he marched through Europe, and none were deemed unimportant, that might affect the issue of a campaign, or a battle; and in this minuteness and accuracy of information, with a capacity to adapt the means at command to the ends in view, was the secret of his success.

We, too, are warriors. And though our contest is spiritual, of mind with mind, and heart with heart, and though our weapons are spiritual, and are made effectual only by divine aid, there is the same demand for inquiry and information, the same scope and necessity for forethought, as in the military enterprises of Napoleon. Indeed, to a very great extent our inquiries relate to the same classes of objects; only they are surveyed from other points of view, and associated by different relations, and estimated by another species of arithmetic and measurement.

The Evangelical Church of our day is laboring more and more on system, with a constant advance in her aggressive movements, and is more and more actuated and sustained in her efforts by the powerful principle of faith. The Evangelical Church is not left, however, to faith alone. How much there is to animate and strengthen her faith in beholding the massive walls, at the very entrance of her promised possession, which had so long shut her out from the pagan world, overthrown at length, like those of Jericho, by the unseen hand of the Almighty. And also in beholding the same infinite power creating marvelous facilities for traversing the globe, and in witnessing, in the uprising Church, what may prove the beginning of that outpouring of the Spirit, — sung by prophets, and longed for by apostles, — which is to arouse every Christian land for the universal and decisive conflict.

The spiritual war for the conquest of the world has certainly begun, and in a manner never seen in any former age. There is not yet, indeed, a popular enthusiasm in the churches, but that will come. What we most need, just now, is deep, calm, untiring principle; for the contest upon which we have entered is vast, having for its object the reign of Christ over all the earth.

And does any one believe that He, who has all power in heaven and on earth, will stop, after so marvelous an opening of the heathen world to the gospel? Does any one believe that the churches, after so many organizations for the spread of the gospel, after so much exploring of heathen tribes and nations, and after occupying thousands of posts, will ignominiously retire from the field? Will Christian people, will the Christian ministry, will the Christian churches never feel a stronger interest in the triumphs of the Redeemer's kingdom through the world, than they do now? It cannot, it will not be. The churches will not always be lukewarm in this work, and they may not be so long. Who can tell but that a vast revolution in the views and feelings of God's people is near? Who can tell but that the outpouring of the Spirit upon all flesh, foretold by the prophet Joel, is at hand? God's people and his ministers will then be made willing, beyond all they now deem possible. They will delightfully awake to the claims of Christ upon them. Vastly higher will be their aims; vastly broader their plans; and vastly greater their ability to feel, pray, and consecrate their all to him.

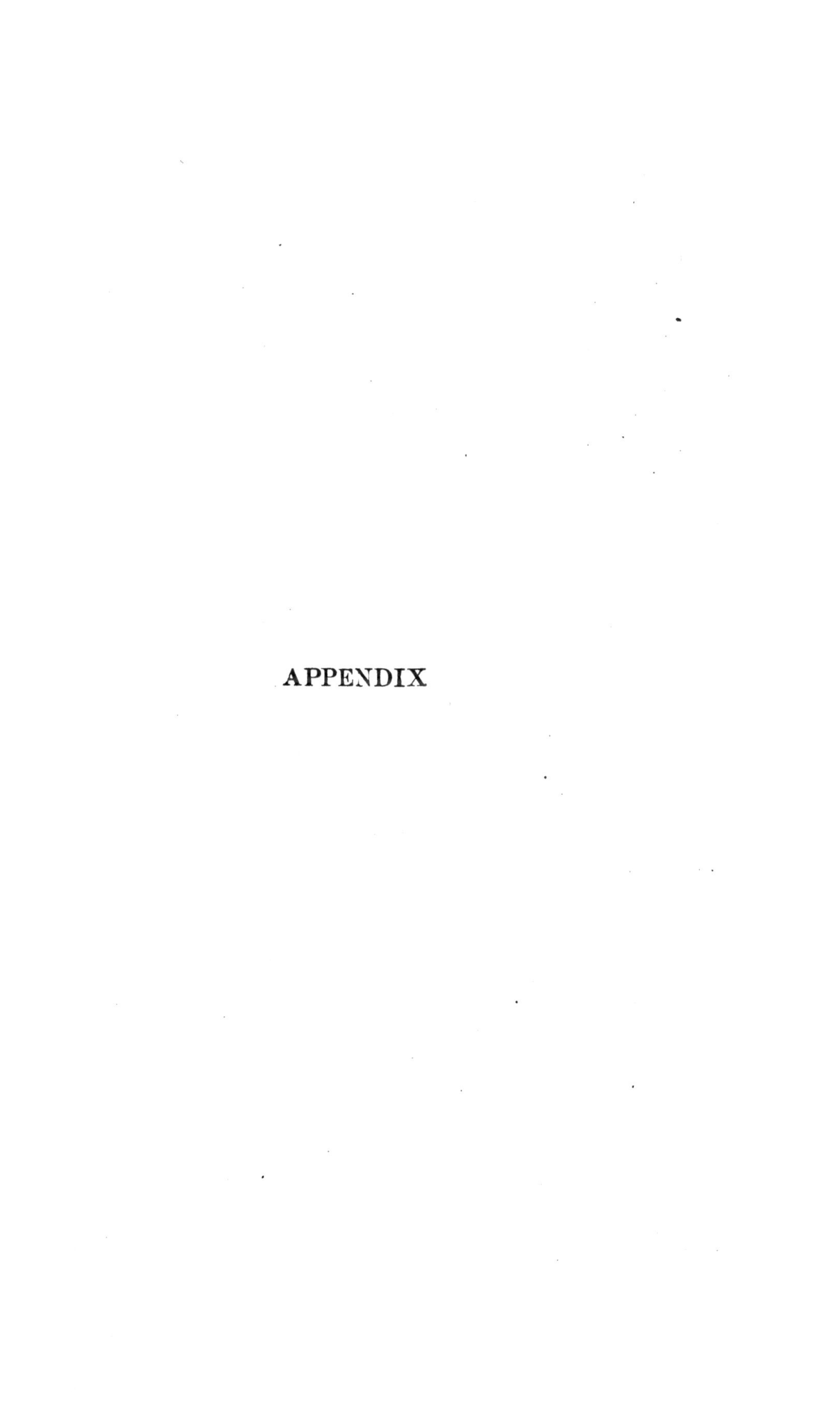

APPENDIX

APPENDIX.

I.

COMPETENCE OF MISSIONARIES TO TESTIFY CONCERNING MISSIONS.

[From a speech of Rev. Dr. Norman Macleod, of the Established Church of Scotland, after returning from an official visit to the Missions of that Church in India.]

"But you may say, 'You have come to tell us about India; how do you know your facts are correct?' I met a man the other day at a dinner party, a man who had been in India, and who told me the missionaries there had done nothing. Now those mysterious men are always turning up; men who have been in India, and who tell you missionaries have done nothing. I have often met this remarkable phenomenon. Well, in order to ascertain all we could, Dr. Watson and myself put ourselves in communication with men of all classes, and first of all with missionaries. And with reference to the missionaries, I will maintain this: that they know more of India, that their knowledge is more correct, and their accounts are more fair regarding India, than you can get from any other source. But we do not confine ourselves to missionaries. We had letters, I need not say, from government, which gave us access to many sources of information among civilians, — men who had long been in the country, men who had intelligence and knowledge. We did not confine ourselves to Christians, but went to natives also. We had access to what I may call the representative men, and the kindness and courtesy we met with from these gentlemen I shall never forget. We heard all their opinions frankly and fully. We did more than that; we called two great meetings, one at Madras, the other at Calcutta. They were attended by the first men in the country: in Calcutta, by the viceroy, the commander-in-chief, the governor of Bengal, and all the heads of departments. The same in Madras. We asked missionaries of all denominations to come upon the platform and read a *vidimus* of their work; what they had done, each in their own department, what the Baptists had done, what the Independents had done, what the Church Missionary Society had done, the Society for the Propagation of the Gospel, the Free Church, and so on. And upon the platform in Madras and Calcutta I stated this, that one great reason why we requested the meeting was, that after we had labored and worked, and thought we had a thorough understanding of the state of matters, some man, knowing no more about it than a European who had been in India, might pass the claret at table, and say, 'I assure you, missionaries are doing nothing. I know all about it.' Yet this man might not know, perhaps, a single mission in the parish in which he lived. I said that in the presence of editors of European papers in India; in the presence of editors of native papers: in the presence of intelligent Hindus: in a meeting as crowded as this, we asked those reports, and challenged contradiction on the spot. We challenged it in Madras and Calcutta, and if the missionaries were not true, we wished to have that contradiction there, if we could have it. We did not go to India to get up a fine story; we did not go to gather facts only agreeable to ourselves, and put them aside. In God's name we wished to know the truth, and nothing but the truth; and could we do more than I have mentioned to find out the facts? Now, I ask you, is it not a very hard thing, after we have gone, not to one spot, not to a civilian who has stuck in one spot, not to a missionary who has stuck in one spot — but after we have gone through all the Presidencies, and met with a great many missionaries and other people, trying to find out the real facts, and after, too, we have called meetings and challenged contradiction, that all this should be put aside as nothing, as the mere talk of ministers? Ask the man who says that missions in India have done nothing, what mission station he ever visited. Ask him if he ever spent an hour in his life trying to understand missions. Ask him what interest he takes in, or what knowledge he has, of missions at home. You will invariably find that the man who lives in Glasgow, and talks in the manner I have indicated concerning missions abroad, is just as ignorant about them as a man at Calcutta is of what the Free Church, or the United Presbyterian Church, or the Episcopal Church, or the Established Church, are doing for the advancement of religion in Glasgow. This, then, in answer to the heckling question, 'What have you done to ascertain facts, and on what ground do you ask us to have any confidence in you?'"

II.

SECULAR NEWSPAPERS AND RELIGIOUS INTELLIGENCE.

(See Chapter XI.)

SINCE delivering his lectures, the author has seen a brief memoir of the Rev. Austin Dickinson, from which the following statement, by Mr. Dickinson himself, is extracted: —

"From my connection with the press, and intercourse with editors of various classes, for some twenty years, the desirableness of making common secular newspapers the channels of a decided religious influence, often occurred to my mind. But it was not till after a more particular investigation of their numbers and vast controlling influence, that I felt urged by an imperative sense of duty to volunteer in a special effort for their improvement. Early in 1844 I ascertained, from minute inquiry, that there were then printed in New York City alone nearly a million of newspapers a week, and that some editors sent out weekly from ten to sixteen hundred exchange papers to other editors throughout the country, besides many to distant countries; and that there were then published in the United States about four hundred million single newspapers annually, which number has since been rapidly increasing. So that, if a column only of interesting religious matter could be introduced into each of these papers, it would be equivalent to the annual distribution of more than sixteen hundred million tract pages; and this in a form most likely to be read by the whole community — by millions who never see a religious journal, and many of whom would only despise a tract. Previous to this undertaking, the editors of secular papers, generally, scarcely noticed religious movements, or seemed to feel any interest in them. Much delicacy and prudence were, therefore, necessary, in any attempt so to change their views and tastes, that political journals might, without exciting prejudice, be made the heralds of sacred truth and religious instruction."

III.

ENGLISH MISSION SCHOOLS.

(See Chapter VII.)

SINCE the delivery of the lectures, a valuable work by Dr. Mullens has been received, entitled, "London and Calcutta, comparing their Heathenism, their Privileges, and their Prospects; showing the Claims of Foreign Missions upon the Christian Church." The following is an extract bearing on the success of missions: —

"It was during this period that the English mission schools in the great towns sprang into existence, and began to form a prominent and most useful feature of Christian usefulness. Nowhere more completely than in India has the ingenuity of Christian men vigorously applied itself to the production of forms of agency adapted to the work to be accomplished. General schemes had been tried and adopted, in order to overcome that most formidable opponent of Christianity, the caste system; but the right thing had not been discovered. Now it is evident, that nothing will completely overthrow it but that large-hearted enlightenment which gives broad views of human life, of the connection between man and man, between race and race, and which tends to multiply the ties of sympathy between one heart and all others. Many agencies are needed for an end so vast. A just government for all ranks of society, public law, union of separated provinces, railways, abundant employment and abundant trade, and a true, large education of the entire nature, of the intellect, the feelings, and the conscience, — each and all have an important share in the great service. Under these powerful influences, the narrow social exclusiveness, which is the essence of caste, must be swallowed up in broad convictions and generous love. These influences, it may be added, are at the same time the only true cure for the narrow and apparently hopeless bigotry and exclusiveness of the Mohammedan mind. As soon as the English schools were tried, they were found at once to supply a great want, and to exercise a powerful influence in this direction. Boys were seen speedily to acquire a contempt for idolatry, for temples, and for legends, which long labors had with difficulty produced in grown men. What wonder, then, that, in spite of warm controversies, the English mission schools have multiplied, have tended to feed and strengthen the three Indian universities, and have contributed a fair share towards the development of that great school of educated and enlightened native scholars, who, theists in religion, have strongest sympathies with the elevation of their country, and are the only native gentlemen who are striving to secure it. As suitable to this class, a system of

Christian lectures in English has been largely adopted by missionaries in the great cities, and a special literature has been prepared for their use. From the men thus educated have come forth many strong and steadfast converts, who have added greatly to the strength and resources of native churches, and several of whom have been ordained to the ministry of the gospel."

IV.

THE BRAHMO SAMAJ.

(See Chapter VII.)

A SOCIETY of educated natives has grown up in Calcutta, called the *Brahmo Samaj*. It contained, a few years since, about two thousand members; and Dr. Duff regards it as the result of English high schools, and, so far as the more promising and better part of it is concerned, the result in no small degree of the high schools sustained by the Free Church of Scotland. Not long since, a party of progress, desirous of acting out their anti-idolatrous convictions, and relieving themselves from the anti-social trammels of caste, separated and formed a distinct society, at the head of which was a young man of remarkable powers of intellect, named Babu Keshub Chandra Sen, a native gentleman of independent means. Dr. Murray Mitchell, a venerable missionary of the Scotch Free Church, writing from Calcutta, represents the junior section of the Brahmo Samaj as full of life and zeal.

"They have planted societies," he says, "churches, as

they call them, throughout Bengal, in the Northwest provinces, the Punjaub, Bombay, and Madras, in which, as they say, hundreds congregate week after week to worship the holy God in spirit and truth. And theirs, they think, is the church — at least the Indian Church — of the future. They think that their own society will exhibit a purified Christianity — the very essence of the gospel; and while they earnestly say that the future church of India will not be anti-Christian, they are equally strenuous in declaring that it will not be Christian, as Christianity has yet been understood." [1]

This Brahmist school of thought may be said to have originated with Rammohun Roy, fifty or sixty years ago, who undertook to reform Hinduism on the basis of a pure theism, which he held to be the religion of the Vedas. The name by which they are now known appears to have been adopted about the year 1830, when many had joined the sect, who, in passing through the government schools, had unlearned idolatry, without having the void filled by religious instruction. There has been a manifest intellectual progress. They made the discovery, about the year 1846, that the Vedas taught neither a personal God, nor the grand distinctions between virtue and vice. The Vedas were consequently rejected, and the Brahmos betook themselves to External Nature. Not being able to find a God there to suit them, they next turned to Internal Nature — to Intuition; and called in the aid of Francis Newman and Theodore Parker. Here, too, they have found the ground giving way under them; and this discovery, it probably was, that led to the recent division into two sects.

[1] *Monthly Record of the Free Church of Scotland*, 1868, p. 195

A very few have found their way to the revealed Word, and the incarnate Saviour, and his atonement; and there is hope for more."[1]

It is yet to be seen, how far there will be greater readiness in young deistical India to bow to the cross of Christ, than there is in pagan India.

V.

PREACHING AND EDUCATION.

(See Chapter VII.)

DR. MACLEOD, of the Established Church of Scotland, in his recent report of his visit as a deputation to the missions of that church in India, referred to the experience of the Rev. George Bowen, the excellent and long time self-supported American missionary at Bombay, who had been engaged in open-air preaching more than a score of years, without the happiness of knowing that he had made any converts. This was adduced as an illustration of what Dr. Macleod regarded the paramount importance of schools and education, as a means of evangelizing India.

The same point was also illustrated by the Rev. William Miller, of the Free Church of Scotland mission at Madras, in a paper lately published in Scotland, on the "Principles of Missionary Work in India." Mr. Miller regards the Hindus as bound together in a state of interdependence so intimate as to form an organic unity; so that the influence exerted on individuals is largely determined by the corpo-

[1] *Report of Chh. Miss. Soc.*, 1867-8, p. 80; *Chh. Miss. Intel.*, 1868, p. 222.

21

rate life which each one shares. He regards the Shanars and Mahars, among whom the great numerical success of missions has hitherto been, as outside the real Hindu race, and forming no part of it, so that nothing effected among them reaches the inner life of the great Hindu community. "Such," he says, "were the state and prospects of the Christian cause in India, when the Scottish Church began to plant her missions there." After describing the educational work of those missions, he declares that mode of operation to be "the most hopeful way, if not the only one, of reaching and affecting the inner life of the community."

Mr. Bowen's attention was naturally drawn to the reference made to his experience by Dr. Macleod, and the "Bombay Guardian" of March 6, 1869, edited by him, contains an editorial that is well deserving of thoughtful attention. The editor writes thus: —

"There is an organic unity in society; a corporate life in which all participate; we are members of one another; we are in our measure affected by whatever affects the corporate whole; influences that tell upon individuals, terminate not with them, but radiate through the community. Now we submit that this great fact constitutes just as cogent a reason for addressing ourselves to individuals, in the ministry of the gospel, as for seeking to work upon the mass. The fact of the interdependence of men one upon another, is just as much an encouragement in laboring directly to bring one man to Christ, as it is in laboring to pour Christianizing influences into the community at large. For there is no mightier Christianizing influence, than that which is brought to bear upon a community when a member of it is persuaded to consecrate himself, body, soul, and spirit, to the service of Christ. Again, the educational missionary is not laboring for the masses, more than the open-air missionary, who, year after year, continues to address the general population. Here in Bombay there are, at any one time, say one thousand boys and young men in mission schools, out of a population of eight hundred thousand. We have no intention of denying the usefulness of those institutions. Their importance may be overestimated by Mr. Miller, when he intimates that they afford probably the only hopeful way of affecting the inner life of the community; but we readily concede that they occupy a very important place in the work of Indian missions. Yet we do not agree that they are more certainly working upon the inner life of the community than open-air preachers of the gospel are, or than are religious tracts and books in the vernacular. Dr. Macleod, in his recently published lecture on Indian missions, refers to a missionary in Bombay, who has been preaching the gospel for more than twenty years in the open air, without gathering any converts. We were told, the other day, by a gentleman at the head of one of the largest of our mission educational institutions, one where a number of devoted and able missionaries have successively labored, that, during thirty years, there had been from it only two converts, the institution being carried on at an average expense of £1,000 a year. Now we believe that neither the missionary first mentioned, nor the others, have spent their strength for nought, or labored in vain; and we believe, that when the day of fruition comes, it will be found that the one class of laborers told just as truly on the inner life of the community, as the other did. It is admitted that very great changes have taken place, and are taking place, in this community; and God knows that *we* can very imperfectly conjecture what work has tended to bring about those changes; but we fail to see that the secular and religious instruction given in these schools, tends more effectually to influence the common life of the community, than other kinds of missionary work do.

"But let us consider what the New Testament has to tell us of the methods of those who planted the first Christian churches. Our Lord Jesus Christ had before him the problem of winning to himself, and to the service of God, the people of Judea. He went about preaching the Word, and doing good. In the open air, in the synagogues, everywhere, we find him setting forth the great truths of the kingdom, and enduring the contradiction of sinners. We also find him laboring with individuals, and gathering converts. His disciples were not converted Pharisees or Sadducees, scribes or elders, but chiefly men of the people, fishermen, tax-gatherers; and they were Galileans, whose provincial speech was held in contempt by the higher classes, just as Shanars and Mahars are despised by the people of high caste here. Through these individuals he wrought upon the body politic, and wrought effectually. The nation, as a nation, was not converted, but many myriads were. In this way, and by this despised instrumentality, he acted upon the Gentile world. The conversion of one individual, Paul, proved to be like the conversion of a considerable community. Paul went everywhere, seeking to save some — 'if by any means I might save some,' he says. He and his associates believed that the most hopeful way of influencing the organic whole, the community at large, was to show them what God could do in the way of converting, redeeming, elevating individual souls.

"We beg to dissent from what Mr. Miller says, regarding the position of the classes from whom a large proportion of the converts have been made. The Mahars, for instance, are as truly a portion of the Hindu community as the Brahmins are. They are the *imtyuj*, the lowest-born, at the bottom of the scale; but none the less do they belong to the scale. We have seen Mahar converts, whose maharism had so effectually disappeared with their costume, that people of all castes listened to them without being able to discover that they had not been originally 'of good caste;' a fact which, in itself, goes far to dispose of Mr. Miller's theory. And when we consider that the grandest revolution the world has ever seen, was brought about by 'foolish things of the world,' chosen of God to confound the 'wise,' 'weak things of the world, to confound the mighty, and base things, and things despised, and things which are not, to bring to naught things that are,' we feel reluctant to acquiesce in Mr. Miller's proposition, that the Scottish mission school work is 'the most hopeful way, perhaps the only one, of reaching and affecting the inner life of the community.'"

VI.

THE CHRISTIAN MINISTRY.

(See Chapter IX.)

The relations of the gospel ministry to the work of foreign missions, are of sufficient importance to justify the author in appending a brief article on the subject, slightly modified, which was communicated by him, in 1865, to one of the religious newspapers.

"The writer's connection with missions and mission churches, has led him to suppose there would be important advantages gained in apprehending the ecclesiastical *status* of the apostolic age, were we to contemplate it as an age of missions (for such it was), to be illustrated by the missions of the present age. Not being aware that such a thing has been attempted in good earnest by the writers on ecclesiastical history, he makes the following suggestions.

"It will be conceded, that the basis of the Christian ministry is the commission, 'Go ye into all the world and preach the gospel to every creature, baptizing them in the name of the Father, and of the Son, and of the Holy Ghost.' The ministry, thus constituted, was evidently designed for the world, and for all time. This is the generic view of that ministry. It was not until about twelve years after the ascension, that we have any mention of the ordination of pastors. Then Paul and Barnabas, two of the most eminent of the 'prophets and teachers' at Antioch, were, by direction of the Holy Ghost, set apart for a mission to unevangelized peoples. They were evidently accredited ministers of the Word before this time, and there is no conclusive evidence that their setting apart as missionaries (or ordination, as it is improperly called), involved any formal act of the church of Antioch as such; it seems rather to have been done by their fellow 'prophets and teachers;' though it is stated that the two missionaries made report to the 'church' on their return. (Acts xiii. 1–3; xiv. 27.)

"These missionaries appointed pastors (presbyters) of the churches which they had gathered in Lystra, Iconium, and elsewhere, and those churches were what we now call mission churches, and the pastors were what we call native pastors. They were such churches and pastors as missionaries are now constituting in those same regions. Later, we read of Titus, a convert of the Apostle Paul, and employed by him in the missionary work, left in Crete to set in order the churches planted in that island, and appoint pastors (presbyters) in them; with instructions to join the apostle at Nicopolis, as soon as he had completed that work. Timothy, who was also a convert of the apostle and a missionary under his direction, was employed in a similar service in parts of Asia Minor. These ecclesiastical acts are neither more nor less than our missionary brethren in Turkey are now performing in those regions.

"Such is the view we take of the Christian ministry and Christian churches in the apostolic age. That ministry, as ultimately developed in that age, was composed of both missionaries and pastors, — the demand for pastors growing out of the successful labors of missionaries. The missionaries were for the planting of churches, and the pastors for the edification of those churches, and for securing the conquests. A small number of the missionaries, called apostles, were recognized by the rest, and by all the churches, as having extraordinary revelations and authority conferred upon them by the Head of the Church.

"Now if we restrict our attention to the churches planted by the apostles, we have no difficulty in admitting that the only officers in those churches were presbyters and deacons. What other office-bearers could churches so situated have needed? Those infantile churches were no more able to institute foreign missions than were the churches of our fathers in the seventeenth century. The church in the great city of Antioch may have been an exception. But the churches planted by the first missionaries, to which their letters were addressed, were persecuted, impoverished, and feeble, not very unlike the mission churches of our age. Their strength was absorbed in maintaining an existence. They had no foreign missionaries, no missionary societies, colleges, or theological schools, and consequently no occasion for clerical secretaries, professors, and presidents. In these respects they fell short of some of our modern mission churches.

"The New Testament narrative closes in the midst of the missionary age of the primitive churches; and the best illustration of its ecclesiastical development is probably to be found in those modern Protestant missions, which have for their object the raising up of self-governing, self-supporting churches; though, as might be expected, there would seem to be somewhat more of ecclesiastical organization in the modern missions, than there was in the ancient.

"The writers on Congregationalism of the seventeenth century appear to have lost sight of what is certainly the prominent object of the Christian ministry, as set forth by our Lord in the great commission. The view they took of the object and duty of the churches and ministry, is altogether too limited. In their anxiety for the orderly development of the churches, they seem almost to have forgotten the unevangelized world. This was not strange considering their circumstances. But such an oversight is impossible with us, since the entire world, now become accessible, appeals loudly to our Christian sensibilities. And it is now admitted that ordained ministers of the gospel ought to become missionaries, as well as pastors. Experience has shown, too, that foreign missionaries (as in ancient times) ought very seldom to become pastors of the churches they gather from among the unevangelized, but should ordain pastors for them from among the native converts. Nor is it found to be possible to carry forward the work of Christ's kingdom at home and abroad, on an extended scale, without also setting apart clergymen to educate the ministry, to correspond with the missionaries, and to perform the other needful agencies which none but clergymen can perform so well. Though missionaries, presidents, professors, secretaries, and clerical editors are not officers in local individual churches, they belong as really to the ministry of the denomination as if they were, and are as really office-bearers in the denomination. There can be no other conclusion educed from the inspired record in the New Testament

"Thus we have a ministry of the Word, meeting all the exigencies of the case; all on an ecclesiastical parity under the great commission; but existing for different ministerial services, — as missionaries, pastors, etc., etc., — members of one and the same body, the head of which is Christ, and alike claiming his promised presence.

"In this view of the subject, the Evangelists of the New Testament, however gifted they may have been, were only missionaries. The apostles were also missionaries, but with an extraordinary inspiration and authority peculiar to themselves. The ἐπίσκοποι, overseers, superintendents, bishops, contemporaries with the apostles, were the same as presbyters, elders, pastors. The ruling, spoken of in the New Testament, is a thing understood in the mission churches of our day (though perhaps not exactly in the ancient form), where pastoral authority is just as needful in the infancy of those churches, as parental authority is in the early years of a family. Among the churches on the Hawaiian Islands, for instance, the missionaries felt it necessary to exercise authority in the native churches for a course of years, and what of authority remained in the year 1863, and was deemed to be still necessary, was then transferred to the Associations and Presbyteries, — the former intending to relinquish it to the local churches, as soon as the native pastorate had made advances to render it a safe deposit."

VII.

SUCCESS OF MISSIONS.

(See Chapter XII.)

ALTHOUGH enough has been said to demonstrate the fact of God's blessing upon the missions of the Protestant churches, in the unevangelized world, the following statement, from the valuable new work of Dr. Mullens, entitled "London and Calcutta," is too suggestive to be omitted.

"A mere description of the range of labor, the number of agents, and of the annual sum expended in these foreign missions, does little to indicate what the missionary efforts of the churches in foreign lands really include. Around each laborer cluster a variety of agencies, which contribute greatly to the efficiency of his own. Missionary life has its tools of trade, as well as other employments. Everywhere they have been secured with wonderful completeness, in great variety, and have been wisely adapted both to the place of work and to the duty to be done. To any one who is well acquainted with many fields of missionary effort, nothing appears so striking as the way in which the frame-work of effort, the power of agency, and the mode in which they are applied, have been fitted to the varied spheres for which they have been required. Long since, dwelling-houses, chapels, school-rooms, press-rooms, have been provided, suited to climate, country, and people. In some lands the chapel, in others the school, occupies the most prominent place. Here boats have been secured for island visiting; there canoes for inland creeks; in another station palankin chairs, or bullock carriages, are most required. How much labor has been concentrated on the translation of the Bible, on the small libraries of Christian books, on the dictionaries, grammars, and vocabularies of the many tongues employed! Discussions for the learned, simple papers for the villager, comments for the native teachers, English lectures for the educated, vernacular tracts for the plain reader, — all find their place among these literary agencies. Arguments that have been found effective, illustrations which strike attention, modes of agency which draw hearers, plans that suit heathen and Christian, — all have been noted, tested, and laid up as experience for the use of others. And as years have gone by, as younger missionaries have based their efforts on the toil of their predecessors, what wonder that their teachings have become more effective, and that the soil previously prepared gives promise of early and abundant harvests! How steady, also, and patient the toil has been!

"Yet, putting all together, — taking the sum of all the men, and agencies, and funds employed at the present time in foreign missions, — how small the total appears! It is for itself, for its intrinsic worth, for the enterprise which it undertakes, and the prospects which it contemplates, that missionary worth has excited so deep an interest, and takes so prominent a place before the Christian world. It is not for the number either of the agencies or of the men. Putting these all together, they are few and small. The hundred missionaries in China, with their wives and children, would not fill an ordinary lecture-room. Yet they are all the Christian agency given to that great empire by the Church of Christ. The whole band of foreign missionaries sent forth by Europe and America to other races than their own, Jewish, heathen, and Christian, numbers only two thousand and thirty-three individuals. And for the entire undertaking is expended every year only the sum of ONE MILLION STERLING."

VIII.

TABULAR VIEWS.

(See Chapter XII.)

I. BENEVOLENT SOCIETIES, AS THEY WERE IN THE YEAR 1820.

THE view here presented was prepared by the author for the first number of the "Christian Almanac," published in the year 1821, of which he was the editor; being then a member of the Theological Seminary at Andover. It indicates the development of benevolent enterprises in the evangelical churches, as they were fifty years ago. The "Christian Almanac" was soon after adopted by the American Tract Society, and immense numbers have been published. Only two copies of the first number are now known to the author. The tables are copied without alteration.

1.—*Principal Bible Societies in the World.*

EUROPE.

	INSTITUTED		INSTITUTED
British and For. Bib. Soc.	1804	Hungarian Bible Society	1812
Basle Bible Society	1804	Wurtemburg Bible Society	1812
Ratisbon Bible Society	1805	Koenigsberg Bible Society	1812
Berlin Bible Society	1805	Finnish Bible Society	1812
Swedish Bible Society	1809	Chur Bible Society	1813
Zurich Bible Society	1812	Schaffhausen Bible Society	1813

	INSTITUTED
Russian Bible Society	1813
St. Gall Bible Society	1813
Bern Bible Society	1813
Lausanne Bible Society	1814
Geneva Bible Society	1814
Berg Bible Society	1814
Cologne Bible Society	1814
Hanover Bible Society	1814
Hambro-Altona Bible Soc.	1814
Lubeck Bible Society	1814
Prussian Bible Society	1814
Thuringian Bible Society	1814
Saxon Bible Society	1814
Danish Bible Society	1814
Aargovian Bible Society	1815
Strasburg Bible Society	1815
Bremen Bible Society	1815
Pomerania Bible Society	1815
Brunswick Bible Society	1815
Eichsfield Bible Society	1815
Icelandic Bible Society	1815
Sleswick-Holstein Bib. Soc.	1815
Neufchatel Bible Society	1816
Waldenses Bible Society	1816
Koenigsfeld Bible Society	1816
Hesse-Homburg Bible Soc.	1816
Nassau Bible Society	1816
Frankfort Bible Society	1816
Kreutznach Bible Society	1816
New Wied Bible Society	1816
Lippe-Detmold Bible Soc.	1816
Lauenburg-Retzeburg B. S.	1816
Mecklenburg Schwerin B. S.	1816
Rostock Bible Society	1816
Norwegian Bible Society	1816
Polish Bible Society	1816
Netherlands Bible Society	1816
Hesse-Darmstadt Bible Soc.	1817
Waldeck & Pyrmont Bib. S.	1817
Eutin Bible Society	1817
Rendsburg Bible Society	1817
Malta Bible Society	1817
Hanau Bible Society	1818
Hesse-Cassel Bible Society	1818
Gottingen Bible Society	1818
Hildensheim Bible Society	1818
Eisenach Bible Society	1818
Anhalt Bible Society	1818
Paris Protestant Bible Soc.	1818
Glarus Bible Society	1819
Montauban Bible Society	1819
Ionian Bible Soc. at Corfu	1819
Athens Bible Society	1819

ASIA.

	INSTITUTED
Calcutta Auxiliary Society	1811
Columbo Auxiliary Society	1812
Bombay Auxiliary Society	1813
Java Bible Society	1814
Amboyna Bible Society	1815
Astrachan Bible Society	1815
New South Wales Aux. Soc.	1817
Tobolsk Bible Society	1817
Sumatra Bible Society	1817
Smyrna Bible Society	1817

AFRICA.

	INSTITUTED
Mauritius & Bourbon Auxiliary Society	1815
Caledon Auxiliary Society	1815
Sierra Leone Auxiliary Soc.	1816

AMERICA AND THE WEST INDIES.

	INSTITUTED		INSTITUTED
Nova Scotia Auxiliary Soc.	1813	Niagara Auxiliary Society .	1816
Pictou Auxiliary Society .	1813	Liverpool Auxiliary Society	1817
Quebec Auxiliary Society .	1813	Prince Edward's Island Auxiliary Society	1817
Berbice Auxiliary Society .	1815	Upper Canada Aux. Society	1817
Antigua Auxiliary Society .	1815	Honduras Auxiliary Society	1818
American National Bib. Soc.	1816	Barbadoes Auxiliary Society	1818
Yarmouth and Argyle Auxiliary Society	1816	Bermudas Auxiliary Soc. .	1819

A large proportion of these societies have branches and auxiliaries. The British and Foreign Bible Society has 637; the Russian Bible Society, 120; the Prussian, 23; the Sleswick-Holstein, 101; the American, 228, etc. The whole number of Bible societies in the world exceeds one thousand five hundred. These have all been instituted since the year 1804. The British and Foreign Bible Society may be considered as the parent of all the others, as it was the means, directly or indirectly, of establishing them, and is the patron of most of them. Since its foundation, it has assisted in printing the Bible in forty-nine languages and dialects, in which it was never before printed, and is now assisting in translating and printing it in thirty-eight other languages and dialects, into which it has never yet been translated. The whole number of languages and dialects, in which this noble institution has aided in translating, printing, and distributing the Word of God, is one hundred and twenty-seven! Its income for the year 1811, was four hundred and nineteen thousand one hundred and forty-one dollars. During the first fifteen years of its existence, it expended three million one hundred and thirty-two thousand six hundred and twenty-two dollars for the simple purpose of disseminating the Bible through the world.

2. — *Foreign Mission Societies.*

Societies.	Countries.	Founded.	Missionaries.	Income in 1818–19.
Soc. Prop. Gos.[1] . .	England . .	1647	1	$61,350 00
Soc. Prom. Christian Knowl.[2] . . .	England . .	1701	8	247,250 00
Soc. Prop. Gos. N. Am. Ind. . . .	Scotland . .	–	5	–
Danish Mission Col.	Denmark . .	1715	2	–
United Brethren . .	–	1732	84	22,912 00
Methodist Miss. Soc.	England . .	1786	66	101,839 00
Baptist Miss. Soc. .	England . .	1792	72	29,547 00
London Miss. Soc.[3] .	England . .	1795	84	94,614 29
Scotch Miss. Soc.. .	Scotland . .	1796	12	32,703 93
Church Miss. Soc. ..	England . .	1800	74	121,958 65
London Jews Soc.[4] .	England . .	1809	1	40,871 26
Am. B. C. F. Miss. .	United States	1810	35	34,166 68
Baptist B. F. Miss. .	United States	1814	5	18,942 17
United F. Miss. Soc.	United States	1817	3	–
Negro Conver. Soc. .	England . .	–	6	–
Total			458	$806,154 08

[1] The exertions of this society are confined chiefly to the British Provinces in North America.

[2] Of the income of this society, $172,573 was expended on the *destitute at home.* Among other things, this society is engaged in giving a religious education to more than 100,000 poor children.

[3] This society has several auxiliary societies among the converts from heathenism in Africa, and three in the islands of the Pacific Ocean. At the last annual meeting of one of these, nearly 6,000 natives were present, and voted. King Pomare is president.

[4] A Jews Society was some years since formed by ladies of Boston, and another, more recently, by ladies in Portland. The former has annually contributed $444 to the London Jews Society, and $100 for the education of Jewish children at Bombay.

3. — *Geographical View of the Missionaries employed by each Society, and of the Missionary Stations occupied by them.*

Countries.	Societies.	Missionaries.	Missionaries.	Stations.
West Africa	Church Miss. Soc.	15	17	10
	Methodist Miss. Soc.	1		
	Soc. for Prop. Gospel	1		
South Africa	London Miss. Soc.	21	37	1
	United Brethren	12		
	Methodist Miss. Soc.	4		
Mauritius Island	London Miss. Soc.	1	1	1
Madagascar	London Miss. Soc.	1	1	1
Malta	Church Miss. Soc.	2	3	1
	London Miss. Soc.	1		
Ionian Islands	London Miss. Soc.	1	1	1
Palestine	American Board	2	2	1
Constantinople	Church Miss. Soc.	1	1	1
Polish Jews	London Jewish Soc.	1	1	1
Russia in Asia	Scotch Miss. Soc.	12	18	5
	United Brethren	3		
	London Miss. Soc.	3		
Thibet	Church Miss. Soc.	1	1	1
Farther India	London Miss. Soc.	7	9	3
	American Baptists	2		
Hindostan	English Baptists	64	152	46
	Church Miss. Soc.	43		
	London Miss. Soc.	26		
	Christian Knowl. Soc.	8		
	American Board	5		
	Methodist Miss. Soc.	4		
	Danish Missions	2		
Ceylon	Methodist Miss. Soc.	14	27	12
	American Board	7		
	Church Miss. Soc.	4		
	English Baptists	2		
Asiatic Islands	English Baptists	5	6	4
	London Miss. Soc.	1		
New Zealand	Church Miss. Soc.	5	5	1

Geographical View — Continued.

Countries.	Societies.	Missionaries.	Missionaries.	Stations.
Society Islands . .	London Miss. Soc. .	16	16	4
Sandwich Islands . .	American Board . .	8	8	1
Guiana	United Brethren . .	7	14	4
	London Miss. Soc. .	5		
	Methodist Miss. Soc.	2		
West Indies . .	Methodist Miss. Soc.	41	81	38
	United Brethren . .	29		
	Conv. Negro Sl. Soc.	6		
	Church Miss. Soc. .	3		
	English Baptists . .	1		
	London Miss. Soc. .	1		
Cherokee Indians .	American Board . .	7	9	5
	United Brethren . .	1		
	American Baptists .	1		
Choctaw Indians . .	American Board . .	4	1	1
Arkansas Indians .	American Board . .	2	2	1
Ind. tr. in N. Y. & N. J.	Soc. for Prop. Gospel	5	5	2
Osage Indians . . .	United For. Miss. Soc.	3	3	1
Illinois Indians . . .	American Baptists .	2	2	1
Delawares & Chippewas	United Brethren . .	2	2	2
Labrador	United Brethren . .	19	19	3
Greenland	United Brethren . .	11	11	3
			455	156

4. — *Religious Tract Societies.*

Societies.	Instituted.	Income, 1819.	Whole No. issued.
London Relig. Tract Soc.	1799	$27,477 00	$30,000,000 00
New England Tract Soc.	1813	-	2,240,000 00
New York Tract Society	-	-	-
Church of Eng. Tract Soc.	1813	2,006 00	-

5. — *Societies for Educating Pious Young Men for the Ministry.*

Societies.	Instituted.	Income, 1820.
Maine Education Soc. aft. Aux. to Am. Ed. Soc.	1813	-
Massachusetts Baptist Education Society . .	1814	$1,372 00
American Education Society [1]	1815	13,490 00
New York Baptist Education Society . . .	1818	565 00
Maine Baptist Education Society	1819	-
Presbyterian Board of Education	1819	-

An association existed in Holland as early as 1633, for educating pious men for the ministry.

[1] The American Educational Society has assisted 277 students in their preparatory studies. The income in 1819 was $21,291 00.

6. — *Other Societies for Improving the Rising Generation.*

Societies.	Instituted.	Income.	No. of Schools.	No. in School.
National Education Soc. Eng.	1813	$21,099 00	1467	200,000
British & Foreign School Soc.	–	10,269 00	–	–
Sunday School Union, Eng. .	–	–	2029	237,584
Sabbath School Union, Scot. .	–	–	480	34,000
Sunday School Soc. for Ireland	–	–	–	84,147
N. Y. Sunday School Un. Soc.	–	–	36	3,500
Boston Soc. for Religious and Moral Instruction of Poor .	–	–	8	700
Total			4020	559,931

The British and Foreign School Society exerts a salutary influence over schools in France, Spain, Russia, Germany, Italy, Malta, the United States, Nova Scotia, Hayti, and the East Indies.

7. — *Institutions for Africans.*

African Institution, Eng., instituted 1791. American Colonization Society, instituted 1817. Benezet's African School in Philadelphia, instituted 1782. School for educating young men of color for preachers and teachers to the African race, instituted 1816. This school is established in New Jersey. In 1819, seven young men of color were there preparing for the ministry. It is under the management of a Board of Directors annually appointed by the Synod of New York and New Jersey. In

1792, the African Institution transported more than a thousand blacks from Nova Scotia to Sierra Leone. At that colony there were "many thousand" negroes, liberated from slave ships. The American Colonization Society has planted a colony at Sherbro, east of Sierra Leone.

II. — Societies for Foreign Missions, at the Present Time.

The tabular views now to be given of the operations of foreign missionary societies, as they exist at the present time, may be found to differ somewhat from each other, and not to correspond entirely with statements in the body of the work. Perfect accuracy is not easily attainable.

1. — *Societies in the United States of America.* 1868.

Instituted.	Societies.	Expenditures.	Missionaries.	Native Agents.	Stations.	Communicants.
1810	A. B. C. For. Miss.	$530,885 00	140	965	98	25,538
1814	Am. Baptist Miss. Union . . .	214,411 00	42	400	18	19,908
1819	Methodist Epis. Miss. Society[1].	275,866 00	130	256	50	7,468
1832	Bd. of Reformed (Dutch) Church	90,745 00	12	58	15	1,140
1833	Free Will Baptist For. Miss. Soc.	69,955 00	8	10	4	134
1833	Presbyterian Bd. Foreign Miss. .	312,828 00	79	101	49	1,616
1835	Epis. Bd. of Miss.	79,929 00	17	14	22	628
1837	Evang. Lutheran Missionary Soc.	15,509 00	–	30	4	633
1844	Bd. of Reformed Pres. Church .	9,951 00	2	–	2	–
1844	Bd. of Associated Pres. Church }	Merged in the	Board Churc	of Uni h.	ted P	resb.
1844	Bd. of Associated Ref. Church }					
1845	Southern Baptist Convention. .	14,832 00	11	–	11	1,500
1846	Am. Miss. Ass.[1] .	25,824 00	10	2	11	–
1849	Am. and Foreign Christ. Union[1]	Not known.	–	–	–	–
1859	United Pres. Ch.	68,053 00	18	55	14	239
1861	Southern Pres. Bd. For. Miss..	18,000 00	12	4	12	1,200
	Total . . .	$1,726,788 00	481	1,895	310	60,004

[1] Proportion for foreign missions.

2.—*Great Britain and Ireland.* 1868.

Instituted.	Societies.	Expenditures.	Missionaries.	Native Agents.	Stations.	Communicants.
1701	Soc. for Prop. the Gospel	$249,310 00	125	–	–	–
1792	Baptist Missionary Society	163,970 00	62	–	–	–
1795	London Missionary Society	526,445 00	159	720	81	29,847
1800	Church Missionary Society	754,320 00	198	1987	155	15,523
1816	General Baptist Missionary Society	24,900 00	7	18	9	433
1817	Wesleyan Missionary Society	584,260 00	175	104	157	47,480
1824	Church of Scotland	26,185 00	7	–	–	–
1840	Welsh Calvinistic Methodist Miss.	14,865 00	4	–	–	–
1840	Irish Presb. Church	19,080 00	8	–	–	–
1841	Edinburgh Med. Miss.	5,400 00	3	–	–	–
1842	Reformed Presb. Ch.	10,000 00	7	–	–	–
1843	Free Church of Scotland	159,145 00	24	146	36	1,674
1844	South Am. Mission	36,675 00	10	–	–	–
1847	United Presbyterian Mission	110,805 00	38	–	–	–
1854	Turkish Missions Aid Society	8,295 00	–	–	–	–
1860	United Methodist Free Church	25,015 00	25	–	–	–
	English Presb. Ch.	36,780 00	10	–	–	–
	Moravian, English Branch	24,275 00	–	–	–	–
	Foreign Evangelist	7,215 00	–	–	–	–
	Garrow Mission	2,185 00	2	–	–	–
	Methodist New Connection	9,020 00	4	–	–	–
	Total	$2,798,145 00	868	–	–	–

3. — *Societies for Jewish Missions.* **1867.**

[From Dr. Mullens' "London and Calcutta."]

Societies.	Amount expended.	Missionaries, Ordained and Lay.
1. London Society for Promoting Christianity among Jews	**$173,415**	**51**
2. British Society for Promoting Christianity among Jews	**37,395**	**26**
3. Church of Scotland Mission	**17,225**	**5**
4. Free Church Mission	**20,795**	**6**
5. Irish Protestant Mission	**8,995**	**4**
6. Jerusalem Society, Berlin	**4,460**	**1**
7. Basle Union	**2,925**	–
8. Netherlands Union	**1,780**	**3**
Total	**$266,990**	**96**

4.—*Continental Missionary Societies.* 1867.

[From Dr. Mullens' "London and Calcutta."]

No	Societies.	Amount expended.	No. of European Missionaries.	Countries.
1	United Brethren	$90,140	160	Various.
2	Berlin Missionary	40,510	19	S. Africa.
3	Rhenish Missionary	62,480	36	S. Africa.
4	Evangelical Missionary (Berlin)	21,450	22	Coles, Bengal.
5	N. German Missionary (Bremen)	18,750	15	W. Africa.
6	Leipsic Lutheran Missionary	41,235	19	S. India.
7	Basle Mission	171,770	92	Various.
8	Paris Missionary	52,290	26	S. Africa.
9	Netherlands Missionary Society	35,000	12	Java.
10	Netherlands Missionary Union	11,860	5	–
11	Utrecht Miss. Soc.	16,290	15	E. Islands.
12	Netherlands Reform'd Miss. Society	5,000	3	Java.
13	Danish Miss. Soc.	–	1	E. India.
	Total	$566,775	425	

SUMMARY.

Societies in the United States	$1,723,788
Societies in Great Britain and Ireland	2,798,145
Societies for Jewish Missions	266,990
Continental Missionary Societies	566,775
Grand Total	$5,355,698
Number of Missionaries	**1,870**

5. — *Summary View of Protestant Missions.*

[From Dr. John C. Lowrie's "Manual of the Foreign Missions of the Presbyterian Church," 1868.]

In the different Mission Fields.

Mission Fields.	Ordained Missionaries.		Assistant Missionaries.		Communicants.	Scholars.
	Foreign.	Native.	Foreign.	Native.		
American Indians . .	105	16	135	14	8,192	1,766
Spanish Amer. States .	32	1	39	2	928	483
Guiana & West Indies	217	81	250	–	79,879	17,047
Africa — N. and E., and Madagascar . . .	28	97	41	–	4,718	2,335
Western Africa . .	132	29	115	99	14,093	8,408
South Africa . . .	277	6	323	14	30,402	16,448
Asia — Western . . .	89	113	92	237	3,115	7,353
India and Ceylon .	533	203	563	2,769	35,440	92,476
Burmah and Siam .	35	106	37	250	9,237	1,516
China and Japan .	133	10	119	178	3,577	1,532
Islands — China Sea and Pacific . . .	196	12	180	209	61,447	55,541
Total . . .	1,777	674	1,894	3,772	251,028	204,905

By the different Ecclesiastical Bodies.

CONGREGATIONAL. — American Association, etc.	10	
American Board	102	
American Baptist Union	41	
Southern Baptist	14	
Free Will Baptist	4	
Canadian	2	
English Baptist	60	
English General Baptist	9	
English Independent London Missionary Society	156[1]	
English Jews Society	1	
	—	399
EPISCOPAL. — American	19	
Canadian	2	
English Church Missionary Society	204	
English Gospel Propagation Society	108	
London Jews Society	7	
	—	340
LUTHERAN. — American	4	
German	13	
	—	17
METHODIST. — American	69	
American, Southern	3	
American United Brethren in Christ	2	
English, Wesleyan	176	
English, United Free	15	
English, New Connection	4	
English, Lady Huntington Connection	10	
	—	279
MORAVIAN. — One half of "laborers of all classes"		158
PRESBYTERIAN. — Old School, Board of Foreign Miss.	71	
Old School, Southern	8	
Old School, American Board	2	
New School, American Board	43	
New School, at Kolapore	1	
Carried forward	125	1,193

[1] The whole number, but some of them are Presbyterians

Brought forward	125	1,193
United Presbyterian	14	
Reformed Presbyterian, N. S., connected with Presbyterian Board	4	
Reformed Presbyterian, O. S.	2	
Reformed (Dutch)	14	
Nova Scotia Church	6	
English	9	
French	21	
German	275	
Irish	10	
Scotch, Free	28	
Scotch, Established	12	
Scotch, United	46	
Welsh, Calvinistic Methodist	5	
	—	571
UNKNOWN. — American Association, Christian Union		13
		1,777

SUMMARY.

Congregational	399	
Episcopal	340	
Lutheran	17	
Methodist	279	
Moravian	158	
Presbyterian	571	
Unknown	13	
	—	1 777

IX.

SUMMARY OF ROMAN CATHOLIC MISSIONS.

(See Chapter XIV.)

[From Schem's "American and Educational Almanac." Condensed from a theological journal published by the Jesuits in Paris.]

I. *Missions of the Secular Clergy.* — Under this head six missionary seminaries are mentioned; namely, the "Seminaries for Foreign Missions," at Paris, Genoa, Milan, All Hallows' (Ireland), Brussels, and the "Seminary for African Missions," at Lyons. Statistics are given only of the Seminary of Paris, which entertains two hundred and sixty-four missionaries in East India, Farther India, China, Thibet, Corea, and Japan.

II. *Missions of "Religious Congregations."* — The following table gives the names of the Religious Congregations which send out missionaries, the countries in which they work, and the aggregate number of missionaries supported by each: —

1. *Lazarists* have missions in Abyssinia, Turkey, Greece, Persia, Tripoli, Egypt, China, United States, Brazil, Argentine Republic, Chili, Peru, Guatemala. Number of missionaries, 340.

2. *Picpus Society,* in Polynesia, Chili, Peru; 130.

3. *Oblates of the Immaculate Conception,* in British America, United States, Mexico, Natal, Ceylon; 236.

4. *Marists,* in the United States, Australia, New Zealand, Polynesia; 128.

5. *Congregation of the Holy Spirit and Holy Heart of Mary,* in Western Africa, East India, French Guiana, Hayti; 125.

6. *Congregation of the Holy Cross,* in the United States, British America, East India; 187.

7. *Redemptorists,* in the United States, St. Thomas; 25.

8. *Melchitarists,* in Turkey; 65.

III. *Missions of Monastic Orders.* — 1. *Franciscans,* in Russia, Turkey, China, Egypt, Central Africa, Tripoli, Morocco, United States, Mexico, United States of Columbia, Bolivia, Peru, Chili, Argentine Republic, the Philippine Islands, New Zealand, British America; 1,384.

2. *Dominicans,* in Turkey, China, Philippine Islands, and the United States; 322.

3. *Capuchins,* in Turkey, India, Eastern and Central Africa, Tunis; 210.

4. *Carmelites,* in Turkey, Persia, East India; 50.

5. *Jesuits,* in Turkey, Greece, India, China, British America, United States, Mexico, French Guiana, Ecuador, Guatemala, Chili, Brazil, Paraguay, Argentine Republic, Philippine Islands, Australia; 1,672.

Altogether there are 264 missionaries in the first class of missions; 1,236 in the second class; and 3,639 in the third class; giving a total of 5,138 missionaries.

A recent Report of the Society for the Propagation of the Faith, exhibits the following report of receipts and expenditures for the year 1866: —

Total receipts, 5,145,558 francs, or nearly $1,000,000.

Of this sum France furnished more than 3,500,000, Italy not quite 450,000, Belgium nearly 100,000, Germany

233,000, North America about 190,000, the British Isles not quite 140,000, Holland only 80,000, Switzerland nearly 50,000, Portugal about 40,000, South America 27,000, and Spain a little over 5,500.

Not quite 2,000,000 francs were appropriated to Asiatic missions, more than 1,000,000 each to America and Europe (America taking the precedence by a few thousand francs), nearly 500,000 to Oceanica, and about 450,000 to Africa.

X.

FRANCIS XAVIER AND ROMISH MISSIONS.

(See Chapter XIV.)

ONE of the most valuable contributions to the missionary literature of modern times, is a work by Rev. Henry Venn, B. D., Honorary Secretary of the English Church Missionary Society, entitled "Missionary Life and Labors of Francis Xavier, taken from his own Correspondence, with a Sketch of the General Results of Roman Catholic Missions among the Heathen." London, 1862. It is to this work so frequent reference is made in Chapter XIV. As it has not yet been republished in this country, the reader will be interested in a series of extracts, illustrating the mission of the great Romish missionary, and going to strengthen the positions taken in the chapter on the Romish Missions.

Materials for the History of Romish Missions. — "Our information of Roman Catholic missions is very meagre and unsatisfactory. The sources of information are either various collections of letters of missionaries, or dry compilations from those letters. But these sources of information cannot satisfy any one who desires a clear knowledge of this subject. He will seek for histories of missions written from the field of labor by the laborers themselves, or by those who have witnessed the work abroad; or the journals and collected letters of individual missionaries. Since missions were taken up in earnest by the Protestant Church, at the close of the eighteenth century, the press, in England and America, has teemed with such missionary histories and biographies. Numerous volumes have been written by missionaries themselves, or by their relatives and others. In such books we see the living man and his real work. As soon, therefore, as my attention was turned to the subject of Romish missions, I sought out for some such authentic biographies, memoirs, or histories of Romish missionaries. Wherever I inquired, the Life of Xavier was presented to me, and no second work of that class could be named. I searched public libraries and booksellers' shops without success. I made inquiries personally at the head-quarters of Romish missionaries in France, namely, the Institute of the Faith at Lyons, but was assured that the Life of Xavier was the only biography of any authority; the same answer was returned to a friend, who made the inquiry at the College of the 'Propaganda' at Rome; and my friend was further informed, that it was contrary to the principles of the Romish Church to permit the unauthorized publication of the personal history of its missionaries.

"I was hence led to study the Life of Xavier as the only authentic source from which an internal view of the life and labors of a Romish missionary can be obtained.

"The Life of Xavier has another title to consideration. Many prevailing sentiments of the present day, even in Protestant countries, respecting missions, find their counterpart in some of the most striking features in the history of Francis Xavier, such as a craving for the romance of missions; the notion that an autocratic power is wanted in a mission, such as a missionary bishop might exercise; a demand for a degree of self-denial in a missionary bordering on asceticism. These, and many such sentiments, are often illustrated by a reference to the life and success of Xavier. The delusive character of such sentiments cannot fail to appear on a careful study of the truth of Xavier's history." — *Preface*, pp. i.–iii.

Xavier's Converts. — "It will not escape the notice of an intelligent Christian, that, in the elaborate description which Xavier gives of his conversions, there is no reference to the divine power on the hearts of individuals. Xavier's favorite expression is, 'I have made so many Christians' ('Feci Christianas'), when he had baptized infants, or taught adults to repeat the prescribed formulas. Even when he introduces a notice of the divine power, it is often in a way which exalts human agency, rather than the work of the Holy Spirit." — *Page* 38.

"All his hopes of success rested upon the incessant inculcation of dry formularies, and in the strictness and severity of external discipline. This was the whole of the work, according to his limited views of true religion. But such nominal and deficient Christianity can never bring men out of heathenism, or, at least, enable them to stand in the day of trial. Xavier had light enough to see this.

23

His early acquaintance with Protestants seems to have left on his mind traces of spiritual truth, which soon dissatisfied him with the result of his teaching, and made him tremble with apprehension for the house he had 'built on the sand.'" — *Page* 39.

Xavier's Ideas of Expiation. — "He says to Mansilla: 'God give you patience, which is the first requisite in dealing with this nation.[1] Imagine to yourself that you are in purgatory, and that you are washing away the guilt of your evil deeds. Acknowledge the singular mercy of God in granting you the opportunity for expiating the sins of your youth while you live and breathe, which may now be accomplished by the merit of grace, and at a far less cost of suffering than in the world to come.' This idea of the efficacy of the sufferings in this life, when endured for God's glory, to diminish the pains of purgatory in the next life, strange as it appears to any one who takes his religion from the Bible, is a favorite notion with Xavier, and with Romish writers of his class." — *Page* 49.

Xavier's Use of the Civil Power. — "Severe and magisterial threats were not unusual in Xavier's correspondence. In one of his letters, the Portuguese Governor of Tuticorin, who had opposed Xavier himself, and oppressed the native Christians, is threatened with the Inquisition. 'Tell him that I will write to Prince Henry, the President of the Inquisition at Lisbon, to put the utmost rigors of that ecclesiastical court in force against him as a hinderer of the gospel.' In the same letter he enjoins Mansilla to

[1] He is speaking of India.

keep a sharp and careful watch over the native Malabar teachers (*clerici*) associated with him, saying, 'If you detect anything wrong in them, restrain them, for God's sake, and punish them instantly and severely; for we shall have to bear a dreadful load of guilt, which many stripes will hardly serve to expiate, if we neglect to use the plenary power committed to us, carrying it like a sword in a scabbard, instead of punishing offenses against God, especially such as are a stumbling-block to the multitude.'" — *Page* 54.

He thus wrote to the King of Portugal from Cochin, January 20, 1548: "I very earnestly desire that you should take an oath, invoking most solemnly the name of God, that in case any governor thus neglects to spread the faith, he shall, on his return to Portugal, be punished by close imprisonment for many years, and all his goods and possessions shall be sold, and devoted to works of charity. In order that none may flatter themselves that this is but an idle threat, you must declare as plainly as possible that you will accept no excuses that may be offered; but that the only way of escaping your wrath, and obtaining your favor, is to make as many Christians as possible in the countries over which they rule.

"I could give many instances to prove the necessity of this, but I will not weary your Majesty by what would only be the recital of my past and present anxieties, undergone without any hope of reward. I will only assert this much: if every viceroy and governor be fully persuaded that you have bound yourself by oath to do this, and that you will perform all that you have threatened, the whole island of Ceylon, many kings of the Malabar coast, and the whole promontory of Comorin, will embrace the religion of Christ in a single year. But so long as the viceroys and governors are not urged by the fear of disgrace and fine to make many Christians, your Majesty must not hope that the preaching of the gospel will meet with great success in India; or that many will be brought to baptism, or make any progress in religion. The only reason why every man in India does not acknowledge the divinity of Christ, and profess his holy doctrine, is the fact, that the viceroy or governor who neglects to make this his care receives no punishment from your Majesty." — *Page* 161.

Xavier as a Christian Missionary. — "We have thus brought to a close the first period of Xavier's labors in the East, namely, the three years spent in South India. This review cannot but leave upon the mind a strong conviction of Xavier's inconsistency of character. He was a man of strong impulses, of quick transitions of feeling, liable to pass from extravagant hope to unreasonable despair. This we conceive to be the solution of the contradictions in his letters. He probably wrote from the impulse of the moment. He lacked, in fact, that stable confidence in the enterprise he had taken in hand, which every true missionary derives from a supreme regard to the word of God. It is impossible otherwise to reconcile his sudden abandonment of India, after so short and imperfect a trial, with his previous professions of spiritual comfort and success in his work, — or his sublime appeals to men of learning and science in the universities of Europe to become his associates, with the fact that his chief comfort was the baptism of moribund infants, and the dumb show of a crowd of adult worshippers. It is impossible also to reconcile, on Christian principles, the various offices which he attempted to sustain. At one time he was the preacher of love and peace; at another the agent of the cruel and accursed Inquisition; at another the instigator of a crusade. Compare the two pictures. See Xavier on the Fishery Coast, toiling in the instruction of Christian neophytes, and professing to find his chief joy in divine consolations; he appears as an apostle. See Xavier at Negapatam, on the look-out for the earliest intelligence of a hostile and murderous expedition, which he himself had instigated, for the advancement of true religion: in what did his spirit then differ from that of a Mussulman?

"It will not, indeed, be fair to judge Xavier altogether by the standard of the primitive church, or of the missionary spirit of the present day. We must not forget that he belonged to a church which canonized Charlemagne." — *Page* 78.

"Upon reviewing Xavier's character, it will appear that he possessed in a very high degree some of the essential qualities of the leader of a great enterprise. He was of a generous, noble, and loving disposition, calculated to gather followers, and to attach them firmly to his leadership. But in respect of missions, Xavier was little fitted to direct others. Of the peculiar duties of an evangelist to the heathen, he had no conception. His directions to his missionaries are wholly addressed to their conduct as pastors of Christian communities. In his voluminous 'Instructions,' all that can be gathered of missionary directions amounts to little beyond the general relations of the clergy with their flocks, with each other, and with their ecclesiastical superiors.

"Even if Xavier had better understood the work of missions, there was one great fault in his system, which would have proved fatal to success. He attempted to carry everything by authority. He constantly inculcated the supreme merit and advantage of implicit obedience to himself. The sequel of his history will show how completely this system failed to form an efficient body of coadjutors. Xavier's history will, therefore, afford a useful caution against a notion, too much countenanced at the present day, that an ecclesiastical head of a mission is needed to secure efficiency by uniformity of action, and to counteract the evils which may arise within a mission from the contrariety of individual opinions. Such absolute power may consist with the government of a settled Christian church, where the relation between ecclesiastical authority and the pastoral function has been defined by canons, and by experience. But no canons or regulations have yet been laid down for missions to the heathen. That work is so varied, and its emergencies are so sudden, that the evangelist must be left to act mainly on his own responsibility and judgment. It preëminently requires independence of mind, fertility of resource, a quick observance of the footsteps of Divine Providence, a readiness to push forward in that direction, an abiding sense in the mind of the missionary of personal responsibility to extend the kingdom of Christ, and a lively conviction that the Lord is at his 'right hand.' These qualifications are, like all the finer sentiments of Christianity, of delicate texture; they are often united with a natural sensitiveness; they are to be cherished and counseled, rather than ruled; they are easily checked and discouraged, if 'headed' by authority. Yet these are the qualities which have ever distinguished the missionaries who win the richest trophies, and advance the borders of the Redeemer's kingdom. Among such a body of workmen no formidable difficulties will arise from the contrariety of individual opinions; and such as do arise will be easily composed by affectionate, Christian, and wise counsels, whether offered on the spot, or transmitted from Europe." — *Page* 145.

Xavier's Estimate of his Success in India. — "In a letter to a brother missionary in Travancore, he writes, December, 1548: 'If you will, in imagination, search through India, you will find, that few will reach heaven, either of whites or blacks, except those who depart this life under fourteen years of age, with their baptismal innocence still upon them.'" — *Page* 150.

"The confession of the failure of the work of Romish missionaries in India is rendered still more manifest, by a proposal which Xavier made to the King of Portugal. He solemnly proposed that the conversion of India should be taken out of the hands of missionaries, and put into the hands of the civil authorities!" — *Page* 157.

Xavier as compared with Protestant Missionaries. — "We often hear the name of Xavier put forth as a great hero, to the disparagement of Protestant missionaries. Reduce his history to its true dimensions, and Protestant missions have no need to shun a comparison. His pretensions fall short of those of Samuel Marsden and his two European catechists in New Zealand, spending their first Sunday amidst a crowd of warlike cannibals, upon a coast which had been shunned for many previous years by every merchant ship; or of Henry Martyn, the solitary witness for the word of Christ in Shiraz, disputing with the most learned Mohammedans in their own tongue, and winning their admiration for his person, notwithstanding their bitter enmity to his religion; or of Williams, in his visits to the islands of the Pacific, where no European before himself had landed, and persevering in his efforts to impart to them the gospel of Christ, till his life was sacrificed at their hands; or of Judson in the prisons of Burmah; or of many other names which might be selected from the list of Protestant missionary heroes. And when this list shall be exhausted, we have a reserve of heroic deeds in a class which has no existence in the Church of Rome. Let us compare Xavier with the missionary's wife, Rosine Krapf, who accompanied her husband, Dr. Krapf, into the heart of Abyssinia, shared his flight when expelled through the intrigues of Romanists, reëntered with him the wilderness of Shoho to regain the province of Tigré, though with the prospect before her of the birth of her first-born child in that wilderness. See her comforting her husband under the shade of a wilderness tree, as he took the dying babe in his arms to dedicate it to the Father, Son, and Holy Ghost. Hear her, while he hesitated for a name, pronounce the Amharic term for 'a tear!' And then she was forced by the savage natives to pursue her journey after three days' rest. See the same valiant lady accompanying her husband through the perils of shipwreck in native boats, till they reached the more civilized settlement of Mombas, an island lying off the east coast of Africa, as Sancian lies off the coast of China, each island within sight of the land sought to be evangelized. There listen to the last accents of this genuine female missionary, while sinking into the arms of death, enjoining her husband to carry her body to the opposite continent of Africa, and to bury her on the sea-shore, that the pagan Wanikas, who passed by her tomb, might be reminded of the object which had brought her to that country; and that her grave might be the starting-point for future missionaries to carry the light of the gospel through the Galla country into inhospitable Abyssinia. How does the romance of Xavier's last scene at Sancian, off the coast of China, and of the transfer of his remains to the chapel at Goa, sink in the presence of this parallel story of a missionary's heroic wife!" — *Page* 255.

Failure of the Romish Missions. — "The historical review now given will establish the conclusion, that the brightest prospects and the most confident hopes of Romish missions to the heathen have vanished sooner or later, by one catastrophe or another; that they have not contained within themselves the principles of permanent vitality. Where they are not upheld by the sword, they are overborne by opposition. Their apparent success for a time has been the result of favorable wordly circumstances; and when those circumstances have changed, the mission has come to nothing. This conclusion is based upon the history of three centuries; during the greater part of which period the Church of Rome had the fields to itself. Rome put forth missionary agencies to reap them far more numerous than the Protestant Church has yet been able to command. But Rome failed to gather in the harvest, and the fields are all now still unreaped, and open for the entrance of Protestant evangelists. Romanists boast of Francis Xavier as the apostle of the Indies; they erect altars and chapels for his worship; they invoke his aid in their missionary efforts; and 'verily they have their reward.' The blight of Xavier's missionary principles has rested upon them ever since; and the disappointment which pursued Xavier to his last breath has been the portion of many a sincere, able, and zealous Romish missionary." — *Page* 319.

The Japanese Mission. — "The mission, after Xavier's death, was carried on with great vigor, and was abundantly supplied with laborers, other denominations besides the Jesuits entering upon the field. Vast numbers of the natives are reported to have professed the Christian faith, but I have in vain sought for any reliable accounts of these successes. No such contemporary history or biographies exist of the Japanese mission as the letters of Xavier. I have looked into various collections of Epistolæ Japonicæ, but, like the Epistolæ Indicæ, they are filled with legends; and it is impossible, after reading Xavier's letters, to open those pages without the conviction that we have passed out of the regions of truth into those of exaggeration, supression, and fiction. At the close of the sixteenth century, a fierce and bloody persecution commenced against Christianity, on the part of the political emperor, upon the old plea of persecutors, that the peace of the state was endangered. From the great number of influential persons said to have been involved in this persecution, it may be inferred that the profession of Christianity had been widely extended; and from the length of time, amounting to forty years, for which the struggle was continued, it is evident that multitudes firmly held to their adopted faith. In the year 1637, the reigning emperor discovered, as he affirmed, a traitorous correspondence for dethroning him, between the native Christians and the King of Portugal. He there fore issued orders for the butchery of the remnant of Christians, estimated at 37,000. This order was barbarously carried into effect. Thus the mission planted by Xavier was extinguished in blood, after existing for nearly ninety years; and this *through the political power on which Xavier had leaned in all his missionary enterprises.*" — *Page* 209.

INDEX.

www.ingramcontent.com/pod-product-compliance
Lightning Source LLC
LaVergne TN
LVHW020120110826
845151LV00001B/219

* 9 7 8 1 4 2 5 5 4 1 6 7 5 *